ANALYTIC NARRATIVES

ANALYTIC NARRATIVES

Robert H. Bates

Avner Greif

Margaret Levi

Jean-Laurent Rosenthal

Barry R. Weingast

PRINCETON UNIVERSITY PRESS   PRINCETON, NEW JERSEY

Library of Congress Cataloging-in-Publication Data

Analytic narratives / Robert H. Bates . . . [et al.].
    p. cm.
    Includes bibliographical references and index.
    ISBN 0-691-00128-6 (cloth : alk. paper). — ISBN 0-691-00129-4 (pbk. : alk.
paper)
    1. Political stability.   2. Economic history.   3. International relations.   4. Game
theory.   5. Rational choice theory.   I. Bates, Robert H.
    JC330.2.A45   1998
    320.1'1—dc21   98-9624

To Douglass North ————————————————

MENTOR AND FRIEND

Contents

Acknowledgments ─────────────────────────────

WITH financial support from the National Science Foundation (grant SES-9022192), the Center for Advanced Study in the Behavioral Sciences sponsored this project, enabling us to work together for the academic year 1993–94. In the mornings, each of us labored on his or her own project; in the afternoons, we met, seeking to identify and elaborate upon the intersection of three fields: economics, economic history, and political science. Our discussions increasingly centered on political economy, institutions, and the uses of game theory. This book is the result.

Discussions constitutes too neutral a word. Explorations, debates, arguments: these hit closer to the mark. Indeed, by the end of the year, we had achieved no consensus. We therefore continued to meet and to "discuss" for two more years, dismembering and reassembling drafts of the manuscript. David Featherman employed the Presidential Fund of the Social Science Research Council to defer a portion of the costs of these meetings. We also received support from our departments at Stanford and Harvard Universities and the Universities of Washington and California and from the Harvard Institute for International Development.

Once we sensed convergence, we sought to draw others into our debates. A panel at the 1996 annual meetings of the American Political Science Association provided one forum. A workshop sponsored by the Weatherhead Center for International Affairs at Harvard University provided another. In our letter of invitation to this workshop, we stressed that "good friends can be good critics." Our very good friends include John Aldrich, Charles Cameron, Gary Cox, Jorge Domínguez, James Fearon, Jeff Frieden, Peter Hall, Ira Katznelson, Gary King, Edgar Kiser, David Laitin, Mark Lichbach, Ian Lustick, Lisa Martin, Ronald Rogowski, Fritz Scharpf, Kenneth Shepsle, Theda Skocpol, Steven Solnick, and Margaret Somers. Alison Alter, Smita Singh, and Jeremy Weinstein provided valuable research assistance; Kenneth Schultz and Richard Tucker directed us to several relevant literatures; David Collier, Mihir Desai, Geoffrey Garrett, Roberta Gatti, and Leonard Wantchekon provided valuable commentary.

Besides expressing our gratitude to Philip Converse and Robert Scott of the Center for Advanced Study, we also thank the skilled and supportive staff and the other members of the Class of '94. We offer special thanks to Jorge Domínguez of the Weatherhead Center for International Affairs, Harvard University, whose sponsorship of the workshop contributed so much to the evolution of this project. Robert, Margaret, and Jean-Laurent wish to thank the

Weingast and Greif families, and especially Esti and Susy, for welcoming us to Stanford, and Margaret Bates, Bob Kaplan, and Paula Scott for tolerating our periodic journeys to Palo Alto.

ANALYTIC NARRATIVES

Introduction _____

THIS VOLUME addresses issues of substance and method. Focusing on institutions, the chapters explore the sources of political order; the origins of conflict, both international and domestic; and the interaction between international and domestic political economy. They also raise methodological issues, particularly concerning the use of game theory in the study of political economy. In doing so, they advance a method of analysis that we call "analytic narratives."

The issues we address, both substantive and methodological, cut across fields of scholarship. Students of development join economic historians in seeking the political foundations of growth (World Bank 1997). Institutions increasingly preoccupy not only sociologists and political scientists but also students of industrial organization (Hall and Taylor 1996). The use of game theory has spread from economics to political science and into anthropology as well. The chapters in this volume thus engage the concerns of many disciplines and should therefore command a broad audience.

The case studies in this volume are motivated by a desire to account for particular events and outcomes. For those committed to the close analysis of particular events, the chapters seek to demonstrate the benefits to be gained from the systematic use of theory. For those committed to the development and use of theory, we seek to demonstrate the returns to be reaped from a close dialogue with case materials. The phrase *analytic narrative* captures our conviction that theory linked to data is more powerful than either data or theory alone.

When we refer to theory, we refer to rational choice theory and, most often, to the theory of games. Our advocacy could apply to other forms of theory as well, however. A range of models could serve as the basis of analytic narratives: those derived from the new institutionalism (Hall and Taylor 1996) or from analytic Marxism (Przeworski 1985; Roemer 1986), for example. Because of our understanding of institutions and the sources of their power over collective life—and because four of the five authors in this volume marshal game theoretic reasoning!—we focus on the strengths and limitations of that genre.

Substantive Themes

Political Order

Contemporary events remind us that stability in political communities cannot be assumed; it must be achieved. The chapters in this volume therefore return to one of the classic themes in the social sciences: the sources of political order.

Avner Greif, himself an economist, joins anthropologists, such as Gluckman (1965), Bailey (1969), and Colson (1974), in examining the construction of polities from family systems. Much as in contemporary Africa, the Caucasus, and South Asia, in twelfth-century Genoa, Greif reveals, powerful clans competed for wealth and sought to use public power to advance their private fortunes. Competition among them sparked civil wars. Greif explores the way in which a political institution, the *podestà,* maintained peace between clans. In doing so, he examines the political foundations for economic growth in Genoa, exploring how it was able to extend its political influence and commercial hegemony throughout the Mediterranean.

Genoa was a maritime city-state; the United States is a continentwide federation. As Genoa sought to dominate the markets of the Mediterranean, so too did the United States seek to incorporate the territories of North America. And just as Genoa succeeded, so too did the United States, resulting in the creation of the largest common market on earth. Addressing the politics of the nineteenth-century United States, Barry Weingast plumbs a theme previously explored most closely by Karl Deutsch (1957) and William Riker (1964): the creation of federal systems. It was Riker who stressed the importance of collective gains, such as the occupation of territory, in motivating the construction of federal systems; it was Deutsch who highlighted the role of beliefs, stressing that centers of power can combine only when convinced of the peaceful intentions of their partners. Weingast uses his study of the United States to examine the institutional foundations for federalism. Exploring the well-known balance rule and using a form of strategic reasoning, Weingast demonstrates how the rule facilitated the achievement of political stability and territorial expansion.[1] Just as the *podestà* kept peace by enhancing the security of threatened clans in Genoa, the balance rule prevented civil war by protecting the security of regional blocs.

Bates also addresses the sources of order, this time at the international level. Joining regime theorists (Krasner 1982; Keohane 1984), Bates explores the way in which sovereign states forged a binding agreement at the global level. Focusing on the international market for coffee, he examines the origins, operations, and impact of the International Coffee Organization (ICO), a political institution that regulated global trade in coffee. By governing the market, Bates argues, the ICO restrained competition among producers, thereby securing for them collective benefits: higher coffee prices and the redistribution of income from consumers to producers of coffee (see also Bates 1997).

In exploring the sources of order in clan-based societies, the foundations of federalism, and the origins of international regimes, these chapters address subjects examined at length by others. Distinguishing our work is a central

---

[1]The rule required that when a nonslave state was admitted to the Union, it was to be balanced by the admission of a slave state.

concern with institutions—for example, the *podestà,* the balance rule, and the ICO—and our approach to their analysis. We join those, such as Huntington (1968), who place institutions at the core of the analysis of political order. However, we differ from many in our understanding of them. Institutions, these chapters argue, do not impose constraints; the order they provide emerges endogenously. Institutions rest upon credible promises, of either reward or punishment. They therefore can, and should, be analyzed as the equilibria of extensive-form games—a theme to which we will shortly return.

Interstate Relations

The chapters in this volume also address the study of international relations. In particular, they focus on the relationship between the pursuit of international security and the performance of the domestic political economy.[2]

The chapter by Bates focuses on international politics. Twice, he documents, political organizations replaced market forces in the international coffee market: once during World War II and again during the cold war. On both occasions, the United States, the largest consumer of coffee in the world, cooperated with producers to stabilize market prices. During times of global tension, he argues, economic agents were able to provide political services to the guardians of international security. When the guardians of international security no longer required the services of the economic agents, the guardians defected from the agreement; in so doing, they precipitated the collapse of the political institution that underpinned the cartel. By focusing on the relationship between security interests and trade alliances, Bates contributes to a theme explored perhaps most directly by the contemporary "neorealists" in the field of international relations (Baldwin 1993; Gowa 1994). The international political system is characterized by conflict, they contend; the pursuit of security shapes the behavior of nations. Large powers, they argue, find it in their private interests to provide collective benefits, including institutions at the global level. The chapter both supports and critiques these arguments, and in so doing engages a well-established literature.

Central to Bates's analysis is the impact of international events on domestic politics: clearly the threat of nazism and communism rendered security considerations more persuasive, and security specialists more powerful, in the domestic policy process. Levi amplifies and extends this theme. Exploring broad but nuanced comparisons, she investigates the ways in which various states at various times have levied manpower for their military forces. By studying the comparative politics of conscription, Levi highlights the domestic transformations precipitated by war.

---

[2]Note the important symposium that addresses many of the following issues: Elman and Elman (1997); see especially Levy (1997).

Jean-Laurent Rosenthal also explores the impact of war upon the domestic economy. Stressing the economic costs of absolutism, Rosenthal argues that the search for taxes fed the growth of bureaucracy. Resources attempted to flow from the portions of the economy controlled by adventurous kings to the portions controlled by the more pacific parliaments. The division of fiscal authority therefore led to distortions in the allocation of resources and to the growth of a regulatory bureaucracy, as the executive sought to stem the depletion of his tax base.

The impact of external threat need not be solely negative, however. Thus Greif argues that external threat reduced the value of political domination, thereby relaxing the constraints on interclan cooperation and promoting private contributions to the furtherance of long-distance trade. Given the threat of war, clans found political domination less valuable; they therefore devoted fewer resources to challenging each other militarily and devoted them instead to commercial expansion. Economic cooperation was less constrained by the need to maintain self-enforcing restraints on domestic political rivalry. Changes in the external environment thus led to a transformation in domestic political and economic organization, but in a way that promoted the growth of the economy.

The chapters by Bates, Levi, and Rosenthal contribute to a second literature in the field of international relations: one that focuses on the domestic impact of international competition. Cameron (1978) and Katzenstein (1985), for example, have studied the political transformation brought on by the need to compete in international markets, whereas Skocpol (1979) and Trimberger (1972) have focused on those brought on by the need to survive in a hostile political world. The chapters in this volume thus address "the second image reversed," in the phrasing of Peter Gourevitch (1978), or the international determinants of domestic politics.

Levi and Rosenthal also explore the interaction between the global and the national from the domestic perspective. Highlighting the variation in the institutional structure of states, they stress how differences in domestic political structures promote differences in the likelihood and the nature of warfare. Military policy, like any policy, results from a process of bargaining, they argue; and the outcome of such bargains is shaped by the structure of political institutions.

In exploring the domestic origins of international conflict, Levi's and Rosenthal's chapters can be read as contributions to the literature on "two-level games," which addresses the interplay between politics in the international and domestic arenas (Putnam 1988; Evans et al. 1993). Too often this literature has merely offered a metaphor for politics. Rosenthal, it should be noted, goes further, providing an explicit model and deriving from it specific propositions about politics. Stressing that monarchs placed a higher priority on warfare than did parliaments, Rosenthal distinguishes among autocracies, in which the monarch had near total control over war and taxes; parliamentary systems, wherein the civilian elite held power; and absolutism, under which kings and legislatures shared control. In parallel with this progression, Rosenthal finds a declining willingness to engage in warfare. He also finds a "selection effect": parliamentary governments, for example, fight fewer wars. They are willing to fight only those wars that are profitable, and they are more willing to finance adequately, and therefore more likely to win, the wars they choose to sponsor. His conclusion is reinforced by the argument of Levi, which explores the impact of increased democratization and industrialization on military mobilization. Faced with an increase in both variables, she argues, governments must invest more in convincing their populations of the importance of the war and in winning their consent to fight. The chapters thus build links between the literature on two-level games and that on the "democratic peace"[3] and identify mechanisms that render democracies distinctive in their choice of security policies.

Political Economy

The chapters address a third set of themes: the interaction between politics and economics. Recent decades have witnessed the resurgence of political economy.[4] Within the voluminous literatures engendered by this revival, those originating from economic history and development economics are most germane. Inspired by the writings of Douglass North (1981, 1990), economic historians have increasingly addressed the role of the state in the securing, or violation, of property rights (Rosenthal 1992); the lowering, or increasing, of transaction costs (Hoffman 1988); or the management, or failure to manage, of capital markets (Root 1994). Development economists have also focused on the role of the state (Harris et al. 1991; Meier 1991), such as by studying its role in promoting growth in Asia (World Bank 1993; Fishlow et al. 1994) or in retarding growth in Africa (Findlay 1991). We join with both economic historians and development specialists in focusing on the political foundations for economic prosperity. Greif, for example, examines the role of political stability in the commercial expansion of Genoa; Weingast explores the federal underpinnings of the economic expansion of the United States. We join economic historians and development specialists as well in exploring the political origins of property rights (Weingast's study of slavery and Levi's of the draft), of taxation (Rosenthal's study of France), and of trade policy (Bates's study of the coffee

---

[3]For statements of this thesis, see Doyle (1983) and Russett (1993). For debates, see Gowa and Farber (1995) and Spiro (1994), and the rebuttal by Maoz (1997).

[4]The references are too numerous to list. Indicative, however, is the creation of new journals, such as *Economics and Politics,* and book series, such as the influential Political Economy of Institutions and Decisions, edited by James Alt and Douglass North and published by Cambridge University Press.

market). Economic historians and development specialists who focus on the role of the state will thus find much of interest in these studies.

What distinguishes our work is not the themes we address; rather it is the assumptions we make in addressing them. The chapters are distinguished by the way in which they analyze coercion. We do not treat force as exogenous to economic life; it does not intrude from a separate political domain. Nor do we approach political economy as a mere interplay of economic and political factors, or as the intrusion of "the state" upon "the market." Instead the chapters presume that coercion is as much a part of that life as are production, consumption, and exchange.

Our recognition of the pervasive presence of coercion represents a rejoinder to others, largely political scientists, who criticize rational choice theory for "taking the politics out" of political science.[5] We do, of course, focus on choice and explore gains from voluntary exchanges. But we also explore the role of threats, constraints, and force. We look at territorial expansion, conquest, state-building, and war. Although based on models of rational choice, our work is *not* apolitical.

How can coercion be structured and organized? How can it be made to underpin economic growth? It is to address such questions that the chapters focus on the role of political institutions.

Institutions

Institutions, we argue, induce choices that are regularized because they are made in equilibrium. In equilibrium, no actor would unilaterally choose to alter his or her behavior, given the options, the payoffs, and expectations regarding the choices of others; nor would that actor have reason to revise or alter his or her expectations.[6] Should exogenous factors remain the same, we would expect behavior to remain unaltered (see the appendix). Behavior becomes stable and patterned, or alternatively institutionalized, not because it is imposed, but because it is elicited.[7]

There are, of course, other conceptions of institutions. Sociologists who follow Weber focus on patterns of authority; economists and political scientists point to legal conventions and coercive structures (Hall and Taylor 1996). Although it draws upon the writings of others, our notion is distinguished by its reliance upon micro-level reasoning. Based upon the premise of rationality

---

[5]See the debates summarized in Almond (1988, 1990).

[6]For further elaboration of the concept of equilibrium, see van Damme (1987), Rasmusen (1989), Dixit and Nailbuff (1991), and Gibbons (1992), as well as the appendix.

[7]Andrew Schotter (1981) was perhaps the first to base the notion of institutions on game-theoretic notions of equilibrium.

in choice, it derives most directly from the reasoning of those who focus on exchange in nonmarket settings. Included would be such game theorists as Milgrom and Roberts (1992); students of the firm, such as Oliver Williamson (1985); and economic historians, such as North (1981, 1990). Equally significant would be the work of political scientists (Shepsle 1979; Ostrom 1990; Kiewiet and McCubbins 1991; Krehbiel 1991) and others who employ microlevel reasoning to study legislatures, parties, and other political institutions. Important differences exist among these approaches, and we neither desire nor intend to summarize the broader literature.[8] The following discussion and the appendix should suffice for present purposes.

In analyzing institutions we utilize concepts drawn from the analysis of games in extensive form.[9] The purposes that underlie the volume motivate this selection. Because we seek to explore concrete, historical cases, we wish to examine the choices of individuals who are embedded in specific settings. We wish to trace the sequences of actions, decisions, and responses that generate events and outcomes. The individuals we study possess preferences and expectations; they are not isolated, but rather are locked in patterns of strategic interdependence. The extensive form explicitly highlights these features of our case materials.

Because we focus on extensive-form games, we conceive of equilibria in terms of subgame perfection. In extensive-form games, a subgame, roughly speaking, is any part of the game in which behavior can be analyzed independently from that in any other portion (see the appendix).[10] A strategy combination consists of a complete listing for each player of the choices that he or she will make at each point in every subgame. A strategy combination is a Nash equilibrium if no player can benefit from altering his or her choices, given the choices of the other players. A strategy combination that constitutes a Nash equilibrium thus captures, in a sense, each player's expectation of the choices that will be made by other players. A strategy combination is subgame perfect if it is a Nash equilibrium in every subgame, including those that will never be reached along the path of play (see the discussion in the appendix).

Note the subtle distinction between Nash and subgame-perfect equilibria. In each case, the equilibrium choice of strategies defines the resulting path of play, that is, the decision nodes at which one actually arrives. A Nash equilibrium imposes a weak restriction on the choice of actions at nodes that lie off the path of play: that the choices maximize the player's payoffs, given the expected

---

[8] A variety of excellent texts review the theory of games and decisions and their applications to economics (Tirole 1988) and politics (Hinich and Munger 1997). These books should be read to gain a more precise understanding of the concepts we employ.

[9] As have others; see, for example, Gates and Humes (1997).

[10] Hence it is any part of the game that runs from an information set that is a singleton and extends to, and incorporates, all subsequent nodes and payoffs. Note that the game as a whole thus constitutes a subgame.

behavior of the other players and the expectation that the game will not actually reach these nodes (i.e., that it will remain on the path of play). A subgame-perfect equilibrium imposes an additional restriction. It requires that in every subgame, including those never actually reached (i.e., those that lie off the path of play), the player's actions constitute a best response to the actions taken by others in that subgame. The notion of subgame-perfect equilibrium thus requires that threats or promises be credible. The players remain on the equilibrium path of play because it would be in the best interests of others to fulfill their threats or promises should they stray off it. Subgame-perfect equilibria thus constitute a subset of Nash equilibria; they exclude those strategy combinations that form Nash equilibria that include threats or promises that are not credible.

Credible threats of punishment thus constitute an essential feature of subgame-perfect equilibria. A player refrains from straying off the path because he or she anticipates being made worse off, given the expected response of other players. Fears of the consequences that await those who stray encourage adherence to equilibrium behavior. Credible threats therefore play a significant role in generating institutionalized patterns of behavior.

The chapters in this volume thus address the sources of political order, warfare, and interaction between the international and the domestic in the political economy of nations. In doing so, they explore the interplay between politics and economics and stress the role of institutions. They consider fundamental themes in modern political economy. What is distinctive is their use of a particular methodology, analytic narrative, to blend rational choice analysis and narration into the study of institutions and of their impact upon political and economic behavior.

Analytic Narratives

We call our approach analytic narrative because it combines analytic tools that are commonly employed in economics and political science with the narrative form, which is more commonly employed in history. Our approach is narrative; it pays close attention to stories, accounts, and context. It is analytic in that it extracts explicit and formal lines of reasoning, which facilitate both exposition and explanation.

The chapters in this volume constitute in-depth investigations of events that transpired in particular periods and settings. In this sense, the volume contributes to the ideographic tradition in the social sciences (McDonald 1996a,b). The chapters trace the behavior of particular actors, clarify sequences, describe structures, and explore patterns of interaction. Thus they contribute to the "historical turn in the social sciences," in the words of Terrence McDonald, which is based "first and foremost on a commitment . . . to producing understanding via richness, texture, and detail" (1996a:10, quoting from Ortner 1996).

In addition to probing the narrative record, the chapters seek "parsimony, refinement, and (in the sense used by mathematicians) elegance"—the very qualities that McDonald explicitly counterpoises to those characteristic of the "historic turn" (1996a:10, quoting from Ortner 1996). Each constructs, employs, or appeals to a formal model. Greif, Rosenthal, and Weingast construct their models; Bates takes existing models "off the shelf"; and Levi mobilizes formal lines of reasoning.

William Riker, who pioneered the application of rational choice to the study of politics, turned to the theory of games in order to move, he stated, from "wisdom" to "political science" (1962:viii), by which he meant a body of related generalizations "deduced from one set of axioms, which . . . [offer] a coherent theoretical model" (1962:3). Riker saw in rational choice theory the promise of a universal approach to the social sciences, capable of yielding general laws of political behavior. Critics of rational choice likewise point to the abstract and logical character of game theory, but do so in order to condemn it. The failures of rational choice theory, Green and Shapiro declare, are "rooted in the aspiration of rational choice theorists to come up with universal theories of politics." The result, they argue, is a preoccupation with theory development, accompanied by a striking "paucity of empirical applications" (1994:x). Research "becomes theory driven rather than problem driven"; its purpose is "to save or vindicate some variant of rational choice theory, rather than to account for . . . political phenomena" (1994:6).

Clearly the chapters in this book are problem driven, not theory driven; they are motivated by a desire to account for particular events or outcomes. They are devoted to the exploration of cases, not to the elaboration of theory. In these ways, they counter the charges raised by Green and Shapiro. By the same token, neither do the chapters conform to Riker's vision of the role of theory. Although informed by deductive reasoning, the chapters themselves seek no universal laws of human behavior.[11]

Where possible, we make use of formal arguments. In particular, we analyze games, since we find them useful in order to create and evaluate explanations of particular outcomes. We identify agents; some are individuals, but others are collective actors, such as elites, nations, electorates, or legislatures. By reading documents, laboring through archives, interviewing, and surveying the secondary literature, we seek to understand the actors' preferences, their perceptions, their evaluation of alternatives, the information they possess, the expectations they form, the strategies they adopt, and the constraints that limit their actions. We then seek to piece together the story that accounts for the outcome of interest: the breakdown of order, the maintenance of peace, the decision to fight or collude. We thus do not provide explanations by subsuming

---

[11]Indeed, as with those of McDonald, we consider Riker's claims to be based on an "over-confident" and naive vision of the sciences (McDonald 1996a:5).

cases under "covering laws," in the sense of Hempel (1965). Rather we seek to account for outcomes by identifying and exploring the mechanisms that generate them. We seek to cut deeply into the specifics of a time and place, and to locate and trace the processes that generate the outcome of interest.

The chapters thus build narratives. But the narratives are analytic narratives. By modeling the processes that produced the outcomes, we seek to capture the essence of stories. Should we possess a valid representation of the story, then the equilibrium of the model should imply the outcome we describe—and seek to explain. Our use of rational choice and game theory transforms the narratives into analytic narratives. Our approach therefore occupies a complex middle ground between ideographic and nomothetic reasoning.[12]

At least since the writings of Thucydides (1951), the narrative form has been the dominant form for explaining human behavior. Recognition of its limitations, however, led to the adoption of other modes of explanation. Narratives, it was recognized, embody explanations. But they often mobilize the mythology and hagiography of their times, mixing literary tropes, notions of morality, and causal reasoning in efforts both to justify and to explain (Dray 1964; Stone 1979; Danto 1985; White 1987; Fry et al. 1989; Goldthorpe 1991; Lustick 1996). Social scientists therefore found it difficult to extract defensible propositions from these complex mixtures. In the face of such difficulties, some, like Robert Fogel, urged the abandonment of narrative accounts of particular events and the exploration, through statistics, of regular and systematically generated events: births, deaths, and market transactions, for example (Fogel and Elton 1983).

As have others, however, we seek to return to the rich, qualitative, and descriptive materials that narratives offer.[13] And, as have others, we seek an explicit and logically rigorous account of the events we describe. Modernization theorists (Lipset 1963), Marxists (Lefebre 1924), world system theorists (Wallerstein 1974), and others (such as the Whig historians, e.g., Trevelyan 1938) have composed compelling accounts of qualitative materials. In two respects, however, we differ in our approach.

First of all, others sometimes offer metanarratives that document the ascendance of political ideas or the emergence of political forces. We pursue a more modest objective. We seek to locate and explore particular mechanisms that shape the interplay between strategic actors and that thereby generate

---

[12]As is recognized by Tetlock and Belkin (1996:5).

[13]See the symposia in *Social Science History* 16 (3) (Fall 1992), *Sociological Methods and Research* 20 (4) (May 1992), and *Journal of Mathematical Sociology* 18 (2–3) (1993). Relevant contributions include Aminzade (1993) and Somers (1992). Others are engaged in projects resembling ours, for example Abbott (1993), Abell (1993), and Kiser (1996); see also Goldthorpe (1996). Also germane are the comments of Donald McClosky (1990). For a far less successful effort, see Ferguson (1996).

outcomes.[14] Second, most of these literatures are structural: they focus on the origins and impact of alignments, cleavages, structures, and institutions. Our approach, by contrast, focuses on choices and decisions. It is thus more micro than macro in orientation. By delineating specific mechanisms and focusing on the determinants and impact of choices, our work differs from that of our predecessors.

However, it is important to clarify and emphasize that we view our approach as a complement to, rather than as a substitute for, structural and macro-level analyses. As seen, for example, in the work of Bates, Levi, and Rosenthal, we too explore the impact of large-scale political forces: of bipolarity and communism in the twentieth century, of democratization in the nineteenth, or of absolutism in the Early Modern period. But we focus on the mechanisms that translate such macrohistorical forces into specific political outcomes. By isolating and unpacking such mechanisms, analytic narratives thus contribute to structural accounts. They also draw upon them. The models that we mobilize presume that some variables are constrained, whereas the values of others can be chosen; they presume that alternatives have been defined, as well as the linkages between actions and outcomes. Analytic narratives and macrostructural analyses therefore stand as complementary approaches to explanation.

Building Narratives

When students learn research methods, they typically start by learning principles of case selection.[15] Like them, we resist this point of departure. As have many of our students, we too have been impelled to "do social science" by our fascination with particular cases: World War I, the French Revolution, or the U.S. Civil War. In effect, our cases selected us, rather than the other way around.

So compelling do we find our cases that we wish to immerse ourselves in them. But we also want to construct logically persuasive and empirically valid accounts that explain how and why events occurred. In seeking to build such accounts, we follow Alexander George in tracing the historical processes that characterized the unfolding of the events of concern (George 1979; George and Bennett 1998; see also Lijphart 1971; Eckstein 1975). We identify the actors, the decision points they faced, the choices they made, the paths taken and shunned,

[14]We are of course aware that we may unwittingly be participating in a metanarrative, be it of the extension of rationality or the scientific method. Through vigilance and self-awareness, we have sought to defend against that possibility.

[15]Collier and Mahoney (1996) and King et al. (1994) define the state of the arts. See the symposium on this work in *American Political Science Review* 89 (2) (June 1995): 454–70. Przeworski and Teune (1970) endures as a major contribution to this literature, which of course extends back a century or more.

and the manner in which their choices generated events and outcomes. In the words of Richard Fenno (1990), we "soak and poke." In the phrasing of Clifford Geertz (1973), we seek "thick" description. In these ways, we respond to the call of Lawrence Stone (1979) to return to the narrative tradition or to the urging of Terrence McDonald (1996b) to take the "historic turn" in the social sciences.

But we do not stop there. In an effort to move from apprehension to explanation, we move from "thick" accounts to "thin" forms of reasoning. We seek to highlight and focus upon the logic of the processes that generate the phenomena we study. In doing so, we use rational choice theory. We find game theoretic models particularly useful ways of exploring the validity of narrative accounts. The theory is actor-centric; in extensive form, games explicitly take sequence into account and highlight its significance for outcomes. They capture the influence of history, the importance of uncertainty, and the capacity of people to manipulate and strategize, as well as the limits of their ability to do so. The structure of extensive-form games thus readily accommodates the narrative form. To distill the essential properties of a narrative, we seek to construct the game that provides the link between the prominent features of the narrative and its outcome.

A narrative possesses a background or setting, a beginning, a sequence of scenes, and an ending. The construction of an analytic narrative involves mastering the elements of the drama. Narratives fascinate, however, in part because, like dramas, they can be elusive; many possible explanations can exist, and many possible interpretations. How then are we to evaluate our accounts?

Evaluating a Narrative

Once made explicit and recast as a model, the interpretation of the narrative can be subject to skeptical appraisal. Rendering explanations explicit enables us to put them at risk. Do their assumptions correspond to what is known?[16] Do their conclusions follow from their premises? Do their implications find support in the data? How well do they stand up by comparison with other explanations? And how general is the explanation: does it apply to other, analogous cases? By compelling explanations to respond to such challenges, we gain the opportunity to evaluate them.

To illustrate from the chapters in this volume:

1. *Do the assumptions fit the facts, as they are known?* Motivated by this question, scholars might challenge Bates's assessment of the views of the Department of State; Levi's claim about the importance of fairness; Rosenthal's portrayal of the preferences of the French elite; or Weingast's account of the

---

[16]Milton Friedman (1953) has challenged this criterion. We disagree with his position.

beliefs of Southern politicians in the 1850s. Should Bates, Levi, Rosenthal, and Weingast successfully rebut such challenges, then their explanations gain greater credibility.

2. *Do conclusions follow from premises?* Addressing this question involves appraising the logic of the model. This is more easily done when the model is formalized. Note, for example, that the relationship between international threat and political cooperation can be more readily checked in Greif's exploration of the politics of Genoa clans than in Bates's examination of the ICO or in Levi's analysis of conscription. One need only check Greif's math! Because neither Bates nor Levi provides a mathematical model, their logic is less readily subject to scrutiny.

It is important to point out that the issue is not fundamentally one of mathematics, however; it is one of correct reasoning. The explanations provided by the chapters in this volume employ the reasoning of rational choice theory. To account for outcomes, game theorists seek to explore whether the choices will occur in equilibrium. Anticipating the behavior of others, would a rational actor behave in the way that generated that outcome? Would his or her expectations of the behavior of others be confirmed by their actual choices? Do the choices represent best responses, given the alternatives and information available at the time of decision? To satisfy, the logic must yield implications that are formally true but also consistent with the reasoning that underlies the theory. It is this reasoning that transforms narratives into analytic narratives.

It is important to stress that such explanations cannot be based upon theory alone. Theory is not adequate in itself. Repeated games, for example, can yield a multiplicity of equilibria.[17] To explain why one outcome occurred rather than another, the theorist must ground his or her explanation in empirical materials, seeking the forces that shaped the selection of a particular equilibrium. The existence of multiple equilibria thus compels the analyst to combine theory and empirics. Deductive theory thus becomes an engine of empirical discovery.

Explicit attention to theory strengthens explanation. An explicit appeal to the narrative is required for the completion of that explanation. In analytic narratives, the empirical content of the narrative is as important as the logical structure of the model.

3. *Do its implications find confirmation in the data?* In addressing this question, the contributors again came to recognize the role of theory as a tool for empirical discovery. For in the process of constructing explanations, they were forced to recognize the existence and importance of factors that hitherto had escaped their attention. In search of explanations consistent with cartel

---

[17]The famed folk theorem states that for a suitable rate of time preference, any outcome can be secured as a subgame-perfect equilibrium in an infinitely repeated game or in a finitely repeated game of uncertain duration (Fudenberg and Maskin 1986).

theory, Bates, for example, was compelled to recognize the significance of the long-term contracts between producers and roasting firms. To determine why nonelite landholders first preferred and then withheld support for a policy of purchased exemptions, Levi discovered the existence of complex forms of insurance against losses arising from military service in rural France and the practice of substitution in the United States. And in search of an explanation of the timing of Genoa's political reform and economic expansion, Greif gained an appreciation of the significance of the threat posed by the emperors of the Holy Roman Empire. The search for theoretically consistent explanations thus animated the process of empirical discovery.

Note that in responding to this third challenge, the authors again blur the conventional distinction between deduction and induction. They also depart from conventional notions of hypothesis testing. The authors derive implications from theory; but when the case materials do not confirm their expectations, they do not respond by rejecting their models. Rather they respond by reformulating them and by altering the way in which they think about the problem. Thus Bates moves from one form of cartel model (that of the Chicago school) to another (that of Oliver Williamson), and Greif incorporates into his model the impact of missing, foreign policy variables. As recognized by Kuhn (1962) and Lakatos (1970), the dominant response to disconfirmation is thus reformulation, not falsification.

In responding to challenge (2)—Do conclusions follow from premises?— we stressed that the theory places constraints upon the narrative; the account is constrained by the logic of the theory. In responding to challenge (3)—Do the implications of the theory find confirmation in the data?—we find the theory being shaped by the case materials. On the one hand, the response highlights once again the interplay between deduction and empiricism characteristic of analytic narratives (George and Bennett 1998). On the other, it underscores the contrast between analytic narratives and interpretation. Like all narratives, analytic narratives are grounded on empirical detail; like all narratives, they provide interpretations of the data. But being based on rigorous deductive reasoning as well as close attention to empirical detail, analytic narratives are tightly constrained. They are more vulnerable than other forms of interpretation. They are disciplined by both logic and the empirical record.

Looking back, we can see that the construction of analytic narratives is an iterative process, resembling George's method of process tracing (George 1979; George and Bennett 1998). Like George, we seek to convert "descriptive historical" accounts into "analytic ones" that are couched in "theoretically relevant" language (George and Bennett 1998:14). Like George, we move back and forth between interpretation and case materials, modifying the explanation in light of the data, which itself is viewed in new ways, given our evolving understanding. What differentiates our approach from the method of process tracing is a greater emphasis on theory.

Initially the theory is formed from the data; it is selected because it appears to offer a good fit. Rendered explicit, the theory then becomes vulnerable; it can be subject both to logical appraisal and to empirical testing. Its logic, moreover, renders it a source of new insights, leading to the gathering of new data and placing the theory at further risk. The richer the theory, the greater the number of testable implications, and thus the greater the risk of being found wanting.

In the end, we, like George, achieve a match between theory and case materials (but see below). Unlike George, we achieve that outcome in a way that renders the process not just a means of tracing but rather a means of testing. Moreover, the finished product does not just report our final account; rather it "shows our work," rendering our process more transparent and our conclusions more open to scrutiny.

We stop iterating when we have run out of testable implications. An implication of our method is that, in the last iteration, we are left uncertain; ironically perhaps, we are more certain when theories fail than when they fit the case materials.[18] To reduce further the level of uncertainty, we therefore seek further challenges and pose two additional questions.

4. *How well does the theory stand up by comparison with other explanations?* Thus far we have discussed our response to failures of prediction. But how are we to respond to models that appear to fit? The problem is troubling because several models can fit the data generated by a particular case. Charles Taylor (1985) has stressed that multiple interpretations can exist for a given observation, each internally coherent and each fitting the facts as they are known (but see Ferejohn 1991). So too has Kuhn (1957).

Selecting among theories is easier the more explicit and logically coherent they are. Explicit theories render anomalies easier to detect. As seen in chapter 5, for example, the contrast between theory and outcome, starkly highlighted because of the explicit nature of the theory, impels Bates to assess a variety of alternative theories. Thus our preference for analytic narratives, which rest upon explicit and logically rigorous models.

As already discussed, however, it is naive to believe that the answer lies in falsification. Even with explicit and logically rigorous accounts, multiple explanations will persist; as they are observationally equivalent, we will not be able to choose among them. One response is that of Greif. He offers a political-economic rather than a cultural account of cooperation in Genoa because it can account for periods of cooperation *and* discord, which, he notes, a cultural account cannot. Greif thus chooses the theory that is the more powerful.

Levi and Weingast follow an alternative strategy. Rather than arbitrating among alternatives, they instead subsume them. They endorse their explanations because of their ability to reconcile alternatives. Levi finds that standard

[18]This discussion draws heavily upon comments offered by Gary King (personal communication).

rationales for the end of "buying out"—one economic, the other political—provide only partial explanation. She therefore offers a synthetic model, in which the growth of the electorate is combined with variation in the opportunity costs of military service to account for changes in the means of military recruitment. Weingast's approach enables him to explain why traditional historians have pointed to slavery as the dominant national issue of mid-nineteenth-century U.S. politics, while the new political historians consider the issue to play but a minor role. Levi and Weingast thus respond to the existence of multiple explanations by seeking a more general explanatory framework, capable of subsuming the competing approaches.

5. *How general is the explanation? Does it apply to other cases?* This last question merits extended discussion. It is the stuff of which conclusions are made. We therefore return to it, following presentation of the chapters.

References

Abbott, Andrew. 1993. "Measure for Measure: Abell's Narrative Methods." *Journal of Mathematical Sociology* 18 (2–3): 203–14.

Abell, Peter. 1993. "Some Aspects of Narrative Method." *Journal of Mathematical Sociology* 18 (2–3): 93–134.

Aldrich, John H., and Kenneth A. Shepsle. 1997. "Explaining Institutional Change: Soaking, Poking, and Modeling in the U.S. Congress." Paper presented at a conference in honor of Richard Fenno, University of Rochester.

Almond, Gabriel. 1988. "Separate Tables: Schools and Sects in Political Science. *P.S.: Political Science and Politics* 21: 828–42.

———. 1990. *A Discipline Divided.* Newbury Park, Calif.: Sage.

Aminzade, Ronald. 1993. *Ballots and Barricades.* Princeton, N.J.: Princeton University Press.

Bailey, F. G. 1969. *Stratagems and Spoils.* Oxford: Basil Blackwell.

Baldwin, David, ed. 1993. *Neorealism and Neoliberalism: The Contemporary Debate.* New York: Columbia University Press.

Bates, Robert H. 1997. *Open-Economy Politics: The Political Economy of the World Coffee Trade.* Princeton, N.J.: Princeton University Press.

Cameron, David R. 1978. "The Expansion of the Public Economy: A Comparative Analysis." *American Political Science Review* 72: 143–61.

Collier, David, and James Mahoney. 1996. "Insights and Pitfalls: Selection Bias in Qualitative Research." *World Politics* 94 (2): 56–91.

Colson, Elizabeth. 1974. *Tradition and Contract.* Chicago: Aldine.

Danto, Arthur. 1985. *Narratives and Knowledge.* New York: Columbia University Press.

Deutsch, Karl. 1957. *Political Community and the North Atlantic Area.* Princeton, N.J.: Princeton University Press.

Dixit, Avinash, and Barry Nailbuff. 1991. *Thinking Strategically.* New York: Norton.

Doyle, Michael W. 1983. "Kant, Liberal Legacies, and Foreign Affairs," Parts 1 and 2. *Philosophy and Public Affairs* 12: 205–54, 323–53.

Dray, William. 1964. "Conflicting Interpretations in History: The Case of the English Civil War." In *Hermeneutics: Questions and Prospects,* edited by Gary Shapiro and Alan Sica. Amherst: University of Massachusetts Press.

Eckstein, Harry. 1975. "Case Study and Theory in Political Science." In *Handbook of Political Science,* vol. 7, edited by Fred I. Greenstein and Nelson W. Polsby. Reading, Mass.: Addison-Wesley.

Elman, Colin, and Miriam Fendius Elman, eds. 1997. "Symposium on Diplomatic History and International Relations." *International Security* 22 (1): 3–85.

Evans, Peter, Harold Jacobson, and Robert Putnam, eds. 1993. *Double Edged Diplomacy: International Bargaining and Domestic Politics.* Berkeley: University of California Press.

Fenno, Richard. 1990. *Watching Politicians: Essays on Participant Observation.* Berkeley: Institute of Governmental Studies, University of California.

Ferejohn, John. 1991. "Rationality and Interpretation: Parliamentary Elections in Early Stuart England." In *The Economic Approach to Politics,* edited by Kristin Monroe. New York: HarperCollins.

Ferguson, Niall, ed. 1996. *Virtual History.* London: Picador.

Findlay, Ronald. 1991. "The New Political Economy: Its Explanatory Power for LDCs." In *Politics and Policy Making in Developing Countries,* edited by G. M. Meier. San Francisco: International Center for Economic Growth.

Fishlow, Albert, Catherine Gwin, Stephan Haggard, Dani Rodrik, and Robert Wade. 1994. *Miracle or Design: Lessons from the East Asian Experience.* Washington, D.C.: Overseas Development Council.

Fogel, Robert, and G. R. Elton. 1983. *Which Road to the Past.* New Haven, Conn.: Yale University Press.

Friedman, Milton. 1953. "The Methodology of Positive Economics." In his *Essays on Positive Economics.* Chicago: University of Chicago Press.

Fry, Brian, Eugene Ol Golob, and Richard Vann, eds. 1989. *Louis O. Mink: Historical Understanding.* Ithaca, N.Y.: Cornell University Press.

Fudenberg, Drew, and Eric Maskin. 1986. "The Folk Theorem in Repeated Games with Discounting or with Incomplete Information." *Econometrica* 54: 533–54.

Gates, Scott, and Brian Humes. 1997. *Games, Information, and Politics.* Ann Arbor: University of Michigan Press.

Geertz, Clifford. 1973. *Interpretation of Cultures.* New York: Basic Books.

George, Alexander L. 1979. "Case Studies and Theory Development: The Method of Structured, Focused Comparisons." In *Diplomacy: New Approaches in History, Theory and Policy,* edited by Paul Gordon Lauren. New York: Free Press.

George, Alexander L., and Andrew Bennett. 1998. *Case Study and Theory Development.* Cambridge, Mass.: MIT Press.

Gibbons, Robert. 1992. *Game Theory for Applied Economists.* Princeton, N.J.: Princeton University Press.

Gluckman, Max. 1965. *Politics, Law and Ritual in Tribal Societies.* Oxford: Basil Blackwell.

Goldthorpe, John H. 1991. "The Uses of History in Sociology." *British Journal of Sociology* 42 (2): 220–52.

———. 1996. "The Integration of Sociological Research and Theory." Paper presented at the ICS International Conference, University of Groningen, June.

Gourevitch, Peter. 1978. "The Second Image Reversed: The International Sources of Domestic Politics." *International Organization* 32 (4): 881–913.

Gowa, Joanne. 1994. *Allies, Adversaries, and International Trade.* Princeton, N.J.: Princeton University Press.

Gowa, Joanne, and Henry Farber. 1995. "Politics and Peace." *International Security* 20: 13–46.

Green, Donald P., and Ian Shapiro. 1994. *Pathologies of Rational Choice Theory.* New Haven, Conn.: Yale University Press.

Hall, Peter A., and Rosemary C. R. Taylor. 1996. "Political Science and the Three New Institutionalisms." *Political Studies* 44 (5): 936–57.

Harris, John, Janet Hunter, and Colin M. Lewis, eds. 1991. *The New Institutional Economics and Third World Development.* London: Routledge.

Hempel, Carl G. 1965. *Aspects of Scientific Explanation.* New York: Free Press.

Hinich, Melvin J., and Michael C. Munger. 1997. *Analytic Politics.* Cambridge: Cambridge University Press.

Hoffman, Philip. 1988. "Institutions and Agriculture in Old Regime France." *Politics and Society* 61 (2–3): 241–64.

Huber, John D. 1996. *Rationalizing Parliament.* Cambridge: Cambridge University Press.

Huntington, Samuel P. 1968. *Political Order in Changing Societies.* New Haven, Conn.: Yale University Press.

Katzenstein, Peter J. 1985. *Small States in World Markets.* Ithaca, N.Y.: Cornell University Press.

Keohane, Robert. 1984. *After Hegemony.* Princeton, N.J.: Princeton University Press.

Kiewiet, D. Roderick, and Mathew D. McCubbins. 1991. *The Logic of Delegation.* Chicago: University of Chicago Press.

King, Gary, Robert Keohane, and Sidney Verba. 1994. *Designing Social Inquiry.* Princeton, N.J.: Princeton University Press.

Kiser, Edgar. 1996. "The Revival of Narrative in Historical Sociology: What Rational Choice Can Contribute." *Politics and Society* 24 (3): 249–72.

Krasner, Stephen D., ed. 1982. *International Regimes.* Ithaca, N.Y.: Cornell University Press.

Krehbiel, Keith. 1991. *Information and Legislative Organization.* Ann Arbor: University of Michigan Press.

Kuhn, Thomas. 1957. *The Copernican Revolution: Planetary Astronomy in the Development of Western Thought.* Cambridge, Mass.: Harvard University Press.

———. 1962. *The Structure of Scientific Revolutions.* Chicago: University of Chicago Press.

Lakatos, Imre. 1970. "Falsification in the Methodology of Scientific Research Programs." In *Criticism and the Growth of Knowledge,* edited by Imre Lakatos and Alan Musgrave. Cambridge: Cambridge University Press.

Lefebre, Georges. 1924. *Les Payasans du Nord Pendant la Révolution Française.* Paris: Rieder.

Levy, Jack. 1997. "Too Important to Leave to the Other: History and Political Science in the Study of International Relations." *International Security* 22 (1): 22–34.

Lijphart, Arend. 1971. "Comparative Politics and the Comparative Method." *American Political Science Review* 65 (3): 622–93.

Lipset, Seymour Martin. 1963. *The First New Nation.* New York: Basic Books.

Lustick, Ian. 1996. "History, Historiography, and Political Science." *American Political Science Review* 90 (3): 605–18.

McClosky, Donald. 1990. "History, Differential Equations, and the Problem of Narration." *History and Theory* 30 (1): 21–36.

McDonald, Terrence J. 1996a. "Introduction." In *The Historic Turn in the Social Sciences,* edited by Terrence J. McDonald. Ann Arbor: University of Michigan Press.

———, ed. 1996b. *The Historic Turn in the Human Sciences.* Ann Arbor: University of Michigan Press.

Maoz, Zeev. 1997. "The Controversies over Democratic Peace." *International Security* 22 (1): 162–98.

Meier, Gerald M., ed. 1991. *Politics and Policy Making in Developing Countries.* San Francisco: International Center for Economic Growth.

Milgrom, Paul, and John Roberts. 1992. *Economics, Organization and Management.* Englewood Cliffs, N.J.: Prentice Hall.

North, Douglass C. 1981. *Structure and Change in Economic Life.* New York: Norton.

———. 1990. *Institutions, Institutional Change, and Economic Performance.* Cambridge: Cambridge University Press.

Ortner, Sherry B. 1996. "Resistance and the Problem of Ethnographic Refusal." In *The Historic Turn in the Human Sciences,* edited by Terrence J. McDonald. Ann Arbor: University of Michigan Press.

Ostrom, Elinor. 1990. *Governing the Commons.* Cambridge: Cambridge University Press.

Przeworksi, Adam. 1985. *Capitalism and Social Democracy.* Cambridge: Cambridge University Press.

Przeworski, Adam, and Henry Teune. 1970. *The Logic of Comparative Social Inquiry.* New York: Wiley-Interscience.

Putnam, Robert. 1988. "Diplomacy and Domestic Politics: The Logic of Two-Level Games." *International Organization* 42: 427–60.

Rasmusen, Eric. 1989. *Games and Information.* Oxford: Basil Blackwell.

Riker, William H. 1962. *The Theory of Political Coalitions.* New Haven, Conn.: Yale University Press.

———. 1964. *Federalism.* Boston: Little, Brown.

Roemer, John. 1986. *Analytical Marxism.* Cambridge: Cambridge University Press.

Root, Hilton. 1994. *Fountain of Privilege.* Berkeley: University of California Press.

Rosenthal, Jean-Laurent. 1992. *The Fruits of Revolution.* Cambridge: Cambridge University Press.

Russett, Bruce. 1993. *Grasping the Democratic Peace.* Princeton, N.J.: Princeton University Press.

Schotter, Andrew. 1981. *The Economic Theory of Social Institutions.* Cambridge: Cambridge University Press.

Shepsle, Kenneth A. 1979. "Institutional Arrangements and Equilibrium in Multidimensional Voting Models." *American Journal of Political Science* 23: 27–59.

Skocpol, Theda. 1979. *States and Social Revolutions.* Cambridge: Cambridge University Press.

Spiro, David E. 1994. "The Insignificance of the Liberal Peace." *International Security* 19 (2): 50–86.

Stinchcombe, Arthur. 1963. *Constructing Social Theories.* New York: Harcourt Brace and World.

Stone, Lawrence. 1979. "The Revival of Narrative." *Past and Present* 85: 3–24.

Taylor, Charles. 1985. *Philosophy and the Human Sciences.* Cambridge: Cambridge University Press.

Tetlock, Philip, and Aaron Belkin. 1996. "Counterfactual Thought Experiments in World Politics." In *Counterfactual Thought Experiments in World Politics,* edited by Philip Tetlock and Aaron Belkin. Princeton, N.J.: Princeton University Press.

Thucydides. 1951. *History of the Peloponnesian War,* translated by John H. Finley, Jr. New York: Modern Library.

Tirole, Jean. 1988. *The Theory of Industrial Organization.* Cambridge, Mass.: MIT Press.

Trevelyan, Macaulay George. 1938. *The English Revolution.* London: Oxford University Press.

Trimberger, Kay Ellen. 1972. "A Theory of Elite Revolutions." *Studies in Comparative International Development* 7: 191–207.

Van Damme, Eric. 1987. *Stability and Perfection of Equilibria.* Heidelberg: Springer-Verlag.

Wallerstein, Immanuel. 1974. *Capitalist Agriculture and the Origins of the European World Economy.* New York: Academic Press.

———. 1987. *The Content and the Form.* Baltimore: Johns Hopkins University Press.

Williamson, Oliver. 1985. *The Economic Institutions of Capitalism.* New York: Free Press.

World Bank. 1993. *The East Asian Miracle.* New York: Oxford University Press.

———. 1997. *World Development Report: The State in a Changing World.* New York: Oxford University Press.

One

Self-Enforcing Political Systems and Economic Growth: Late Medieval Genoa

AVNER GREIF

THIS CHAPTER analyzes the political institutions of the commune of Genoa during the late medieval period. By the end of the thirteenth century, Genoa stood second, perhaps, only to Venice among the Italian maritime cities in terms of wealth and power. In seeking a better understanding of the rise of Genoa, the chapter addresses several broader themes, most notably the process of state formation, the determinants of political and economic performance, and the politics of resource mobilization and of goal attainment by political communities. Mobilizing theoretical argument and empirical evidence, the chapter seeks to cut more deeply still, to explore the factors that rendered Genoa's political institutions self-enforcing. By exposing these factors, the chapter identifies the conditions under which political actors follow the rules that govern the political order, rather than ignoring them or resorting to other means, such as violence. It determines as well the conditions under which the rules will change, leading to the rise—or collapse—of the political system.

A key finding of this chapter is that the degree to which Genoa's political system was self-enforcing depended on the degree to which its economic system generated appropriate political incentives. In the early period of Genoa's rise, economic growth would have eroded, rather than enhanced, the economic foundation for its maintenance. It was only after a long period of learning and experimentation, and because of particular historical circumstances, that the Genoese altered their political system and introduced a political innovation

I gratefully acknowledge the support of the National Science Foundation (grants 9009598-01 and 9223974) and the Center for Institutional Reform and the Informal Sector at the University of Maryland at College Park. I have benefited from the comments of James Alt, Masa Aoki, Robert Bates, Margaret Levi, Paul Milgrom, Boaz Moselle, Jean-Laurent Rosenthal, Barry Weingast, and participants in a joint Harvard-MIT economic history–development seminar, an all-department seminar at Tel Aviv University, an all-department seminar at Northwestern University, and the Social Science History Workshop at Stanford University. Some of the ideas expressed in this paper were formulated while I was a fellow at the Center for Advanced Study in the Behavioral Sciences, Stanford, California; the Center's kind hospitality greatly facilitated this study. As always, Debbie Johnston provided effective and indispensable assistance.

that enabled them to render political stability consistent with strong economic growth.[1]

The particular historical period examined in this chapter is of interest to economists and political scientists in and of itself. During and after the twelfth century, the economic development of the northern Italian cities was of such magnitude that it had a lasting impact on the economic development of Europe as a whole. This economic ascendancy was accompanied by political events that were extraordinary in a world characterized by a feudal political system. The residents of northern Italy voluntary established, organized, and governed city-republics, also known as communes. In the process, some maritime cities, notably Venice and Genoa, emerged as the main commercial centers linking Europe and the more advanced civilizations of Byzantium, the Muslim world, and the Far East, in the process taking their place among Europe's largest cities.

Yet neither the manner in which these political units became self-enforcing, nor the interrelations between these endogenous political systems and economic changes, have been explored by political scientists or economic historians.[2] In particular, the Italian communes have been viewed as manifestations of the economic needs of their merchants. As the eminent historian of the Commercial Revolution Robert Sabatino Lopez, has asserted, "the Italian communes were essentially governments of the merchants, by the merchants, for the merchants—an ideal platform for the Commercial Revolution" (Lopez 1976:71). Similarly, students of the relations between institutions and growth did not explore the relations between self-enforcing political systems and economic development. North and Thomas (1973:11), for example, stated that early on in the medieval period feudal lords "fought amongst themselves; but gradually, . . . the strife declined." Peace enabled population growth and the realization of gains from "commerce between different parts of Europe" that "had always been potentially of mutual benefit" (p. 11).

Indeed, if one examines the commune of Genoa, its early days are marked by internal tranquility. It had been established around 1096, headed by elected consuls, and until 1164 there were no internal military conflicts. Yet the extent to which this history supports the view that the Genoese commune was an expression of the economic needs of its members is controversial, and historians of Genoa are divided on this matter. Some have argued that the internal tranquility prior to 1164 indicates that the commune was a political manifestation of Genoa's mercantile community. Hence, as conjectured by Lopez, the lack of an "exogenous" benevolent ruler and the reliance on a self-enforcing political system did not constrain economic growth by limiting

---

[1]For a more detailed exposition of the historical and theoretical issues discussed in this chapter, see Greif (1999). For a recent first-rate account of Genoa's general history, see Epstein (1996).

[2]However, such political historians as Vitale (1955), Lane (1973), and Tabacco (1989) have narrated the political and economic development of various cities.

intracommune cooperation. Other historians, however, have noted that during this time Genoa's prominent merchants were nobles, members of the same clans that were at the center of the bitter civil wars that were frequent from 1164 to 1194. They have conjectured that although we have no record of conflicts, interclan antagonism prevailed even before the outbreak of the civil war, implying that Genoa's self-enforcing political system may have hindered economic development by restricting political cooperation between the large clans that dominated Genoa's politics and economics (for a recent statement, see Day 1988). In other words, there is disagreement regarding the extent to which the commune's self-enforcing political system constrained growth, and there is a lack of understanding of the reasons for the breakdown of political order. Although there is an agreement regarding the historical facts, there is disagreement regarding their meaning.

Similar disagreement also exists with respect to the interrelations between economic and political factors following the civil wars. In 1194 Genoa abolished the consulate and instituted an alternative political system, the *podesteria*. At the center of this political system was a *podestà*: a non-Genoese hired by the city to be its military leader, judge, and administrator for a relatively short period of time, usually a year. Under the *podesteria* Genoa enjoyed a long period of relative political stability and rapid economic growth. Political historians have debated how the *podestà* was able to pacify and unite Genoa (compare with Vitale 1951:9; Heers 1977:206). Vito Vitale, Genoa's eminent historian, argued that the *podestà* was merely an administrator and that his institutionalization reflects the need for professional administration and the desire to limit competition over consular posts. Internal tranquility under the *podesteria* was sustained by the gains from cooperation. Yet if this was the case, why were these gains insufficient to guarantee cooperation under the consulate? Why was there a need to alter the political system to foster cooperation? Other scholars consider the *podestà*'s military ability a key to enabling cooperation, since he was able to impose peace on Genoa's rival clans. Yet if this was so, why did the *podestà* not become a dictator? Once again, although the historical facts are not in dispute, their interpretation is.

Narrative alone has been insufficient to comprehend the interrelations between economics and politics in Genoa's case. One cannot infer from the internal tranquility that prevailed from 1096 to 1164 whether or not interclan economic cooperation had been achieved. The absence of civil wars can signal either cooperation or mutual deterrence, in which neither clan finds it beneficial to attack the other. Behavior does not help us answer the following questions: Was the Genoese commune, as conjectured by Lopez, a self-enforcing response to the needs of trade? Or was Genoa's ability to advance its economy constrained by the extent to which intracommune political order was self-enforcing? Similarly, the historical narrative does not indicate the role of the organizational innovation of 1194—the *podesteria*—in facilitating cooperation. Could peace have been achieved without a *podestà,* as conjectured by Vitale? What was the role of the *podestà* in enhancing the extent to which Genoa was a self-enforcing political unit? How did the *podesteria* itself became a self-enforcing political system?

Narrative cannot answer these questions since they relate to events that *did not* occur and the motivation for *not* behaving in a particular way. Addressing these questions requires an appropriate model for linking what we observe with what we do not observe, namely analyzing the relations between expectations regarding off-the-path-of-play behavior and on-the-path-of-play outcomes. The model developed in this chapter enables us to consider these issues by providing a framework for the empirical analysis of the factors determining the extent to which Genoa's political system was self-enforcing.

The following section narrates the relevant historical background. The next section provides the foundations for the appropriate theoretical framework. This framework is then extended to examine the political and economic history of Genoa, discussing how economic factors, the clans' military strength, and the international environment provided the foundations for Genoa's self-enforcing political system. The final section examines, theoretically and historically, the role of the *podesteria* as a self-enforcing political organization that provided yet another foundation for Genoa's political system, thereby altering the city's course of political and economic history.

Narrative: Potential Economic Gains and Interclan Political Cooperation

During and after the second half of the eleventh century, several northern Italian cities became major emporiums whose traders bought and sold goods throughout the Mediterranean. The large political units whose navies had previously dominated the sea either collapsed or declined, and this political transformation enabled these cities to benefit from piracy, raids, and long-distance commerce (e.g., Lewis 1951). Yet history indicates that the key to an Italian maritime city's long-term economic growth was commercial expansion. Such expansion, in turn, was fostered by political exchange through which overseas possessions (commercial privileges in foreign territory) were acquired. In such an exchange, one political unit provided another with possessions in return for an alliance guaranteeing naval and military protection or neutrality. To illustrate the nature of political exchange and possessions, consider the relations between Genoa, the Crusaders, and Saladin (the ruler of Egypt who confronted the Crusaders). In return for past and promised future assistance to the Crusaders, the Genoese received between 1098 and 1110 the right to trade freely within the Crusaders' states without paying a tax, plus storehouses, churches, residential buildings, ports (or parts thereof), castles, and extensive plots of land in various trade centers (for discussion see Heyd 1885:1:149–50; Byrne 1920, 1928; Day 1984). In 1167 and 1170, the Pisans assisted the Crusaders in attacking Egypt in return for possessions in Tyre and promises of possessions in the captured area of Egypt. In 1170 Saladin gained control over Egypt after fighting against the Crusaders and, rather than retaliating against the Italians, he granted, first to Pisa and then to Genoa and Venice, various possessions, including the right of free trade and security throughout Egypt and additional trade privileges in Alexandria, Egypt's main Mediterranean port (*Annali* 1177, vol. 2; for discussion see Heywood 1921:111–13; Day 1984).

The commercial importance of various Italian cities rose and fell depending on their possessions, since possessions substantially reduced the risk and cost of commerce, enabling their holders to crowd out unprivileged traders (e.g., Hicks 1969:49–50). For example, a watershed in Venetian commercial history was a grant from Byzantium rewarding Venice for its naval assistance against the Normans by providing Venetian traders unlimited freedom of trade throughout Byzantium, release from any taxes and customs duties, and the right to possess shops, warehouses, and a landing stage in Constantinople (e.g., Norwich 1989:73). Genoa's trade in North Africa began to prosper after 1161, when the local ruler signed a fifteen-year agreement securing the property rights of the Genoese merchants. Before 1160, the annual volume of trade with North Africa never exceeded 500 lire, but it more than doubled on the eve of this agreement and remained at the higher level in later years (*Annali* 1161:1:84; *Giovanni Scriba* 1154–64; for discussion see Krueger 1932, 1933).

Hence, to expand its commerce, Genoa had to mobilize the resources required for the naval and military apparatus that would enable it to raid and acquire possessions. The Holy Roman Empire, which controlled Genoa de jure, was too fragmented at the time to rule it de facto. It did not assist the Genoese in acquiring possessions; instead, Genoa's residents had to cooperate and to mobilize their own resources. Indeed, the historical records indicate the importance of economic gains in motivating the Genoese to organize themselves politically (see discussion in Greif forthcoming).

After 1099 Genoa's political, administrative, and military leaders were four to eight *consoli del comune* (communal consuls; henceforth, consuls) who were "publicly elected in *parlamentum*," the gathering of all Genoese with "full rights" (CDG, vol. 1, no. 285).[3] The historical sources do not provide any further explicit information regarding the consuls' election process. Implicit evidence, however, indicates that the elected consuls were representatives of the Genoese clans that cooperated through the consulate, that is, those clans whose resources the commune of Genoa was able to mobilize (Hughes 1978:108–10). The consulate—like Genoa itself—was a manifestation of interclan cooperation.

[3]For the development of the Genoese consulate see Vitale (1955), Pertile (1966), and de Negri (1986). The earliest consuls'oath is from 1143 (CDG vol. 1, no. 128).

Genoa's main clans were feudal landholders who, after forming the communes, sought to be involved in any (potentially) profitable activity possible at the time. They supplied the commune with its admirals, Crusaders, raiders, largest landholders, and most prosperous merchants. Clans became the basic unit of Genoa's social and political organization during the years of weak central authority preceding the establishment of the commune (e.g., Herlihy 1969). Arguably, two specific clans, the Maneciano and Carmadino viscountal clans, were the most important in Genoa in the early days of the commune.[4] These clans' centrality in Genoa's political and economic life is reflected, for example, in their relative share in the consulate. From 1099 to 1164, members of 61 families served on the consulate, but the Carmadinos and the Manecianos held 59 of 282 consular posts, or 20.9 percent (*Annali* 1154–64, vols. 1 and 2; Olivieri 1861). In the two main periods before 1170 during which Genoa obtained possessions, circa the First Crusade and from 1154 to 1162, members of both clans served on the consulate and were very active in obtaining possessions.

The importance of the Manecianos and Carmadinos seems to have its roots in the days of their ancestor, Ido, who was a viscount in Genoa under the old Carolingian administrative system. Although by the end of the eleventh century imperial control was nowhere to be found in Genoa, the viscountal clans kept various economic feudal rights in Genoa. Hence they had the military ability and economic resources required for raids and the acquisition of possessions. The extent of their combined resources and the nature of interclan cooperation were evident in 1154, when the commune was practically bankrupt. The four consuls, of whom one was a Maneciano and another a Carmadino, built war galleys to protect Genoa's commercial activity and spent more than 15,000 lire to pay the commune's debt (*Annali* 1154:1:48).

These clans' expenses on the behalf of the commune—their willingness to mobilize their resources on behalf of the commune—were not necessarily an uncalculated investment, since for each of Genoa's main clans the commune was a means for advancing its own political and economic interests.[5] Vitale (1955), in his classic study of the Genoese commune, has noted that the consuls expropriated income from Genoa's possessions. The consuls appointed holders for many lucrative positions, in particular granting licenses for tax collecting and overseas administration, and this power enabled them to favor their kin and friends (Vitale 1955:29–30; see also Lopez 1938:129–30). Probably more important, participation in the consulate enabled a clan to establish special relations with rulers of other political units, which implied political and economic benefits (CDG, vol. 1, nos. 27, 128, and 144; see also Abulafia 1977:62–64;

---

[4]For their genealogy, see Belgrano (1873). Byrne (1920:200–201), Cardini (1978), and Day (1988:74) recognized their political importance.

[5]As noted by Day (1988:128), "for the great men of the twelfth century commune of Genoa, the government [was] little more than a businessmen's consortium."

Day 1988). These benefits were bestowed by rulers of other political units to influence Genoa's political process in their favor.[6]

That each of Genoa's main clans used the consulate to advance its own interests implies a conflict of interest. Income expropriated by one clan could not be expropriated by another, and policy that advanced one clan's interest could harm another. Indeed, the historical records provide more direct evidence for the existence of such conflict and the clans' willingness to resort to the sword to resolve contentions. The Carmadinos and Manecianos, were (as discussed later in this chapter) at the center—although on opposite sides—of Genoa's two principal civil wars of the twelfth century, from 1164 to 1169 and from 1189 to 1194. A twelfth-century chronicler observed that these wars were fought over political control: Civil discords and hateful conspiracies and divisions had risen in the city on account of the mutual envy of the many men who greatly wished to hold office as consuls of the commune" (*Annali* 1190:2:219–20).

Despite the conflicting objectives of Genoa's main clans, the mere establishment of the commune suggests that, at least in its early days, cooperation had been necessary to advance a clan's interests. Indeed, in the early days of the commune no Genoese clan conducted large-scale raids or obtained overseas possessions by itself, and (as discussed at length later in this chapter) Genoa acquired possessions when members of the Carmadino and the Maneciano clans served jointly on the consulate. It seems that these clans could have gained a great deal from cooperation. Yet their members were men of arms at least to the same extent they were merchants, and there was no state to provide Genoa's clans with political order. Each clan could have used its military ability to gain political dominance in Genoa rather than to advance the city's economy.

Did the need of the Genoese clans to ensure that their political system would be self-enforcing—that no clan would resort to violence against the others, attempting to gain control over the city and its resources—affect political and economic outcomes? In other words, what were the factors fostering or diminishing each clan's motivation to maintain political order and to cooperate in advancing Genoa's economy rather than using military force against the other clans to gain political supremacy over the city? What were the economic and political implications, if any, of the need to ensure that the Genoese commune would be self-enforcing?

A narrative of the political and economic history of Genoa from 1099 and 1162 would not suggest that the need to bring about political order among Genoa's main clans affected the city's politics or economics. During this time, no civil war or major violent political confrontation occurred in Genoa. The observed consulate holdings do not shed much light on this issue either. Table 1.1, which presents a detailed listing of consulate holdings over this time, indicates that members of both clans participated in the political life of the city.

[6]See, for example, Day (1988) for the relations between the Guertius clan and Byzantium.

TABLE 1.1
Rank Order of Families and Clans That Provided at Least 50 percent of Genoese Consuls

Family or *Clan*	1099–1122	1123–49	1154–64
Rustico	2		
Platealonga	3		
Rufus	4		
Roza	5		
Pedicula	6		
Maneciano	1		2
Della Volta		2	1
Carmadino		1	3
Guertius			4
Caschifellone		3	
Mallonus		4	
Gontardus		5	
Bellamutus		6	
Number of consuls	102	111	53

Source: Annali (various years); Olivieri (1861).

Notes: See the text for the reasons that these periods were chosen. If the period 1123–49 were extended to 1153, the list would have also included the Platealonga family. There were 127 consuls during that time, and the rank order is Carmadino, della Volta, Caschifellone, Mallonus, Platealonga, Gontardus, and Bellamutus.

Furthermore, between 1099 and 1164, both the Carmadinos and the Manecianos held prominent roles in the consulate, although not necessarily at the same time. That different factions peacefully gained a dominant role in the consulate at different periods necessarily implies neither political confrontation nor lack of cooperation in advancing Genoa's economy.

Thus, evaluating whether the need to ensure that Genoa's political system would be self-enforcing affected the city's politics and economics prior to 1164 (when political order prevailed) requires resorting to theory able to guide an empirical analysis.

The Economics of Interclan Cooperation: Theory

Each of Genoa's main clans, the Carmadinos and the Manecianos, could have decided the extent of their cooperation in raiding and the acquisition of possessions. At the same time, each could have also initiated a costly military confrontation with the other to gain supremacy over the commune and its expropriatable income. This situation may be depicted as a repetitive, complete information game. (The presentation here is intuitive. For a formal presentation see Greif forthcoming.) The model's specification ignores interperiod considerations and asymmetric information but generates robust, interperiod predictions, enabling an empirical analysis.

The model presented in this section analyzes the characteristics of the set of mutual deterrence (subgame perfect) equilibria (MDEs). (MDEs differ in their distributions.) In such equilibria, interclan military confrontation does not occur; the clans cooperate in raiding and divide the gains from current raids and the possessions they have acquired in the past. Concentration on these equilibria is motivated by two considerations. First, the peace that prevailed until 1164 indicates that each clan was indeed deterred from militarily challenging the others. Second, since interclan war is costly, refraining from military confrontation is economically efficient. Furthermore, since obtaining possessions was efficient, studying whether the need for the Genoese commune to be self-enforcing affected its economy is to examine whether this need constrained cooperation in reaching an MDE with the efficient number of possessions.

Examining whether Genoa's self-enforcing political system reached an MDE with the efficient number of possessions requires analyzing the clans' incentives to cooperate in the acquisition of possessions. For simplicity, the analysis first examines the MDE for a *given* number of possessions; only then is it extended to allow the number of possessions to be determined endogenously. This approach reveals the distinct political and economic characteristics of efficient and inefficient MDE, enabling us to compare the insights gained from the theoretical analysis with the historical evidence.

Model: MDE When the Number of Possessions Is Exogenous

There are two clans, each of whom can decide, during each period, whether to cooperate with the other in conducting a raid and how much of its resources to invest in military strength. (All decisions within a period are made simultaneously unless otherwise noted.) Considering investment in military strength by building fortifications, soliciting military and political assistance from nonclan Genoese is appropriate in this historical episode.[7] After all, an exchange of military support for material benefits was an essential part of the feudal world in which twelfth-century Genoa was embedded. The strength of the Carmadino and Maneciano viscountal clans themselves was a product of such an exchange between their ancestors and the emperor.

A clan's ability to recruit supporters is limited by its resources, consisting of the clan's share in the income from the existing stock of possessions and raids if any, that have been jointly conducted during that period. Note that at this point the analysis assumes that the number of possessions is constant and exogenous. Similarly, the clans' shares in the income are assumed to

---

[7]Hiring outside retainers was not an option (see Munz 1969, p. 299).

be constant and exogenous. The historical records do not provide any clue regarding the process through which the clans' shares were determined. Hence the analysis conducted herein is restricted to that appropriate for any allocation of income.

After investing resources in military strength (henceforth equated, for simplicity, with recruiting supporters), each clan can decide (sequentially) whether or not to challenge the other clan militarily. A clan that has decided to challenge can recruit additional supporters prior to the war. No additional supporters can be recruited once the war has begun. If neither clan challenges, the situation described previously repeats itself. If either clan challenges, an interclan war transpires. The war is costly to each side, and a clan's probability of winning the war depends on its relative military strength: this probability is nondecreasing in the clan's military strength and nonincreasing in the other clan's military strength. A clan that wins an interclan war becomes a "controlling" clan, retaining all the income generated from possessions in each of the subsequent periods.[8]

Note how the assumptions above capture the distinct natures of and the relationship between possessions and cooperation in raids. Raiding can be conducted in every period, and it yields booty only during the period in which it is taken. However, a possession, once it has been acquired, generates income in each subsequent period irrespective of whether the clans cooperated in that period. The reason for this specification is that, after possessions have been acquired, they provide a clan with the resources needed to retain them.[9]

Once a clan acquired the position of controlling clan, Genoa might be subject to an external threat. Such threats were an important element in Genoa's historical reality. In particular, during the second half of the twelfth century, Genoa's autonomy was threatened by the ambitions of the Emperor Frederick I (Barbarossa), who aspired to reimpose his empire's control over Lombardy. Although such a threat could have, and indeed had, transpired prior to interclan conflict, interclan war within Genoa weakened the ability of the Genoese as a whole to deter and confront such threats. Accordingly, and to direct the theoretical analysis toward insights that are empirically relevant, it is assumed that prior to an interclan war, external threat would not transpire. Following an interclan war, however, external threat can transpire, and the controlling clan can militarily confront it, although its military strength is limited by the budget constraint.

---

[8]Allowing a clan to surrender would not alter the analysis. Adding direct benefit from political control to a clan's payoff does not qualitatively alter the analysis. For a model of an arms race see Powell (1993).

[9]Indeed, the Embriachi family of the Maneciano clan was able to send only two galleys on a private expedition in the First Crusade. However, its members were able to gain de facto control over many of Genoa's possessions in the Crusader States and became independent lords toward the end of the twelfth century.

The probability of a controlling clan's war against an external threat increases with the *absolute* military strength of the external threat (e.g., the size of the army Barbarossa was able to recruit) and decreases with the *relative* military strength of the controlling clan (namely, its military strength relative to that of Barbarossa). Similarly, if a war actually occurred, the probability that the controlling clan would win would decrease with the threat's absolute military strength and increase with the clan's relative strength. War against the external threat is costly, and defeat implies a zero-continuation payoff to the controlling clan. If a war did not occur or was won, the game proceeds as before.

If a clan neither challenges or is challenged, its per-period payoff equals the income from possessions and raids minus the expenditure on military strength. On the other hand, if the clan challenges, it incurs the cost of war but can gain (with a probability depending on its military strength relative to that of the other clan) control over the future stream of income from possessions.[10] More precisely, its gains are equal to the net present value of a controlling clan, which increases with the number of possessions but decreases with the extent of the external threat. If the number of supporters of one clan is such that the other clan's net expected gain from challenging is less than the expected gain from not challenging, it can be said that the latter clan is deterred from challenging.

A mutual deterrence (subgame perfect) equilibrium, in which neither clan challenges, exists if and only if the following condition (henceforth, condition 1) is satisfied. Each clan invests in military strength the amount that (1) maximizes its net expected value if no clan challenges (given the other clan's military strength) and (2) is required to deter the other clan from challenging for any investment in military strength that that clan can make.

Model: The Efficiency Attributes of MDE When the Number of Possessions Is Endogenous

To understand the implications of condition 1 for the incentives to acquire possessions, the relations between possessions and raids should be made explicit. Assume that there is some finite number, T^*, of possible possessions and that possessions and raids are substitutes in the sense that once a possession is acquired in a specific principality, the Genoese cannot raid it without losing the possession. Indeed, this tradeoff between raids and possessions was inherent in the nature of the political exchange through which possessions were acquired.[11]

---

[10]The analysis assumes that, following interclan confrontation, the clans can no longer cooperate in raids, but it does not qualitatively depend on this assumption.

[11]Indeed, in 1193, in retaliation for attacks by the Genoese pirate Guglielmo Grasso, the Byzantine emperor revoked all of Genoa's privileges (CDG, vol. 3, no. 35; Day 1988:109–11). The inability of one clan to raid after possessions were acquired (even if this clan lost a civil war)

Since having possessions was efficient, assume that there is a positive number of possessions, τ, that maximizes the (gross) income from possessions and raids. Hence, if the number of possessions is lower than that number, the total income from possessions and raids increases with the number of possessions, but the income from raids decreases with the number of possessions. Note that this specification identifies possessions with economic development that yields expropriatable income and decreases the present value of future interclan cooperation in raids.

The analysis can now be extended to examine the number of possessions in the acquisition of which both clans would find it optimal to cooperate, in other words, to examine the extent of possible mobilization of resources. The analysis addresses the following question: does the efficient MDE also maximize the clans' incomes? If the answer to this question is affirmative, it can be concluded (at least from this static point of view) that the need to sustain Genoa's self-enforcing political system did not theoretically entail economic cost.[12] If the answer to this question is negative, however, it can be concluded that theoretically, the need to sustain Genoa's self-enforcing political system hindered economic efficiency, since the clans would not cooperate in achieving the efficient MDE. If this is the case, we can also use the model to identify the exact sources of this inefficiency.

Addressing these questions requires examining when an MDE implies a positive number of supporters. Condition 1 reveals the equilibrium relations between the number of possessions and the clans' endogenous military strength. When there are no possessions, condition 1 holds for any parameter sets, because challenging implies no gains but entails the cost of war and the loss of future gains from cooperation in raids. Hence, in the absence of possessions, sufficiently patient clans would neither militarily recruit supporters nor challenge each other. As the number of possessions increases, however, deterrence may or may not be achieved without supporters (no matter how patient the clans are). A necessary condition for the existence of an MDE with a positive number of supporters for both clans is that there be a feasible number of supporters of a clan that makes it profitable for that clan to challenge if the other clan has no supporters.

Theoretically, then, the MDE with the efficient number of possessions may be associated with either no supporters or a positive number of supporters. It is more likely that an MDE with the efficient level of possessions be characterized by a positive number of supporters the lower the level of external threat, the

---

reflects the constraints on Genoa's main clans owing to the interests of the other Genoese, who gained from trade using these possessions. This point is further elaborated in Greif (1998).

[12]The analysis assumes that acquiring more possessions entails a transition from one MDE to another. It ignores possible hindrances to efficiency resulting from the difficulties in transition from one equilibrium to another.

(time average) cost of war, and the gains from raids. Since we do not know the relevant functional forms and parameters, we cannot theoretically establish what the number of supporters in the efficient MDE had to be in Genoa.

What can be established, however, is that if the equilibrium number of supporters in the efficient MDE is 0, then the efficient MDE maximizes the clans' incomes. If the equilibrium number of supporters in the efficient MDE is positive, however, then the efficient number of possessions does not maximize the clans' incomes. In other words, the clans would not find it optimal to cooperate in obtaining the efficient number of possessions.

This is the case because, in considering the profitability of acquiring possessions, a clan takes into account not only the economic cost of acquiring possessions but also the political cost, namely the expense entailed by the need to ensure deterrence. When deterrence at the efficient level of possessions requires a positive number of supporters, the marginal political cost is positive, since acquiring more possessions entails substituting away from deterrence based on the value of cooperation in raids and confronting the external threat to deterrence based on supporters.[13] Since deterrence implies cost, the number of possessions each clan would find optimal to acquire *does not* equate the marginal economic benefit with the marginal economic cost. Instead, a clan's optimal number of possessions—the number of possessions that maximizes the clan's net income—equates the marginal economic cost with the marginal economic *and* political costs.

In other words, political cost creates a wedge between the efficient and optimal number of possessions. Although the MDE with the efficient number of possessions maximizes the clan's gross average payoff, it does not maximize its net average payoff. The clan would find it optimal to have an MDE with fewer possessions in which the marginal economic gain from cooperation equals the marginal political and economic cost. Note that this result does not depend on the process through which the allocation of incomes from possessions and raids has been determined. It is a statement about the clan's incentive if a clan's share is such that the related efficient equilibrium entails a positive number of supporters.

This analysis has been motivated by the quest to identify the possible sources for political order in Genoa and their implications, and specifically, by the inability of narrative to resolve two conflicting interpretations of the prevalence of political order in pre-1164 Genoa. Theory indicates that both interpretations can be correct: on the one hand, efficient MDE and peace can prevail, and on the other, inefficient MDE and peace can also prevail. Yet the analysis also enables us to determine which one is indeed correct, thus complementing the narrative. It indicates the conditions under which sustaining political order is likely to hinder the acquisition of possessions and the nature of the economic and political

---

[13]The result also holds qualitatively when there are no raids.

behavior associated with an efficient and an inefficient MDE. In particular, an inefficient MDE is more likely to occur when the degree of external threat is low. It would be reached following a period of cooperation in the acquisition of some possessions, and it would have the following economic and political attributes. Raiding and less than the efficient number of possessions would provide the economic foundations for the self-enforcing political system. Each clan's investment in military strength would provide the military foundations of a political system that would be characterized by interclan tranquility.

Evaluating whether sustaining Genoa's self-enforcing political system hindered its commercial expansion thus requires examining the historical evidence in the light of the theory. The theory should be complemented by the narrative. Were the Genoese clans facing a situation in which an inefficient equilibrium was likely to prevail? Were the economic and political features of Genoa similar to those found to be theoretically associated with an inefficient equilibrium?

Back to Narrative

The Economic and Military Foundations of the Self-Enforcing Political System in Genoa, 1099–1164

From 1099 to 1154 Genoa was not subject to threats by another political unit that endangered its political autonomy. It was involved in a lengthy war against Pisa over Sardinia, but this smaller city did not pose any real threat to Genoa. Hence its external condition was similar to that associated with the existence of an inefficient MDE. Indeed, the political and economic situation in Genoa during this time had the features theoretically associated with an MDE with fewer than the optimal number of possessions. It enjoyed internal peace, yet investment in military strength was aimed at confronting internal threats rather than external ones. It exhibited some cooperation in acquiring possessions, yet raids and the acquisition of relatively few possessions remained important features in the commune's economic life.

As mentioned before, between 1099 and 1162 no civil war or major violent political confrontation occurred in Genoa. Despite this internal tranquility and consistent with the theoretical features of an MDE with fewer than the efficient number of possessions, clans invested resources in building fortifications aimed at protecting them from each other and established patronage networks. By 1143 fortified towers were a dominant feature within Genoa (CDG, vol. 1, no. 128). Clans bought land and constructed walls and houses to form fortified enclaves well protected by defense towers [see, for example, GS342 (January 28, 1158) and GS505 (October 4, 1158); see also the discussions in Krueger 1957:270–71; Hughes 1977:99–100, 1978:110–12]. The role of these fortifications during civil wars is well reflected in the words of the Jewish Spanish traveler, Benjamin of

Tudela, who probably visited Genoa during the civil war of 1164–69 (discussed later in this chapter): "Each householder has a tower on his house . . . at times of strife they fight from the tops of the towers with each other" (Tudela 1159–73:62).

Nonclan members moved into clans' quarters, benefiting from their economic resources and political and legal powers. In return, a clan's clients provided it with military and political assistance in case of need. Their participation in civil wars alongside the clans can be seen, for example, in the case of Primo de Castro and his supporters, who battled the supporters of Rolando de Avvocato in the streets of Genoa in 1164. Similarly, in 1179 the Grillo family and its relatives fought against the consul Ogerius Ventus and his "fellow-men," and in 1192 a fight between the della Volta clan and "part of their [former] adherents" occurred (*Annali* 1164:2:16, 1179:2:192, 1192:2:227).

Theory indicates why—during a period of interclan tranquility—Genoa's clans were pursuing the above policy. It was a manifestation of mutual deterrence, as Genoa's leading clans invested resources to maintain the military balance among themselves. Consistent with the other theoretical predictions, this mutual deterrence also involved fewer than the optimal number of possessions. Raids seem to have remained the most important economic activity of the Genoese, and the city did not acquire many possessions prior to 1154, although it could have. Benjamin of Tudela notes that the Genoese have "command of the sea and they build ships which they call galleys, and make predatory attacks upon Edom [the land of the Christians] and Ishmael [the land of the Muslims] and the land of Greece as far as Sicily, and they bring back to Genoa spoils from all these places" (1159–73:62). At the same time, long-distance trade based on possessions was, in the words of Genoa's historian Gerald W. Day, "unusually slow to develop" (1988:6).

That acquiring possessions was possible during the first half of the twelfth century is indicated by the success of Pisa, Genoa's smaller neighbor to the south. By 1154 it had already acquired many possessions: in Corsica (since 1091), Sardinia (before 1118), the Crusader States, Byzantium (since 1111), Spain [in Catalonia (1113) and Almería (1133)], North Africa [in Bona, Tripoli, Sfax, and Bugia (1133)], Egypt (including a bazaar in Cairo since 1153 and a bazaar in Alexandria, which it had acquired much earlier), and probably various principalities in Provence (1113) (Heywood 1921:46–82, 108–15). In contrast, by 1155 Genoa had possessions only in the Crusader States, Sardinia, Provence, and perhaps Valencia. There is no indication that Genoa had any possessions in important trading areas, such as Byzantium, Egypt, Sicily, or North Africa. (CDG, vol. 1; *Annali*, vol. 1).

The difference between Genoa and Pisa cannot be attributed to exogenous factors such as opportunity, geography, or uneven endowments. Pisa's location is not superior to that of Genoa, and Pisa had no more than 60 percent of Genoa's population throughout the twelfth century. The theoretical framework outlined earlier suggests why a less-endowed city might acquire more possessions. Such a city would be better able to mobilize its resources to acquire possessions if the need to ensure the self-enforceability of interclan relations did not hinder cooperation. Indeed, the available historical sources—although not as complete as those for Genoa—indicate that Pisa's political structure differed from Genoa's. In particular, the sources available for the period prior to 1190 indicate the importance of three clans—the Visconti, Gaetani, and Dodo—which together had provided over 35 percent of the commune's consuls and Vicecomes (*Annales Pisani*, various years; Rossetti et al. 1979; Cristiani 1962). Furthermore, for the period ending in 1153, the hold of the Visconti over the commune leadership seems to have been undisputed: this clan provided 65 percent of the known consuls and Vicecomes (Rossetti et al. 1979).[14] The base of their power seems to have been the feudal rights they held in Pisa. The extent and concentration of these provided them with the resources required to obtain possessions without having to fear the implications of additional possessions for mutual deterrence within the city. Their dominance is also well reflected in the Pisan tradition that the consuls held their posts by "the Grace of God" and had the right to nominate their own successors (for discussion see Heywood 1921:8, 253–54; Waley 1988:35–36).

That a lack of political cooperation hindered Genoa's acquisition of possessions is also suggested by the city's consulate holdings, which, consistent with the theoretical prediction, indicate cooperation in the early days of the commune. From 1102 to 1105 members of both clans served on the consulate, and it was then that Genoa helped the Crusaders conquer Tortosa, Acre, and Gibelletto, in each of which the Genoese gained substantial possessions (*Annali* 1155–60; CDG, vol. 1, nos. 24 and 30).[15] Cooperation during this period is also suggested by the presence of members of both clans in various official documents relating to the acquisition of possessions. After 1105, members of the Maneciano and Carmadino clans were not involved alongside each other in the acquisition of possessions until 1154. Indeed, Caffaro, the author of Genoa's annals, who lived during the first half of the twelfth century, attributed this situation to Genoa's political leadership. He reports that by 1154 "the city was asleep and was suffering from apathy and was like a ship wandering across the sea without a navigator" (*Annali* 1154:1:48).

[14]For the period as a whole, the Visconti provided more than 20 percent of the known leaders of the commune. Their dominance was disputed from 1155 to 1164 (when they did not provide any consuls) but resumed thereafter.

[15]For the period 1099–22, members of the Carmadino clan were also consuls in 1118 and 1119. It should be noted that these seven consular posts were held by Ido de Carmadino. That Ido was a member of the Carmadino clan, as his name suggests, has been concluded by Belgrano (1873) and accepted by Day (1988:71).

Theory provides a stronger prediction than cooperating in the acquisition of a few possessions. In particular, it indicates why one clan may find it optimal to cease cooperating with the other through the consulate. Suppose that clan k expropriates all the income from existing possessions but will expropriate much less from any additional possessions. (For simplicity of exposition, assume that the other clan will expropriate nothing.) When this is the case, acquiring additional possessions is not profitable for that clan. It is *strictly* better off retaining the lower number of possessions, as additional possessions imply that it will need to have a higher number of supporters in the new MDE and a lower net payoff.

Interestingly, the historical records indicate that after 1122 the Manecianos ceased serving on the consulate. As reflected in table 1.1, from 1099 to 1122 they dominated the consulate, holding more consular posts than any other Genoese clan (18 percent of the total). From 1123 to 1149, however, no Manecianos served on the consulate, and the Carmadinos provided more consuls than any other clan (13 percent of the total). The change in leading clans was associated with a broader change in the composition of the consulate, suggesting that when a leading clan dominated the consulate, its supporters held consulate posts as well.

Theory predicts that if the Manecianos were in a position to expropriate much income from existing possessions (even without serving on the consulate) but expected to expropriate relatively little from additional possessions, they would be motivated to cease cooperating through the commune. Was this the case? Before 1122, the Manecianos were able to gain de facto control over the main Genoese possessions. After the First Crusade, members of the Embriachi family of the Maneciano clan became the governors of the Genoese possessions in the Crusader States, thus gaining de facto independent control over these possessions. Throughout the twelfth century they refused to pay an annual lease to Genoa or to return the holdings into the hands of the commune for reinvestiture (*Annali* 1099, vol. 1, also quoted in CDG, vol. 1, no. 9; CDG, vol. 1, nos. 47, 170, and 246–48; for discussion see Heyd 1868, 1885; Rey 1895; Byrne 1920:202–5, 1928; Face 1952; Cardini 1978). The Embriachis' control over these possessions enhanced the Manecianos' ability to control the consulate, and by 1122 the Carmadinos and other Genoese not affiliated with the Manecianos had a reason to be concerned about the Manecianos' ability to gain de facto permanent control over Genoa itself.

In 1122, through a process that is neither reflected in the historical records nor explicitly captured by the theoretical framework, the Genoese altered the *compagna*'s regulations to specify that consuls would be elected for only one year, not for the longer term previously allowed.[16] Otto, the Bishop of

---

[16]This episode seems to reflect the political importance of the Genoese, who were neither militarily strong nor rich enough to replace the main clans during the first half of the twelfth

Freising and a twelfth-century German chronicler, is explicit in stating that the shortening of consuls' terms in Italian cities was intended to prevent domination by a particular clan. Lest the consuls "exceed bounds by lust for power," it was decided that they should be "changed almost every year" (1152–58:127). The year 1122 marked the end of a period in which the Manecianos could have expected to take control in any of Genoa's additional possessions. They no longer had an incentive to lead the commune in gaining possessions; the Carmadino clan then took the lead in attempting to acquire possessions and became very active in the western Mediterranean (CDG, vol. 1, various contracts; *Annali*, vol. 1, various years). They had much to gain from acquiring possessions without the Manecianos, who still retained their control over Genoa's possessions in the Crusader States.

Self-Enforcing Political Systems and International Insecurity

FROM PIRATES TO TRADERS: 1154–1164

The nature of Genoa's economy and its interclan relations before 1154 are consistent with the attributes of an MDE with fewer than the optimal number of possessions. Genoa's politics and economy, however, radically changed in 1154. This section describes this change and views it as reflecting a transition from a self-enforcing political system based on economic and military foundations to one based on the appropriate international environment—specifically, one in which the political costs, implied by economic expansion, that deterred the clans from cooperating in acquiring possessions were reduced by international threat, enabling commercial expansion.[17]

In 1154, members of the Maneciano and Carmadino clans served jointly on the consulate for the first time since 1105, and from 1154 to 1162 the two clans held an almost identical number of consulate posts. As shown in table 1.1, the broader structure of the consulate changed as well. Consulate posts were held neither by the important families of the Maneciano period of domination (1099–1122) nor by the important families of the Carmadino period (1123–49). Four clans—the della Volta (who had also held many consulate posts from 1123 to 1149), the Maneciano, the Carmadino, and the Guertius—held 50 percent of the consulate posts.

To the extent that patterns of consulate holding reflect cooperation in mobilizing resources and that such mobilization was essential for acquiring possessions, one would expect that the co-appearance of the Maneciano and the Carmadino clans in the consulate would be associated with a rapid acquisition

---

century but were concerned about the strong clans' aspirations to political control. This issue is not explicitly captured by the model.

[17]The anachronistic term *national* is used here for simplicity.

of possessions. Indeed, from 1154 to 1162 Genoa gained possessions all over the Mediterranean: it reaffirmed its privileges in the Crusader States and acquired possessions in Spain, North Africa, Byzantium, and Sicily and in various cities on the French coast. Furthermore, members of the four clans that dominated the consulate were very active in acquiring possessions. Consequently, Genoa's long-distance (hence lucrative) trade substantially increased, as shown in figure 1.1, providing further indication of the importance of possessions in trade expansion.

How can we explain this phenomenon? The model discussed in the previous section provides a specific prediction regarding a factor that may relax the constraint on cooperation in a self-enforcing political system based on military and economic foundations. The highest MDE level of possessions up to which both clans find it optimal to cooperate increases with the level of external threat. Such an increase implies a transition from a self-enforcing political system based on military and economic foundations to one based on common threat. Suppose that the clans are at an MDE with less than the efficient number of possessions and the level of external threat increases. The payoff from being a controlling clan declines for each clan, since a controlling clan will recruit more supporters given the higher threat, or will have a lower probability of avoiding or winning a war (or both). The reduction in a controlling clan's average payoff, ceteris paribus, decreases the gain to each clan from challenging. Hence a new MDE with a higher number of possessions can be reached, in which both clans

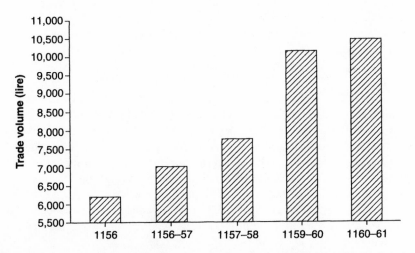

FIGURE 1.1. Genoese export expansion, two-year moving average, 1156–61, based on the cartulary of Giovanni Scriba. The cartulary reflects only exports. It is very fragmented for 1159; hence that year was omitted.

are better off. Note that, although it is well known that rival clans within various Italian city-states often cooperated in confronting external threats, the issue discussed here is the extent of cooperation in the acquisition of possessions.

Theory predicts that if mutual deterrence limits cooperation in the acquisition of possessions, an increase in the level of external threat should enhance cooperation. History indicates that renewed cooperation among the Manecianos and Carmadinos indeed followed a substantial increase in the degree of external threat that the Genoese faced. Specifically, in 1152 Barbarossa became the king of Germany, and two years later—the very same year in which members of the Carmadino and Maneciano clans served jointly on the consulate for the first time in forty-nine years—he crossed the Alps with a large army. Although his military campaign had more than one purpose, it was primarily aimed (or at least has been perceived as primarily aimed) at reimposing the empire's de facto control over the northern Italian cities of Lombardy. Bishop Otto of Freising, Barbarossa's official chronicler, viewed Lombardy as "a very garden of delights [that] surpassed all other states of the world in riches." Yet its residents refused to pay their lord, the emperor, "what is rightfully his own" (1152–58:126–28). Barbarossa demanded a tax from the Italian cities in 1154 and made his intention to impose his control over the cities known in the decrees of Roncaglia in 1158 (Munz 1969:119–20; Waley 1988:88–97).

The Genoese perception of Barbarossa's intentions and the danger he posed are well reflected in a vivid illustration, contained in the Genoese annals, of the city of Tortona after Barbarossa destroyed it in 1155. In haste the Genoese began to build their city's walls (*Annali* 1154, 1155, 1158, 1159, vol. 1). At this point they probably perceived obtaining protection from Barbarossa as more urgent than protecting themselves from each other.

Motivated by the external threat, the Carmadinos and Manecianos attempted to enhance their ability to cooperate by having both clans marry into a third one—the della Volta clan (on political marriage, see Hughes 1978:127–28). From 1123 to 1149 the number of consulate posts held by the della Voltas was second only to that of the Carmadinos, suggesting that the two clans were political allies. Through marriage to both the Carmadinos and the Manecianos, the della Voltas were probably supposed to provide a balance between the two rival viscountal clans (the last section discusses in detail how such a balance may be created) (see figure 1.2). That this was the case is also suggested by an alteration (in an unspecified manner) of the election process in 1155 to ensure that in the future the "best citizens" would be elected. (*Annali* 1155:1:59). Following this alteration, in 1156 two of the four consuls were members of the della Volta clan, and in the following years this clan provided more consuls than any other.

Since Barbarossa had never attacked Genoa, building the walls was probably the largest cost that his actions imposed on the Genoese. Ironically, his threat seems to have enabled the Genoese to cooperate and prosper by relaxing the

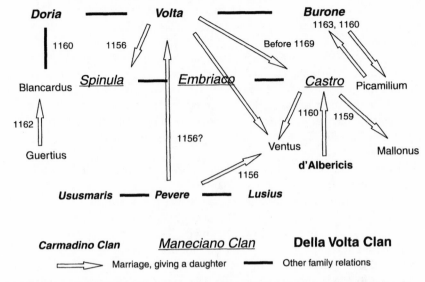

FIGURE 1.2. Family relations among the politically dominant families. *Sources:* See Greif (forthcoming).

constraints ensuring that Genoa's political system would be self-enforcing. Cooperation and attempts to enhance cooperation are reflected in the acquisition of possessions, the building of Genoa's walls, marriages, and the holding of consulate posts. Between 1154 and 1164 the families related by blood and marriage to the della Volta, Maneciano, and Carmadino clans held 73 percent of the consulate posts. The threat imposed by Barbarossa enabled a transition from a self-enforcing political system based on economic and military foundations to one based on the appropriate international environment.

IN THE ABSENCE OF A SELF-ENFORCING POLITICAL SYSTEM:
FROM ORDER TO DISORDER, 1164

The reliance of Genoa's self-enforcing political system on external threat, however, was short lived. In 1164 this threat unexpectedly dissipated. Given the low level of threat and the high level of possessions, neither economic nor military foundations could have enabled the Genoese to maintain political order, and civil war was to be the end result. This eventuality, however, was not foreseen as late as 1164. Two years earlier, the Emperor Barbarossa defeated Milan, which had led the struggle against his attempt to reaffirm imperial control over Lombardy. The Genoese, now directly exposed to the imperial wrath, promised to provide Barbarossa with naval assistance for a campaign to conquer Sicily in 1164 [*Annali* 1162:1:88–90 (Ingo della Volta, Lanfrancus

Pevere, and Rogerone de Ita [de Castro] were among the legates); CDG, vol.
1, no. 308; see discussion in De Negri 1986:289–92; Day 1988:94–95; Waley
1988:33].

Yet in 1164 the emperor's army was nowhere to be seen in Italy. Internal
disarray in Germany and the establishment of the Veronese league in Lombardy
for the purpose of fighting him implied that Barbarossa was no longer a threat,
at least in the short run (e.g., Munz 1969:234–71; Waley 1988:92). That this
development caught the Genoese by surprise is indicated by the fact that by
1164 they had already prepared the navy to assist Barbarossa in the conquest
of Sicily.

By 1164 the external threat to the Genoese had greatly subsided and could no
longer provide the appropriate foundation for Genoa's self-enforcing political
system.[18] Neither could its economy: there was not much the Genoese could
gain from raids, and the possessions acquired in the past made controlling
the consulate a tempting objective. Following Genoa's treaty with Barbarossa
in 1162, his foes, the king of Sicily and the Byzantine emperor, viewed the
agreement as an act of hostility. Pisa, Genoa's bitter rival, took advantage of
this situation and, after attacking and destroying the Genoese compound in
Constantinople, waged war against Genoa. The hostile navies of Sicily and
Pisa blocked the path of the Genoese to the eastern Mediterranean, and most
of the Muslim west was now controlled by the powerful Almohades, in whose
trade centers Genoa held possessions (*Annali* 1162:1:91–98; *Giovanni Scriba*
1162–64; for discussion see Donaver 1890:36–37; Byrne 1916:131, 1920:211;
Krueger 1932:100; Abulafia 1977:127–33). At the same time, the possessions
acquired in the past still made controlling the consulate more tempting than it
had been in 1155. In 1164 Genoa's export trade was more than six times its
1155 value and at 65 percent of its 1161 level.

In sum, in 1164 neither the international nor the economic situations that had
previously provided the foundations for Genoa's self-enforcing political system
were effective. To the extent that the Genoese clans were in an MDE before
1164, theory predicts that this situation could have led to a breakdown of mutual
deterrence. A lower level of external threat and a high income imply a higher average payoff from being a controlling clan, making challenging more attractive,
whereas low gains from raiding imply a lower loss due to challenging. Hence
condition 1 is less likely to hold in this situation. (See the discussion in Greif
[forthcoming] of the relations between parameters in the existence of an MDE.)

If an MDE ceases to exist (for a given allocation of income between the
clans), the model predicts that interclan military confrontation should result. If
an MDE is not an equilibrium, one clan finds it best to challenge the other. A
more elaborate model in which the allocation of income is endogenous would

---

[18]The war with Pisa was conducted on the sea far away from Genoa's shore, or in the
surroundings of Lucca, Pisa's neighbor and Genoa's ally.

have indicated that when a particular MDE ceases to exist, one clan may find it more profitable to agree to a smaller share in the income and to avoid the cost of military confrontation. Yet note that the model also indicates that once a particular MDE (with a particular number of possessions and share of income) ceases to exist, there would not necessarily be another allocation of the income for which an MDE exists and to which both clans would consent.[19]

This is so since the new allocation should be ex ante acceptable by both clans and ex post self-enforcing, despite the link between income and military strength. If, for example, clan 1 finds it profitable to challenge at the existing allocation, it would decline any new allocation that provides it with a lower share of the income, whereas clan 2 will decline any new allocation that would provide it with a share so low that it would prefer a civil war. Any allocation that provides clan 1 with a higher share in the income, however, further militarily strengthens it relative to clan 2. Hence, although clan 1 has less to gain from challenging in the new allocation, it is also more likely to have the upper hand in an interclan confrontation. This implies that there may not be a new allocation that is ex ante acceptable and ex post self-enforcing.

Theory indicates a rationale for an interclan military confrontation in Genoa in 1164. Indeed, a civil war broke out in 1164, to become a semipermanent feature of Genoa's political life. Without going into detail, during at least thirteen of the years from 1164 to 1193 the Genoese were engaged in civil war, namely 43 percent of the time (*Annali,* various years). The very same families that had shared the consulate from 1154 to 1164 and cooperated in the acquisition of possessions fought against each other in these civil wars.

The civil war marked the failure of the della Volta clan to achieve a balance between the Manecianos and the Carmadinos, and it joined forces with the Manecianos against the Carmadinos (the next section will provide a rationale for this failure). The della Voltas had too much vested interest in Genoa and too many interrelations with other Genoese clans. They could not provide an impartial third party with the appropriate incentives to create yet another foundation for Genoa's self-enforcing political system. Providing such a new foundation—one based on self-enforcing political rules—would require a more fundamental change in Genoa's politics.

A Self-Enforcing Political System Based on Political Rules: Changing the Rules of the Game, Political Order, and Economic Growth

The foregoing analytic narrative indicates that comprehending political and economic outcomes in Genoa requires an examination of the foundations of its

---

[19]And note that this allocation differs from that implied if one clan were to renounce its share in the rent.

self-enforcing political system. By 1164, however, this system was in fact no longer self-enforcing, but instead was characterized by disorder, disintegration, and large economic cost. In the civil war of 1189–94, for example, both sides used siege machines to destroy each other's towers, and various cities in Liguria, long controlled by Genoa, asserted their independence. Furthermore, in 1194 the della Voltas' opponents seceded from the commune and established a rival one (*Annali* 1193–94:2:228–30). To revitalize their political and economic system, the Genoese needed a different foundation for their self-enforcing political system—a foundation that would break, in a self-enforcing manner, the link between economic growth and political instability in the absence of an external threat.

By 1194 the future for both rival Genoese factions seemed bleak. Neither faction had control over enough income to enable it to have undisputed control over the city, and the military situation in Genoa itself precluded each faction from devoting resources to acquiring possessions. Furthermore, in 1194 the German emperor, Henry VI, was organizing a campaign to conquer Sicily. The Genoese had much to lose if they did not assist Henry. Refusing to assist or alienating an emperor who might soon control the areas north and south of Genoa and who was supported by Pisa, Genoa's naval rival, would have closed off any prospect of receiving possessions in Sicily. Nevertheless, the Carmadinos and their supporters were unwilling to resume cooperation even in the face of this severe external threat, and their faction seceded from the commune. History might have taught them the fragility of political cooperation sustained by a high external threat. If so, the Carmadinos could have been induced to assist Henry by altering the interclan game in a self-enforcing manner that would have increased their ability to reap ex post the benefit of cooperation even if the external threat subsided.

Indeed, in 1194 the Genoese altered their political system by introducing a new type of organization, the *podestà* (from the Latin *potestas*, "a power"). This transition was influenced by the attempts of Henry VI to use *podestàs* to ensure his control over Italy [e.g., Heywood 1921:214 (Florence), 220 (Pisa); Day 1988:147]. In 1194 Henry, planning to attack Sicily, demanded that Genoa provide him with naval assistance. Genoa, however, could not provide this support as long as it was paralyzed by civil war. Henry's seneschal, Markward of Anweiler, who was present in Genoa to organize the naval support, advised the della Volta consuls to accept a *podestà,* who would rule the city instead of the consuls. Given the deadlock in the fighting on the one hand and the high cost of refusing Henry naval support on the other, the della Volta faction conceded. Oberto de Olivano was nominated to serve as *podestà* for one year, after which the consulate was to resume. Oberto was from Pavia, Henry's capital as the King of Italy, suggesting that his nomination and activities were backed by the emperor and his army. Under the direction of this *podestà*, both Genoese factions cooperated and supported the emperor, who conquered Sicily in 1194 (*Annali* 1194:2:231–32; for discussion see Vitale 1955:1:51–55; Abulafia 1977:204–12; Day 1988:149).

During the Sicilian campaign the Genoese *podestà* died. The Genoese decided to continue the *podesteria* and replaced him with Ottone di Carreto, a Ligurian (*Annali* 1194:2:239, explicitly written "whom the Genoese made *podestà*"). This displeased the emperor, who had probably intended to nominate and motivate the next *podestà* himself, thus providing balance between the Genoese factions. Thus he refused to recognize the legitimacy of the Genoese *podestà* and threatened to destroy Genoa if the Genoese dared to sail the seas (*Annali* 1194:2:240–41). Despite this threat (and most likely motivated by it), the Genoese transformed and organized the *podesteria* in a manner that enabled them to cooperate and make Genoa more economically prosperous and politically powerful than ever before.[20]

The following theoretical discussion explains how and under what conditions a *podestà* can foster cooperation in a self-enforcing manner without becoming a dictator. Conceptually, the introduction of the *podestà* is considered an organizational change: the Genoese altered the relevant rules of their political game. Accordingly, the theoretical analysis in this section concentrates on identifying the nature of the alterations in the rules of the interclan game that were required to ensure the *podestà*'s ability to foster interclan cooperation. A comparison of these alterations to those reflected in the historical records suggests that the Genoese indeed created the conditions that would enable the *podestà* to foster cooperation. Furthermore, it indicates that both of the views regarding the nature of the *podesteria* discussed in the introduction have a grain of truth. They are not as contradictory as they may seem.

Before turning to this theoretical and historical analysis, however, its path-dependent nature should be emphasized. The analysis takes as given the existence of clans, their importance as political decisionmakers, and the strategies they followed in maintaining relations among themselves: namely that each clan would challenge the other if the appropriate opportunity arose. In other words, the starting point of the analysis builds on rather than replaces existing rules and strategies. Hence it takes as given the constraints imposed by Genoa's history on the set of possible alternatives in the political game. Indeed, as discussed subsequently, this position is appropriate, since historically the *podesteria* system seems to have built on the existing clan structure in a manner that perpetuated its importance.

---

[20]For discussion of the Genoese *podesteria,* see Vitale (1951:3–39) and Day (1988:148ff). For a discussion of this system in Italy, see Waley (1988:40–45). A *podestà* was also instituted in 1191; regarding this episode, see Greif (forthcoming). Between 1194 and 1216, the consulate was renewed for several years. It is important to note, however, that from 1194 to 1206 the consulate was renewed only once.

Theoretically, in the context of the interclan game already considered, altering the relevant rules of the game in a matter that limits each clan's incentives to challenge the other entails creating an additional player (the *podestà*) who is motivated to take actions against an aggressor's clan and to assist a clan that stands to lose in an interclan war. If a *podestà* with such motivation is sufficiently strong militarily, he reduces each clan's expected gain from challenging and thereby deters it from doing so. Although the *podestà* should be strong enough to reduce each clan's expected gain from challenging, he should nevertheless be sufficiently weak not to aspire to gain political control. Thus there are three difficulties in implementing such an alteration. First, the *podestà* should be deterred from colluding with one clan against the other. Second, the *podestà* must be motivated to assist the clan that stands to lose. Third, since the *podestà* has to be weak relative to the clans in order not to aspire to gain control, the clan that in the absence of his intervention stands to lose in an interclan war should be motivated to fight alongside the podestà.[21]

To examine how these problems can be mitigated in a self-enforcing manner, it is useful to begin by examining a "collusion game" between a clan and a *podestà*. The question that this game addresses is the extent to which a clan can ex ante commit to reward ex post a podestà who colluded with it against the other clan. The notations used in this game (and the subsequent analysis) are as follows: $v_i(m_j, m_k; m_i)$ is the probability that i will win a war against j and k given the military strengths of m_j, m_k, and m_i. The probability that i will win is declining in m_j and m_k and increasing in m_i. (For ease of presentation, the parameter m_i is omitted in the equations that follow, and the analysis in this section ignores clans' ability to increase their military strength.) If a player participates in a military confrontation, it has to bear the cost c. V_i is the net present value to player i of controlling Genoa, and it is assumed that $V_1 \geq V_p$, namely that a local clan gains more from controlling the city than a *podestà*. (This assumption, as well as the one that the cost of war is the same to all players, is not essential to the result and is made for ease of presentation.)

Using these notations we can examine the ability of a clan and a *podestà* to collude against the other clan. The relevant starting point of such an analysis, presented in figure 1.3, is the situation prevailing after a clan and a *podestà* have colluded against the other clan and gained control over the city. The clan that gained control now has to decide what reward, $R_p > 0$, to provide the *podestà*. Once this reward is announced, the *podestà* can either accept it and not fight the clan for control of the city or can reject it and fight. If he accepts the offer, the payoffs are $V_1 - R_p$ and R_p to the clan and the *podestà*, respectively. If he rejects it and fights, the payoff to each is the probability of winning times the

---

[21]The analysis of this last point can also be expanded to include strengthening the *podestà* through the participation of the Genoese not affiliated with Genoa's main clans. For simplicity, this issue is ignored here.

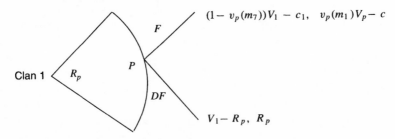

$$(1 - v_p(m_7))V_1 - c_1, \quad v_p(m_1)V_p - c$$

$$V_1 - R_p, \quad R_p$$

FIGURE 1.3. The collusion game.

value of gaining control minus the cost of war, namely $(1 - v_1(m_p))V_1 - c$ and $v_p(m_1)V_p - c$.

The *podestà* will not fight if he will get at least the net expected value of fighting against the clan, namely, $R_p \geq v_p(m_1)V_p - c$. Similarly, the clan will not find it profitable to offer an R_p higher than the one required to make it indifferent between fighting or not fighting, that is, $V_1 - R_p \geq (1 - v_p(m_1))V_1 - c$. Hence, it will be willing to offer $R_p \leq v_p(m_1)V_1 + c$, implying that the clan is willing to pay the *podestà* more than is required to prevent the *podestà* from fighting. Hence in any subgame perfect equilibrium the clan will not offer more than the amount needed to make the *podestà* indifferent between fighting and not fighting, namely $R_p = v_p(m_1)V_p - c$. This finding implies that the only subgame perfect equilibrium is such that the clan offers $R_p = v_p(m_1)V_p - c$ while the *podestà*'s strategy is to fight if paid less than that and not to fight if paid at least that amount. The payoffs associated with this equilibrium are V_p^c to the *podestà*, where $V_p^c = \text{Max}\{0, v_p(m_1)V_p - c\}$, and $V_1 - V_p^c$ to the clan.

The analysis thus implies that after collusion has occurred, the amount by which the clan would reward a *podestà* would depend on the *podestà*'s ability to confront that clan militarily.[22] Specifically, the *podestà* would not get, in any equilibrium, more than his net present value for militarily confronting the clan, $v_p(m_1)V_p - c$. This implies that ex ante—before collusion has occurred—a clan cannot credibly commit to reward the *podestà* ex post by more than this amount. When $v_p(m_1)V_p - c \leq 0$, for example, the clan cannot make its promise to reward the *podestà* credible at all. More generally, the lower the *podestà*'s military ability, the lower the extent to which the clan can make its ex ante promise to reward the *podestà* credible. This implies that by limiting the military ability of the *podestà* relative to that of a clan, the ability to collude can be curtailed. Yet such a reduction in the *podestà*'s military ability implies that it is less plausible to be able to rely solely on the *podestà*'s military might

[22]A similar commitment problem also prevails in the relations between a clan and its supporters, but this problem could be more easily mitigated through their ongoing relations in ways that are not feasible when dealing with an outsider.

to deter a clan from attempting to gain control over Genoa. To see how a clan could nevertheless have been deterred, one must consider the collusion game within the broader context of interclan relations.

To examine this broader context, some additional notations are required. Denote by I_i the income per period for clan i if no clan assumes control, by W the *podestà*'s wage, and by δ the factor used by the clans to discount future income.[23] Using this notation, the broader context of the *podesteria* game can be examined to reveal how the interclan game could have been altered to enhance cooperation by introducing a *podestà*, despite his ability to collude and the limit on his military power required to ensure that he would not become a dictator. This game is presented in figure 1.4.[24] The game begins, without loss of generality, with clan 1 having to decide whether or not to challenge clan 2. If clan 1 challenges, clan 2 can either fight or not. In either case, the *podestà* can respond either by attempting to prevent clan 1 from taking control (an action denoted by p), or by not preventing it (dp), or by colluding with clan 1 (co). If the *podestà* colludes, it is assumed, for ease of exposition, that clan 2 cannot gain control over the city and that the *podestà* and clan 1 are playing the collusion game (figure 1.3). Since the collusion game has a unique subgame perfect equilibrium, figure 1.4 presents only the payoffs associated with this equilibrium.

If clan 1 does not challenge, the payoffs are (I_1, I_2, W) to clan 1, clan 2, and the *podestà*, respectively, and the same game is then played in the next period. If clan 1 challenges and clan 2 *does not fight*, clan 1 becomes the controlling clan and the associated payoffs are as follows: If the *podestà* does not prevent, the payoffs are $(V_1, 0, 0)$. If the *podestà* colludes, clan 1 will reward him by V_p^c (namely, the *podestà*'s payoff in the equilibrium of the collusion game), and hence the payoffs are $(V_1 - V_p^c, 0, V_p^c)$. If the *podestà* prevents, his payoff equals the net expected value of his attempting to gain control, and hence the associated payoffs are $(v_1(m_p)V_1 - c, 0, v_p(m_1)V_p - c)$. If clan 1 challenges and clan 2 *does fight*, the associated payoffs are as follows: If the *podestà* does not prevent, each clan's payoff equals the net expected value of being a controlling clan while the *podestà* gets 0, that is $(v_1(m_2)V_1 - c, (1 - v_1(m_2))V_2, 0)$.[25] If the *podestà* colludes, then, as before, clan 1 assumes control and the payoffs are $(V_1 - V_p^c, 0, V_p^c)$. Finally, if the *podestà* prevents, then clan 1 will either gain control and get V_1 or fail to do so and get only his share in that period's income, I_1. If clan 1 fails to gain control, then clan 2 gets his share in that period's income (I_2) while the *podestà* gets his wage, W. The payoffs are thus $v_1(m_p, m_2)V_1 - c + (1 - v_1(m_p, m_2))I_1, (1 - v_1(m_p, m_2))I_2 - c$, and $(1 - v_1(m_p, m_2))(W - c)$.

---

[23]It is implicitly assumed then that the *podestà*'s reservation utility after assuming the office is 0.
[24]Note that this is not a stage game, but rather a repetitive (but not repeated) game.
[25]The analysis holds if a *podestà* who did not prevent could challenge the clan who won the interclan confrontation.

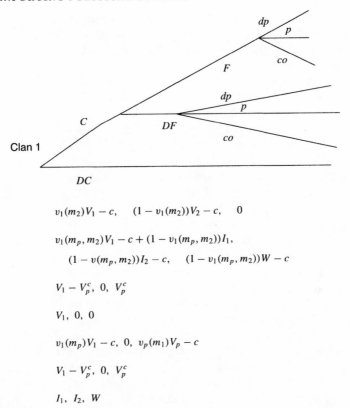

$$v_1(m_2)V_1 - c, \quad (1 - v_1(m_2))V_2 - c, \quad 0$$

$$v_1(m_p, m_2)V_1 - c + (1 - v_1(m_p, m_2))I_1,$$

$$(1 - v(m_p, m_2))I_2 - c, \quad (1 - v_1(m_p, m_2))W - c$$

$$V_1 - V_p^c, \; 0, \; V_p^c$$

$$V_1, \; 0, \; 0$$

$$v_1(m_p)V_1 - c, \; 0, \; v_p(m_1)V_p - c$$

$$V_1 - V_p^c, \; 0, \; V_p^c$$

$$I_1, \; I_2, \; W$$

FIGURE 1.4. The *podesteria* game.

In this game, the strategy combination—specifying that clan 1 does not challenge, clan 2 fights if it is challenged, and the *podestà* prevents if clan 1 challenges and clan 2 fights but, if clan 2 does not fight, colludes if $V_p^c > 0$ and does not otherwise prevent—is a subgame perfect equilibrium if the following conditions hold:

I. Motivating the *podestà* to prevent and not to collude if clan 2 fights: $(1 - v_1(m_p, m_2))W - c \geq V_p^c$

II. Motivating clan 2 to fight: $(1 - v_1(m_p, m_2))I_2/(1 - \delta) \geq c$

III. Deterring clan 1 from challenging: $c(v_1(m_p, m_2)(V_1 - I_1))$

These conditions indicate both how the *podesteria* can provide the appropriate incentives and the delicate balance required to maintain these incentives. Intuitively, condition I implies that the *podestà* is better off preventing if clan 2 fights, although it would not prevent otherwise. Condition II guarantees that clan 2 would fight. Because the *podestà* would not prevent unless clan 2 fights, and since condition II implies that clan 2 prefers to fight rather than not fight if the *podestà* prevents, it is clan 2's best response to fight if challenged. Condition III then implies that clan 1, expecting clan 2 and the *podestà* to fight it, finds it optimal not to challenge.

These conditions and the equilibrium strategy indicate how the appropriate incentives can be provided by the *podesteria* system to overcome the problems that can render the system ineffective. Condition I and clan 2's strategy prevents collusion between clan 1 and the *podestà*. Collusion is curtailed by sufficiently reducing the *podestà*'s military strength relative to his wage so that the highest amount by which clan 1 can credibly commit to reward the *podestà* following collusion is not sufficient to induce him to collude. The *podestà*, expecting clan 2 to fight alongside him, prefers to prevent clan 1 rather than collude. Clan 2 is motivated to fight alongside the *podestà* because the *podestà*'s strategy implies that otherwise the *podestà* would not confront clan 1 either. At the same time, condition II implies that the combined forces of clan 2 and the *podestà*, relative to clan 2's share in the gain (I_2), are such that the clan finds it optimal to fight alongside the *podestà*.

The preceding discussion indicates the delicate balance of power that must be maintained in order for the *podesteria* to provide the appropriate incentives. On the one hand the *podestà* should not be too militarily strong in order to deter him from aspiring to gain control by himself or collude with clan 1. (Both sides of condition I decline in m_p but the right side increases in W.) At the same time, he should be sufficiently strong that his threat to fight alongside clan 2 in case of need sufficiently reduces clan 1's incentive to challenge. (The left side of condition II increases in m_p and the right side of condition II declines in m_p.) This delicate balance, however, provides the *podestà* with an important incentive that is not explicitly captured in the model. The equilibrium is more likely to hold, and hence the *podestà* is more likely to gain W without being involved in a war, the closer is the military strength of the clans. Hence the *podestà* is motivated to prevent fighting but not at the cost of severely weakening any clan. Thus he could credibly commit to impartial behavior toward the clans aimed at maintaining their relative positions.

Therefore the model identifies how the *podestà* could have fostered interclan cooperation using his military ability without being able to become a dictator. He could have achieved cooperation by providing a balance of power between the rival clans. Hence the model lends support to the view that introduction of the *podestà* may have been a self-enforcing organizational change, or a set of political rules aimed at enabling cooperation. To verify whether in fact this was the case requires returning to the narrative and examining whether the Genoese *podesteria*'s rules created the conditions identified in the model as being required to enable the *podestà* to foster interclan cooperation.

As already explained, the *podestà* was a non-Genoese noble, hired to be the main military leader, judge, and administrator of Genoa for a year, during which period he was supported by twenty soldiers, two judges, and servants that he brought with him (Vitale 1951:27).[26] Although the military force brought by the *podestà* was not large in size, it was far from negligible by the standards of the day. In 1170, when the Genoese desperately needed to enhance their military strength, they knighted one hundred men; Barbarossa sailed to the Third Crusade with six hundred knights. The *podestà* was merely intended to provide the military balance between factions, as reflected, for example, in the destruction of the fortified tower of the Castro family after members of this family murdered Lanfrancus Pevere for political reasons (*Annali* 1190:2:220). The *podestà* was militarily important but presumably not strong enough to defeat a significant Genoese clan by himself.

The *podestà* was offered very high wages, which in 1226 amounted to 1,300 lire—a huge sum, given that the annual farm of the toll from Genoa's port was 7,000 lire in about 1200 (Vitale 1951:25).[27] However, as the discussion above indicated, a high wage would not be sufficient incentive for the *podestà* to intervene in interclan war to prevent one clan from defeating the other. Clearly a high wage would be sufficient to compensate him for fighting if the need arose, but for the wage to *prevent* fighting, arrangements would have to be such that he would not be able to receive his wage if he did not intervene. In other words, condition 1 has to hold: the clan that challenges another should not be able to commit credibly to rewarding a *podestà* who colluded with it. The collusion game indicates why such a commitment was not easy. A militarily powerful clan can credibly commit only to a low reward following commitment—a reward that does not merit fighting even the relatively militarily weak *podestà*.

Yet a clan and a *podestà* might try to circumvent this problem though the use of other commitment devices, such as marriages and joint economic ventures. The regulations under which the *podestà* served indeed seem to have been aimed at hindering the ability to employ such devices. The incoming *podestà* was selected by a council, whose members were chosen on a geographic basis to prevent its control by any specific clan, and the selection process for naming a new *podestà* was governed by the outgoing *podestà*. The *podestà*—as well as his relatives to the third degree—was restricted from socializing with Genoese, buying property, getting married, or managing any commercial transactions for himself or others. Until permanent housing was built for the *podestà*, he was obliged to spend his year in Genoa living in several of the city's quarters, to prevent him from associating for too long with the members of any particular clan. To comprehend the meaning of this obligation, one should know that it was Genoa's policy to force Ligurian nobles who recognized Genoa's supremacy

[26]Two exceptions to this rule were Fulco de Castro, a Genoese who was a *podestà* in 1205, and Gioffredotto Grassello from Milan, who was a *podestà* in 1202, 1203, and 1204.

[27]From the mid-twelfth to the mid-thirteenth century, Genoa experienced annual inflation of about 35 percent.

to live in the city for at least several months each year, in order to get them involved in Genoa's public life. The conscious attempt to keep the *podestà* away from the influence of Genoa's main clans is also reflected in those years during which rectors (*rettori*) assisted the *podestà*. It is rare to find a rector who can be identified with one of the major families involved in the factional wars of the twelfth century.[28] Furthermore, the *podestà*, as well as the soldiers who came with him, was required to leave the city at the end of his term and not return for several years, and a *podestà*'s son could not replace him in office.

The credibility of the Genoese promise to reward a *podestà* at the end of his term if no clan had initiated and won an interclan war was probably derived from a desire to retain a reputation for rewarding *podestàs* so that Genoa would be able to hire high-quality *podestàs* in the future. Indeed, Genoese *podestàs* were recruited from a handful of Italian cities, in particular from Milan, and the contract between Genoa and a new *podestà* was read in front of the parliament of the city from which the *podestà* was recruited. This practice does not imply that a *podestà* was given a free hand to mismanage the city's affairs, taking advantage of Genoa's desire to retain its reputation. After the end of his term a *podestà* was required to remain in the city for fifteen days, during which period his conduct was assessed by auditors (*sindicatori*), and deviations from the previously specified rules were punished by fines to be paid before his departure or subtracted from his remuneration (Vitale 1951: 27–28). At the same time, additional incentives for the *podestà* to prevent interclan confrontation were probably provided by the *podestà*'s own concerns about his reputation. At the end of the twelfth century and the beginning of the thirteenth, many communes adopted the *podesteria* system (Waley 1988). Serving as a *podestà* became the profession of many nobles, who competed for these positions in the market for *podestàs*' services.

One should not conclude, however, that the *podesteria* system was necessarily the same in various cities (although its introduction around the same period suggests the importance of several common factors discussed below). An organizational change such as the introduction of a *podestà*, although seemingly similar from one city to the next, can in fact reflect distinct motivations and the functioning of distinct self-enforcing systems if the underlying relations among the clans in those cities are different, for example if one clan has a decisive military superiority over another. Once again a comparison of Pisa and Genoa is instructive. When Emperor Henry VI rose to power in 1190 he nominated Tedici de Gherardesca, the count of Dondoratico or count of Bolghieri (near Pisa), as the *podestà* of Pisa—a post that he held exclusively from 1190 to April 1199. Rather than providing a balance of power between two factions,

---

[28]After 1196 the *podestà* was assisted by eight *rettori* or *consiglieri,* one per district, who functioned as part of the administration and control. See Olivieri (1861) for the years 1196, 1199, 1202, 1203, 1205, and 1206. For discussion see Vitale (1951:11) and Day (1988:150–51).

the Pisan *podestà* during this period seems to have been a means by which the emperor could exert control.[29] By 1199, however, the Visconti clan that had dominated Pisa prior to 1190 was able to reestablish its control. From 1199 to 1129 members of the Visconti clan provided most of the *podestàs*. We know the names of seventeen *podestàs* from these years and ten of them were members of the Visconti clan.[30]

Hence, at least initially, the introduction of a *podestà* in Pisa reflected the domination of a particular faction rather than a balance of power. The Visconti and the de Gherardesca were at the center, but on opposite sides in a civil war that erupted in Pisa in the second quarter of the thirteenth century.[31] It was only after this war that foreign *podestàs* became the rule rather than the exception in Pisa. Prior to 1237 the names of only twenty-seven *podestàs* are reflected in the historical records, but only three of them were non-Pisan. However, after 1237 the position was regularly filled by non-Pisans.[32] In summary, for its first forty-seven years the essence of the Pisan *podesteria* differed from that of Genoa. Although the same term was used in both cities, it reflected different realities. In Genoa, the essence of the office was the creation of a balance of power, whereas in Pisa it was the title assumed by those who held power. Yet the development of Pisa's *podesteria* confirms the interpretation of the Genoese case offered previously: once the two Pisan factions had reached a stalemate and external pressures from Genoa mounted, a foreign *podestà* able to maintain balance of power was introduced.

In any case, the broader movement in Italy to place communes under the administration of *podestàs* suggests the process by means of which an appreciation of the feasibility and working of the *podesteria* emerged in Genoa. The concept of the *podestà*—of an administrator with judicial and police functions who serves for a limited time, after which his actions are assessed according to the law—resembles that of dictatorship as practiced in ancient Rome (Spruyt 1994:143). The Roman dictator enjoyed absolute power for six months, after which time he had to account for his actions in the court of law. Perhaps inspired by this example, several Italian communes experimented during the first half of the twelfth century with a political system guided by a single executive administrator. In 1155, one such administrator, Guido de Sasso, the *rector* or *podestà* of Bologna, met with the Emperor Barbarossa. In 1162, after Frederick had destroyed Milan and subdued the rebellious Lombard communes, he nominated an outsider in each city as an imperial vicar, or

[29]On such use of *podestàs* by the emperor, see Day (1988:147).

[30]In 1223, five (!) *podestàs* held the post at the same time, and among them were two members of the Visconti clan.

[31]But see Cristiani (1962) on the involvement of the people (*popolo*) in this war.

[32]This and the following discussion are based on Heywood (1921), Cristiani (1962), and Rossetti et al. (1979).

podestà, to ensure the cities' obedience and to administer them on his behalf.
Imperial vicars, counts, and *podestàs* are mentioned in such cities as Sienna,
San Miniato, Volterra, and Florence. After 1168, the emperor lost control in
certain cities, yet the historical record indicates that many cities nominated civil
officials—variously called *rectores, dominatores,* and *podestàs*—who seem to
have acted as administrators and were bound to follow the law (Heywood
1921:262; Hyde 1973:100–101; Waley 1988:42). Hence the introduction of
the *podestà* as an organizational innovation in Genoa in 1194 was not merely a
reflection of the incentives associated with particular historical circumstances. It
seems to also have reflected a process of learning and experimentation, resulting
in an awareness of the feasibility of such a change.

In addition to the mechanisms aimed at providing the *podestà* and the clans
with the incentives required to foster interclan cooperation while preventing the
podestà from becoming a dictator, the presence of an administrator controlling
Genoa's finances further reduced the likelihood of civil war. This was so because
limiting the clans' ability to increase their military strength by expropriating
income severed the link between commercial expansion and the clans' military
might.[33] Under the *podesteria,* each of Genoa's possessions was administered by
a consul sent from Genoa. He was appointed for only one year and was required
to return to Genoa as soon as his successor had arrived, on the very same ship.[34]
The consul had to deposit a bond as a guarantee of proper conduct and was
prohibited from receiving donations worth more than half a lira or to undertake
any commercial venture (Byrne 1928). Genoese ambassadors who were sent
to negotiate commercial treaties and to organize the administration of Genoa's
possessions were instructed to prevent any particular family from acquiring or
leasing private properties to an extent that would enable it to achieve de facto
control over that possession.[35] The care taken to prevent any single faction from
gaining control over Genoa's possessions is also suggested by the nomination
as consuls of those possessions of individuals who were not members of any
family of importance within the rival factions.[36]

---

[33]Concern about the *podestà*'s ability to expropriate rent is suggested by the regulation,
discussed previously, requiring that after the end of his term a *podestà* remain in the city for
fifteen days, subject to audit and the possible payment of fines (Vitale 1951:27–28).

[34]Under the consular system, the possessions were leased for prolonged periods of time.

[35]An example would be the Guertius family, which, as a part of the della Volta faction during the
twelfth-century hereditary claim, gained the position of administrators of the Genoese possessions in
Constantinople. In a document dated 1201, a Genoese ambassador to Constantinople was explicitly
instructed to prevent the office of the Genoese viscount of Constantinople from falling into the hands
of Alinerio, the son of Tanto, a member of the Guertius family. That the possessions of the Guertius
family in Byzantium benefited them commercially is suggested by the fact that they invested in
trade with Byzantium more than any other Genoese family (see also discussion in Day 1988:111ff,
122–25, 166). It is interesting to note that this instruction was given despite the fact that a member
of the Guertius family was consul during this year.

[36]This assertion relates only to the partial list of sixteen administrators in Syria (see Byrne
1928:168–70).

Similarly, to limit the clans' ability to establish patronage networks, their hold over the legal system was reduced. As the chief justice of Genoa, the *podestà* was to provide all residents with impartial justice. During the first years of the *podesteria* he was assisted by local nobles, but in 1216 justice became even more impartial when foreign judges chosen by the *podestà* replaced the nobles. To restrict further the power of judges to make arbitrary decisions, Jacopo di Balduino, a *podestà* from Bologna (a city known for its law school), codified the existing common law in 1229 (for discussion see Vitale 1955:1:56).

The *podesteria* regulations were also aimed at ensuring that the rules the *podestà* had to follow would be difficult to manipulate. These rules had to be approved by a large forum, a council having at least eight representatives from each of Genoa's eight districts. Major policy decisions had to be approved by a larger body, the *parlamentum*, that is, the gathering of all Genoese with "full rights" (see discussion in Vitale 1951:32–40). It is likely that in the larger legislative bodies the families unrelated to the rival factions were given enough weight to safeguard them from fights over control of those bodies.

The *podesteria* was an organizational innovation that altered the rule of Genoa's political game in a self-enforcing manner that fostered economic cooperation. The *podestà*'s military strength as well as his administrative role fostered interclan cooperation by weakening the relations between economic growth and political instability and the dependence of political stability on external threat. Furthermore, policy was determined by those who were expected to benefit from the long-run increase in the volume of trade, and a high, yet conditional, monetary reward motivated the *podestà* to follow this policy and to prevent any particular clan from expropriating income.

The Genoese *podesteria* formally lasted about 150 years, during which it faced many challenges as a result of temporary imbalances between factions, the political rise of the *popolo* (that is, the non-noble element), and the conflict between the pope and the emperor that affected Genoa during the thirteenth century. Yet the *podesteria* retained the same basic structure throughout this period, and by enabling cooperation it brought about a period in Genoa's history that Vitale (1955:69) has considered to be *"veramente l'età aurea del Comune genovese"* (indeed the golden age of Genoa). The ability of the Genoese to cooperate, the operation of an impartial political and legal system, and the few limits it placed on individuals' initiatives seem to have been instrumental in Genoa's economic and political growth. Politically, in 1195, Genoa was at peace for the first time in many years, and the Genoese joined together to reaffirm their control over the smaller cities around them. During the next hundred years under the *podesteria,* Genoa completely freed itself from the rule of the Holy Roman Empire; destroyed Pisa, its bitter enemy in the western Mediterranean; and was able temporarily to defeat Venice, its commercial rival in the eastern Mediterranean (for a historical narrative of this period, see, for example, Donaver 1890; Vitale 1955). Under the *podesteria* Genoa acquired extensive possessions in the Mediterranean, including the city of Syracuse in Sicily and other cities on the Black Sea (e.g., Vitale 1951, chapters 2–3). Although each of the available measures of Genoa's economic growth—such as the growth of trade and population—is imperfect, they are consistent in presenting a uniform picture of spectacular economic performance relative to Genoa's past and to the performance of Venice, its last rival for supremacy among the Italian maritime cities (for details see Greif forthcoming).

Conclusion

This chapter has utilized analytic narrative to study a self-enforcing political system. Neither a narrative nor a theoretical approach could, by itself, reveal the nature and implications of the factors that led to political order or disorder and their interrelations with Genoa's economy, social structures, political rules, and external environment. Analytic narrative indicates that although the Genoese commune was a self-enforcing response to gains from cooperation, its subsequent political and economic history was shaped by the extent to which the political system was self-enforcing.

This extent depended on the particularities of Genoa's economy. Gains from raids and the acquisition of possessions motivated initial cooperation, but the acquisition of possessions undermined the extent to which cooperation was feasible. Genoa's main clans reached an MDE in which they refrained from cooperating in the acquisition of additional possessions owing to the political implications that such possessions would have, namely the increased cost to each clan of sustaining Genoa's self-enforcing political system. Under the consulate, the factors that determined the extent to which Genoa was a self-enforcing political system hindered economic development. Sustaining political order in Genoa came at an economic price: preserving an economy based on piracy and raids that provided the economic foundations of a self-enforcing political system.

For a time, the presence of external threat relaxed this constraint on economic development. Yet, in the long run, the induced economic development undermined the sustainability of Genoa's self-enforcing system. Once this threat had subsided, the political system in Genoa was no longer self-enforcing: neither an appropriate economic foundation nor external threat could support a self-enforcing political system in Genoa. Political disorder and the associated economic cost were the result. Both before and after the period of civil war, the relations among economic development, external threat, and the extent to which Genoa's political system was self-enforcing shaped its political and economic history.

The *podesteria* relaxed the constraint on political order and economic development imposed by Genoa's self-enforcing political system, thereby altering the course of Genoa's political and economic history. In particular, it motivated clans to cooperate further in the acquisition of possessions by reducing each clan's motivation to use military force to gain control over the city in a self-enforcing manner. This self-enforcing organizational innovation was a product of a particular historical learning process inside and outside Genoa and of certain historical circumstances. More generally, the transition to the *podesteria* reflects a path-dependent process that constrained Genoa's political rules from evolving significantly away from the forms and functions shaped by their historical origins.[37] The *podesteria* was a viable political organization because it built on the existing factional structure.

Although the *podesteria* provided Genoa with a relatively impartial political and legal system, it was not a democracy. This system was based on a third party—an outsider with military, legal, and administrative powers strong enough to guarantee that the balance of power among Genoa's factions would be maintained. Hence disintegration of the factions that evolved during the twelfth century did not occur, as each faction had an incentive to maintain its integrity and sufficient military strength, and the *podesteria*'s functioning was based on the factions' existence. Indeed, when the interfaction military balance was upset circa 1339, Genoa's political system was altered, and until 1528 the city was ruled by a doge (for discussion see, for example, Donaver 1890:86ff).[38] Genoa was weakened as a commercial and political unit and defeated by Venice in 1381. In a sense, Genoa's defeat in the fourteenth century was foreordained, although not sealed, during the twelfth century.

This study demonstrates the complexity of investigating self-enforcing political systems. Such an investigation requires a detailed examination of the particularities of the time and place under consideration, utilizing a coherent, context-specific model. Thus it may be premature to attempt to generalize based on this study regarding the sources and implications of self-enforcing political systems. Yet it is appropriate to make one general comment.

A general conclusion is that comprehending the sources of political order and disorder, a state's ability to mobilize resources for economic and political ends, and the relations between political rules and the importance of particular social groups requires examining those strategic interactions among the political actors that determine the extent to which the political system is self-enforcing. A self-enforcing political system exhibits particular interrelations between its politics and economy: political order and the ability to mobilize resources are required for economic development. Yet a developed economy does not necessarily provide, in and of itself, a better foundation for a self-enforcing political system. The history of Genoa illustrates that the appropriate political

---

[37]On the theory of path dependence, see David (1988).

[38]It should be noted that prior to 1339 there were short periods of time during which Genoa was not ruled by a *podestà*.

rules may be the key to sustaining political order while pursuing development. However, political rules are but one of the factors sustaining a self-enforcing political system. Hence the same political rules can reflect and lead to distinct political and economic outcomes. Other endogenous and exogenous factors determine the extent to which particular rules will indeed be self-enforcing and hence effective in altering behavior. Evaluating the impact of particular rules requires examining them in the broader context of the factors influencing the extent to which the political system is self-enforcing.

Indeed, many of the other Italian communes of the late medieval period had political rules similar to Genoa's under the consulate and even under the *podesteria*. Yet they had distinct patterns of political and economic history. Their distinct histories, as well as those of other political units, offer the promise that comparative studies of different political units will shed additional light on the process through which various political units were able, or failed, to achieve self-enforcing political systems conducive to the maintenance of political order and economic development.[39]

More generally, the study of Genoa's self-enforcing political system indicates that understanding a state's political and economic history can benefit from examining the factors sustaining it as a self-enforcing political system, their implications, and their historical development. Analytic narrative provides the combination of narrative and theory to facilitate the analysis of the extent to and the manner in which a political system is made self-enforcing on its particular trajectory of political, economic, and social development.

References

Abulafia, David. 1977. *The Two Italies.* Cambridge: Cambridge University Press.

Annali Genovesi di Caffaro e dei suoi Continuatori, vols. 1–4, trans. Ceccardo Roccatagliata Ceccardi and Giovanni Monleone (1099–1240; reprint Genoa: Municipio de Genova, 1923–29).

Annales Pisani (Bernardo Maragone) (1108–ca. 1188; reprint, edited by M. Lupo, in *Gentile in Rerum Italicarum Scriptores,* vol. 6, part 2, Bologna: Nicola Zanichelli Editore, 1936).

Bairoch, Paul, Jean Batou, and Pierre Chèvre (eds.). 1988. *The Population of European Cities from 800 to 1850.* Geneva: Center for International Economic History.

Belgrano, Luigi T. 1873. *Tavole Genealogiche a Corredo Della Illustrazione del Registro Arcivescovile de Genova.* Genoa: Atti della Società Ligure di Storia Patria.

Bonds, W. N. 1968. "Money and Prices in Medieval Genoa (1155–1255)." Ph.D. diss., Department of History, University of Wisconsin, Madison.

Byrne, Eugene H. 1916. "Commercial Contracts of the Genoese in the Syrian Trade of the Twelfth Century." *Quarterly Journal of Economics* 31 (November): 128–70.

---

[39]For such a preliminary study, see Greif (1995).

———. 1920. "Genoese Trade with Syria in the Twelfth Century." *American Historical Review* 25: 191–219.

———. 1928. "The Genoese Colonies in Syria." In *The Crusade and Other Historical Essays*, edited by L. J. Paetow. New York: F. S. Crofts.

Cardini, Franco. 1978. Profilo di un Crociato Guglielmo Embriaco. *Acrchivio Storico Italiano* 2–4: 405–36.

Codice Diplomatico della Repubblica di Genova dal MCLXIIII [sic] al MCLXXXX [sic], vols. 1 and 2, edited by Cesare Imperiale di Sant'Angelo (reprint Rome: Fonti per la Storia d'Italia, 1936, 1938). (CDG)

Cristiani, Emilio. 1962. *Nobilta' e popolo nel comune di Pisa*. Istituto italiano per gli studi storici, vol. 13. Milan: Casa Editrice Einaudi

David, Paul A. 1988. "Path-Dependence: Putting the Past into the Future of Economics." Technical report 533. Institute for Mathematical Studies in the Social Sciences. Stanford, Calif.: Stanford University.

———. 1984. "The Impact of the Third Crusade upon Trade with the Levant." *International History Review* 3 (April): 159–68.

———. 1988. *Genoa's Response to Byzantium, 1154–1204*. Urbana: University of Illinois Press.

De Negri, Teoflio Ossian. 1986. *Storia di Genova*. Florence: G. Martello.

Donaver, Federico. 1890. *Storia di Genova*. Genoa: Nuova Editrice Genovese.

Epstein, S. 1996. *Genoa and the Genoese*. Chapel Hill: University of North Carolina Press.

Face, Richard D. 1952. "The Embriaci: Feudal Imperialists of Twelfth-Century Genoa." M.A. diss., Department of History, University of Cincinnati.

Giovanni Scriba, Cartolare di, vols. 1 and 2 (1154–64; reprint edited by Mario Chiaudano. Turin: Chronicon Estense, 1935). (GS)

Greif, Avner. 1995. "Political Organizations, Social Structure, and Institutional Success: Reflections From Genoa and Venice during the Commercial Revolution." *Journal of Institutional and Theoretical Economics* 151 (December): 734–40.

———. Forthcoming. *Genoa and the Maghribi Traders: Historical and Comparative Analysis*. New York: Cambridge University Press.

Heers, Jacques. 1977. *Parties and Political Life in the Medieval West*. Oxford: Oxford University Press.

Herlihy, David. 1969. "Family Solidarity in Medieval Italian History." In *Economy Society, and Government in Medieval Italy, Essays in Memory of Robert L. Reynolds*, edited by David Herlihy, R. S. Lopez, and V. Slessarev. Kent, Ohio: Kent State University Press.

Heyd, W. 1868. *Le Colonie Commerciali Degli Italiani in Oriente nel Medio Evo*. 2 vols. Venice: G. Antonelli.

———. 1885. *Histoire du Commerce du Levant au Moyen-âge*. 2 vols. Leipzig: Otto Harrassowitz.

Heywood, William. 1921. *A History of Pisa, Eleventh and Twelfth Centuries*. Cambridge: The University Press.

Hicks, John. 1969. *A Theory of Economic History*. Oxford: Oxford University Press.

Hughes, Diane Owen. 1978. "Urban Growth and Family Structure in Medieval Genoa." In *Towns in Societies*, edited by Philip Abrams and E. A. Wrigley. Cambridge: Cambridge University Press.

————. 1977. "Kinsmen and Neighbors in Medieval Genoa." In *The Medieval City*, edited by Harry A. Miskimin, David Herlihy, and A. L. Udovitch. New Haven, Conn.: Yale University Press.

Hyde, John K. 1973. *Society and Politics in Medieval Italy: The Evolution of Civil Life, 1000–1350*. London: Macmillan.

Krueger, Hilmar C. 1932. "The Commercial Relations Between Genoa and Northwest Africa in the Twelfth Century." Ph.D. diss., Department of History, University of Wisconsin, Madison.

————. 1933. Genoese Trade with Northwest Africa in the Twelfth Century. *Speculum* 6 (July): 377–95.

————. 1957. "Genoese Merchants, Their Partnerships and Investments, 1155 to 1164." In *Studi in Onore di Armando Sapori*. Milan: Istituto Editoriale Cisalpino.

Lane, Fredric C. 1973. *Venice: A Maritime Republic*. Baltimore: Johns Hopkins University Press.

Lewis, Archibald R. 1951. *Naval Power and Trade in the Mediterranean, A.D. 500–1100*. Princeton, N.J.: Princeton University Press.

————. 1938. *Storia delle Colonie Genovesi nel Mediterraneo*. Bologna: Nicola Zanichelli.

————. 1976. *The Commercial Revolution of the Middle Ages, 950–1350*. London: Cambridge University Press.

Munz, Peter. 1969. *Frederick Barbarossa*. Ithaca, N.Y.: Cornell University Press.

North, Douglass C., and Robert P. Thomas. 1973. *The Rise of the Western World*. Cambridge: Cambridge University Press.

Norwich, John Julius. 1989. *History of Venice*. New York: Random House.

Olivieri, Agostino. 1861. *Serie dei Consoli del Comune di Genova*. Bologna: Arnaldo Forni Editore. Also published in *Atti della Società Ligure di Storia Patria* 1858, vol. 1, pp. 155–479.

Otto of Freising and His Continuator. *The Deeds of Frederick Barbarossa* (1152–8; reprint, transl. and ann. Charles Christopher Mierow with the collaboration of Richard Emery, New York: Columbia University Press, 1953).

Pertile, Antonio. 1966. *Storia del Diritto Italiano dalla Caduta dell 'Impero Romano alla Codificazione*, 2nd ed. 2 vols. Bologna: Arnaldo Forni Editore.

Powell, Robert. 1993. "Guns, Butter, and Anarchy." *American Political Review* 87 (March): 115–32.

Rey, E. 1895. "Les Seigneurs de Giblet." In *Revue de l'Orient Latin*, vol. 3. Paris: Presses Universitaires de France.

Rossetti G., M. C. Pratesi, G. Garzella, M. B. Guzzardi, G. Guglié, and C. Sturmann. 1979. *Pisa nei secoli XI e XII: Formazione e caratteri di una classe di governo*. Pisa: Pacini Editore.

Spruyt, Hendrik. 1994. *The Sovereign State and Its Competitors*. Princeton, N.J.: Princeton University Press.

Tabacco, Giovanni. 1989. *The Struggle for Power in Medieval Italy*. Cambridge: Cambridge University Press.

Tudela, The Itinerary of Benjamin of (1159–73; reprint Malibu, Calif.: Joseph Simon/Pangloss Press, 1987).

Vitale, V. 1951. *Il Comune del Podestà a Genova*. Milan: Ricciardi.
————. 1955. *Breviario della Storia di Genova*, 2 vols. Genoa: Società Ligure di Storia Patria.
Waley, Daniel. 1988. *The Italian City-Republics*. New York: Longman.

Two

The Political Economy of Absolutism Reconsidered

JEAN-LAURENT ROSENTHAL

L'argent est le nerf de la guerre. [Money is the
sinew of war.]
  Richelieu

J'ai trop aimé la guerre. [I loved war too much.]
  Louis XIV

European Comparative History

Between the mid-seventeenth century and the end of the nineteenth century, Europeans transformed their political and economic institutions to create modern states. Among the many aspects of this transformation, I focus in this chapter on four that played a key role in determining the process by which countries changed. Over these two centuries, there were three key political changes: central governments increased their control over expenditures and taxation, representative institutions became the norm, and expenditures for war increased stunningly. Finally, the key economic institutions were also transformed in that markets in general, and financial markets in particular, lost their medieval or early modern regulations and expanded dramatically. The spread of this dramatic transformation was slow. Indeed nearly two hundred years elapsed between the Glorious Revolution and the unification of Germany in 1870. This dispersion in time is odd at least in hindsight, since the countries that first adopted these new institutions derived considerable political and economic advantages. This fact poses a problem for common theories of long-term change, since they imply that societies that face common challenges should evolve in similar ways. The historical evidence, however, argues that our theories must bear the burden of explaining both evolution and stasis. This chapter argues that the uneven process of political and economic change across European countries can best be explained by focusing on fiscal institutions.

This chapter was begun during a fellowship at the Center for Advanced Study in the Behavioral Sciences. The author gratefully acknowledges the support provided by grants from the National Science Foundation (SBR 9258498 and SES 9022192) and the RBSL Bergman Foundation. I thank Lee Alston, Robert Bates, Gary Cox, Robert Cull, James Fearon, Avner Greif, Philip Hoffman, Edgar Kiser, Margaret Levi, Larry Neal, Paula Scott, William Summerhill, and Barry Weingast for their suggestions.

Within the broad development of political institutions in Europe, this chapter examines how political institutions in England and France came to diverge dramatically in the seventeenth century. Of equal concern is why Old Regime France failed to evolve toward the British institutional model. The political and economic evolution of Britain and France has great prominence in economic and political history because these two countries were the great rivals of the preindustrial period.[1] Economic historians seeking to explain France's institutional immobility relative to Britain have made frequent appeals to political economy (De Vries 1976; Jones 1981; North 1981). These accounts, however, rarely detail which political institutions stifled change in France while encouraging it in England.

I argue that the divergent French and British experiences had their roots in the different outcomes of domestic conflicts over fiscal policy. In these countries elites (henceforth the elite) played a substantial role in determining the Crown's fiscal resources. Indeed, although the Crown usually enjoyed substantial independent revenues, it could not increase taxation without consulting the elite. The Crown sought resources to wage war, whereas the elite would have preferred more pacifist policies. The elite tried to use the power of the purse to influence royal activities in general and war making in particular. Among other things it sought to protect or increase its fiscal authority and reduce that of the Crown. Kings, in turn, tried to use their control of the political agenda either to maintain the status quo or to reduce elite political activities. Until the 1720s French kings' fiscal autonomy grew while their British counterparts lost authority to Parliament in a series of domestic political struggles. In this view political evolution was not the result of bargaining or of cooperative problem solving but of contention.

To make this case I employ an analytic narrative that rests on a specific theory of political negotiation. The theory is implemented in a model of taxation and warfare that illuminates the key factors favoring or restraining changes in the distribution of fiscal authority. Although the model was generated solely to explain the political economy of Old Regime Europe, it applies broadly whenever authority over policy is divided between groups that have significant differences in their policy objectives. The model sidesteps the standard debates about the reasons for war (see Fearon 1995); instead I argue that the cost and benefits of war are sufficiently unevenly distributed in societies that wars—which destroy resources in the aggregate—can be profitable for decisionmakers. The approach is also narrative because it seeks to use history to construct the theory and to flesh out its implications. The mathematics of the model have been relegated to an appendix, to better integrate the historical evidence with the general patterns underscored by the broad results of the theoretical analysis.

[1] The importance of the comparison between the two countries has certainly not been lost on historians (see for instance Miller 1987; North and Weingast 1989).

This approach leads to a synthesis of the political divergence of France and England in the seventeenth century that places taxation at center stage. This emphasis has general implications for theories of long-term change. It thus echoes Levi (1988) and North (1981), who emphasize the importance of taxation in institutional change, yet it goes beyond these previous analyses to construct a specific model of politics and taxation. For Levi and North, differences in tax rates rest in the intrinsic fiscal efficiency of political regimes or in the preferences for revenue of political actors, but in this model taxation depends on the way institutions structure the interactions of political actors. In particular I emphasize the role of corporate, provincial, or parliamentary organizations in choosing tax levels. This approach also echoes the sociological literature on the rise of the state that seeks to understand how classes and states interact (Skocpol 1979; Tilly 1990). Here I seek to show that the rulers may, at times, have an agenda that is different from the agendas of members of dominant classes; in particular, when the executive is staffed by a monarch, the monarch's independence varies depending on the political structure. Thus the apparent levels of tension between the ruler and the elite do not necessarily inform us about the role of divergent preferences.

The new narrative presented here also has implication for the historiography of Early Modern Europe. Most scholars, including those who reject Whiggish historiography, divide nations into two groups: those that adopted or retained representative institutions and those that failed to do so. Since representative institutions are often viewed as socially superior, those countries where kings were able to impose absolutist regimes are perceived as having failed. The literature has yet to draw fully the distinction between failure at a national level and the success of royal policies. The issue remains of why some countries developed representative institutions while others did not. Clearly if political evolution failed it must have been that a coalition that would have suffered under the new rules blocked change. According to this theory, the Crown was the central obstacle, not because it failed to perceive the social gains from Parliamentarism but rather because the Crown's private costs of change outweighed the private gains from change. Thus the goals of different actors were similar in the different countries examined, but differences in the distribution of fiscal authority had long-run implications. Indeed those countries where the Crown had insufficient independence to act alone were the ones that developed representative institutions.

The chapter proceeds as follows. First, I use France's history to construct a model of taxation and warfare. At the same time I use the model to analyze the institutional evolution of France during the two centuries that preceded the revolution of 1789. In the next section I argue that the model fits England with very few modifications and helps us understand why the Stuarts and their opponents were so fixated on fiscal issues. The examination of the historical material then leads me to consider the importance of two factors ignored by the model: domestic political structure and religion. The model is then put to work to reexamine the joint political evolution of France and England. I conclude by turning to a broader set of conclusions.

A Model of French Political Conflict

After the end of the Seven Years War the French Crown had to reorganize its finances. Bringing the state's budget back into balance was achieved through a partial repudiation of the debt and by increasing taxes (Marion 1927–31:1, 222–79). As part of this broad reorganization the Crown solicited funds from a variety of organizations, among them the Burgundian Estates. Burgundian officials had the following reaction to a new loan request:

> Sera néanmoins très humblement representé au seigneur Roi que les impots multiples dont ses sujets ont été acablés pendant la guerre et sous le poid desquels ils continuent de gémir depuis la paix ont dut diminuer considérablement la masse des dettes de l'état, si le produit de ces impots a été employé suivant la destination annoncée par les édits sans nombre qui les ont créés.
>
> Et que si malheureusement ces dettes subsistent encore elles ne sauroient s'éteindre que par une sage économie des revenus de sa majesté, par le retranchement des dépenses, et non par des emprunts fréquents qui ne libèrent point l'état en substituant de nouveaux créanciers à la place de ceux qui sont remboursés. (Archives Départementales de la Côte d'Or, series C4568, 13-3-1771)[2]

Burgundian officials did grant the Crown some financial relief, but, as had been the case since Louis XIV, less than the Crown really desired (Major 1994:344). This was because in Burgundy the king could levy no taxes without the assent of the provincial estates, whose fiscal authority had been recognized since the fifteenth century (Major 1994:21–22). The same officials noted pointedly that the Crown did not appear to be spending the resources it had raised as it had promised. The estates and other Burgundians expected taxes to reduce the debt, which had not been the case. This reflection from officers of the province of Burgundy encapsulates the central elements of the model we need to build: a Crown with limited fiscal authority, but with the ability to spend as it pleases, and public expenditures heavily focused on war.

---

[2]"It shall nevertheless be suggested to the lord King that the many taxes, which have burdened his subjects during the war and which continue to weigh upon them since the peace, should have considerably reduced the debts of the state if the product of these taxes has been used in the way that the innumerable edicts that created them suggested.

"And that if sadly these debts remain today, they will only be paid off by a wise economy of his majesty's income, by the reduction of expenditures, and not by frequent borrowing which does not liberate the state but simply replaces old creditors with new ones."

A quote does not establish a fact, so we must begin by reviewing the evidence that argues that, in Old Regime France at least, the elite and the Crown had separate spheres of fiscal authority. In Early Modern France, the Crown's fiscal authority was limited by a battery of organizations. The Estates General, provincial estates, the assembly of the clergy, municipalities, venal officers corps, and other groups all provided funds to the Crown in separate negotiations (Mousnier 1974; Major 1994: Michaud 1994). The organizations that provided supplementary funds to the Crown were dominated by nobles, clergymen, and urban elites; rural dwellers and the laboring classes were not enfranchised. These organizations controlled taxation over geographical areas, groups of individuals, or economic activities. In each case, the Crown recognized the fiscal authority of the organizations by charter. Although it could and did sometimes revoke the charters, this was a very costly step and one that was largely abandoned after 1660 (Beik 1985; Bien 1987; Potter and Rosenthal 1997a,b).

The institutional complexity and diversity of these organizations leaves many modeling options open. I chose the simplest one and model the public finance process as follows. Taxation is not unified; rather it is decided separately by the elite and the king in the distinct sectors of the economy over which each has fiscal control. For simplicity I assume that the elite is unified, so that a single entity decides taxation in sectors over which the elite has fiscal control. The elite sector contains all the disparate organizations that enjoyed fiscal independence. The royal sector contains the rest of the economy. In particular, the French Crown had significant latitude in fiscal matters because it was able to rely on one or more of the following strategies: changing excise and tariff rates, the sale of offices or titles, manipulation of the currency, and the use of judicial authority to regulate property rights.[3]

What is crucial for the model is that the elite controls taxation in one part of the economy (henceforth the elite sector) while the Crown controls taxation in the rest (henceforth the royal sector). Indeed such separation of fiscal decisions will be the source both of a free rider problem (each party will prefer to have the other raise resources for joint projects) and of the power of the purse (if the Crown's fiscal authority is small enough then the elite can influence policy through its control of funds). Finally, raising resources is a costly enterprise, so that the burden imposed on the country is larger than the revenues raised. Although this last assumption is standard in studies of the economics of taxation, it pertains particularly well to Early Modern Europe, whose bureaucracies were of limited efficiency.

---

[3]For our purposes the Crown's sector yielded two sources of revenue, ordinary revenue and prerogative revenue. The Crown had been able to secure some regular revenues, usually called ordinary revenue, by transforming what had at one time been extraordinary taxation into annual levies; prerogative revenue flowed from the Crown's control of certain property rights (Collins 1988; Hoffman 1994; for England see North and Weingast 1989).

In France, as elsewhere in Early Modern Europe, fiscal resources were used primarily to prepare for and prosecute war (Hoffman and Rosenthal 1997). Kings found their ordinary revenues adequate in peacetime but woefully inadequate in wartime. Thus, in conflicts over domestic policy, as Burgundian officials found out in 1771, the elite could not expect to have much influence on royal decisions.[4] This then allows us to focus on war. The objective of both the elite and the Crown is to maximize their respective returns from war. Whereas in reality both the elite and the Crown probably had much more complex goals, the importance of war in total expenditures means that it must have been the dominant dimension of contention.

When kings wanted to go to war they had to secure resources, because success in warfare was contingent on the availability of funds. Louis XIV, for instance, increased indirect taxation upon the opening of the war of the League of Augsburg in 1689, and he also secured financial commitments from the Church, venal officers, and provincial estates (Michaud 1994; Potter and Rosenthal 1997a,b). If the king could not raise sufficient funds to fight the war he desired, then negotiation was likely to settle the dispute that had created the opportunity for war. If, however, the king succeeded in securing sufficient resources from one or both sectors of the economy, he could then launch his army into battle. Here it is crucial to note that in the model the king makes executive decisions—which seems fitting for an absolutist monarch. By implication, we assume that the elite cannot control the stream of expenditures, and that there is a moral hazard problem between the elite and the king. In other words, the king may use resources for purposes of which the elite does not approve. For simplicity, in the model these purposes are restricted to unpopular wars. It should be noted, however, that the problem of moral hazard would crop up whenever the executive prefers policies of which other members of society do not approve.

In keeping with the history of Europe, where years of warfare could produce only minor changes in territory, I allow for conflicts to end in draws.[5] Winning, losing, or stalemate are uncertain outcomes, but I assume that the odds of success rise as a country invests in arms, provided that other countries do not

---

[4]See the discussion later in this chapter of the frustration of the English elite when faced with the religious policies of Charles I in the 1620s and 1630s.

[5]The existence of draws affords a convenient way to introduce a bias to account for the personal value that the king attaches to a given war. For other ways to translate resource effort into outcomes and achieve an equilibrium, see Hirshleifer (1995). Previous theories of war have focused on rent dissipation. Each period of play features two players with a resource endowment. Each player can use his endowment for either war or production. Output is divided according to the relative magnitude of warfare investment by each party. Although it is possible to introduce a political structure to choose war investment, in that setting it is not possible to distinguish between aggressiveness (which wars get fought) and resource commitment (how hard wars are fought), a central theme of this research.

simply match the increased spending.[6] More important is the question of how the spoils of war were divided.

I assume that the elite and the Crown share the returns from winning and losing according to the extent of their fiscal control of the domestic economy. For instance, the elite's share in victory is simply the value of victory times its share of fiscal control. The elite is also assumed to bear a cost from draws because it is responsible for staffing the army and the administration, both of which are made to work harder during hostilities.[7] What is crucial here is not the precise division of returns between elite and king, but rather that there is a significant difference between the expected profits of the king and those of the elite. This difference creates the key policy tension in the model: there are some wars that the king wishes to fight but that the elite does not. Other ways of creating this difference in preferences, such as a fixed cost of war for the elite or asymmetries in the division of the spoils, do not alter the substantive results of the analysis.

That such significant differences exist presupposes that the Crown and the elite cannot reach a bargain whereby they split the returns from war in a way that mirrors their attitudes toward war. In other words, it assumes that the institutions that govern the division of spoils are not sufficiently flexible that they can adjust to differences in the expected profitability of wars. We cannot ascertain how such institutions worked; however, we can examine the implications of choosing a different assumption. Should the king and the elite always evaluate the profitability of war in the same way, there would be no conflict in objectives and the only difference across countries would involve fiscal divisions. Since fiscal divisions induce free rider problems whereas unified taxation (taxation solely controlled by either the elite or the Crown) is efficient, we would expect regimes to evolve quickly toward unified taxation. Indeed, since efficient taxation increases the resources available for war, countries in which there are no important policy differences should evolve efficient fiscal regimes. Clearly, however, that was not the case for France. Fiscal reform in general, and unified tax authorities in particular, did not emerge from a process of regular bargaining between Crown and elite; rather reform occurred during the French Revolution.[8]

---

[6]As has often been observed, all other things being equal, numerical supremacy significantly improves the odds of success for a combatant. Numerical supremacy on the battlefield can be the result of strategy, organization, or luck, but it is often the result of superior resources.

[7]The remaining cost of draws is borne by the rest of the population. The essence of the problem is that the elite and the Crown *both* bear relatively low costs for war relative to the rest of the population; but the Crown bears a lower cost of war than the elite. Using draws to create war bias is convenient but not fundamental.

[8]We can easily imagine that the Crown could offer to compensate the elite for losses incurred in war. Such promises, however, may not have been credible. Indeed the Crown would have had to increase its transfers to the elite after wars that it lost (in other words, when its coffers were particularly bare).

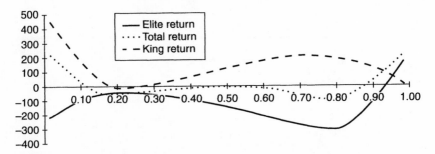

FIGURE 2.1. Returns when the value of winning is close to the value of losing. The model analyzed to arrive at the values in table 2.1 has the following parameters: $Y = 10,000$, $W = 11,000$, $L = -6,000$, $D = -500$, $d = 1,000$. For the functional forms see the appendix.

I therefore assume that the rule for sharing the spoils of war is fixed. Furthermore I assume that spoils were divided according to shares of fiscal power. Although somewhat artificial, these assumptions do serve as reasonable approximations. After all, a king cannot hog the profits from war if he expects support from the elite. In the model, the process of war making unfolds in several steps. First, when faced with a war opportunity, the king decides whether or not to fight. If he decides on war, he calls on the elite to make a contribution and decides how to raise resources in the part of the economy he controls. The war is then fought, followed by a division of spoils.

The appendix offers a mathematical version of the model just described. For purely technical reasons it is not possible to solve the model just outlined in general form.[9] Standard specifications of the impact of taxation and of the relationship between spending and war outcomes have well-behaved solutions. Thus the figures and tables display the result of a numeric example whose results stand up to specification changes. The model has a number of important implications for our understanding of the relationship between fiscal authority and political regimes.

First, according to columns 3 and 4 of table 2.1, when the division of fiscal authority is quite skewed, only one of the two parties contributes to the war effort (in the example, when the elite controls less than 10 percent of the economy, it raises no taxes). Indeed, in these cases the party with little fiscal authority opts

[9]It is possible to solve for equilibria in a general setting, but obtaining comparative static results requires additional assumptions because the tax curve will not always have a unique minimum. Although it has been found to be broadly U-shaped in all cases, when the returns from winning and losing are nearly alike, the return from war for each party has two local minima. In such cases aggregate returns are typically negative, and changes in the tax structure lead to perverse results. In some ranges (as illustrated in figure 2.1), it pays for the Crown to surrender fiscal control, even though the probability of winning declines, simply because it can shift a greater share of the tax burden *and* the consequences of losing onto the elite.

TABLE 2.1
War Resources, Tax Rates, and War Outcomes by Regime Type

		Tax rate		Outcome probabilities	
Regime type	Total effort	Elite	King	P	Q
0.01	604.55	0.00	5.99	0.27	0.27
0.05	577.00	0.00	5.48	0.26	0.28
0.10	542.50	0.00	4.88	0.25	0.28
0.15	518.80	0.02	4.31	0.24	0.29
0.20	508.40	0.08	3.75	0.24	0.29
0.25	500.50	0.18	3.23	0.24	0.29
0.30	494.80	0.31	2.74	0.24	0.29
0.35	490.50	0.48	2.30	0.23	0.29
0.40	487.50	0.69	1.89	0.23	0.29
0.45	486.00	0.94	1.53	0.23	0.29
0.50	485.10	1.22	1.20	0.23	0.29
0.55	485.70	1.55	0.92	0.23	0.29
0.60	487.20	1.92	0.67	0.23	0.29
0.65	489.70	2.32	0.46	0.23	0.29
0.70	493.70	2.77	0.30	0.23	0.29
0.75	498.90	3.25	0.16	0.24	0.29
0.80	506.30	3.77	0.07	0.24	0.29
0.85	516.00	4.34	0.01	0.24	0.29
0.90	545.30	4.91	0.00	0.25	0.28
0.95	579.50	5.51	0.00	0.26	0.28
0.99	606.90	6.01	0.00	0.27	0.27

Note: The model analyzed to arrive at the values in the table has the following parameters: $Y = 10,000$, $W = 18,000$, $L = -6,000$, $D = -500$, $d = 500$. For the functional forms see the appendix.

to let the other side pay for all war costs. The implication is that when the Crown is dominant in taxation, the elite has no real power and does not contribute to war efforts.[10] Conversely, if the elite's fiscal authority is dominant it can control war making. The Crown in such cases free rides by not levying any taxes on the limited sector it controls. France, before 1789, clearly corresponds to a regime of divided taxation in which neither party is dominant because elite groups did contribute to the budget, and their contributions increased in wartime.[11] Second,

[10]This problem perpetually plagued the British Empire, from the Stamp Act crisis of the American colonies to discussions with Australia, Canada, New Zealand, and South Africa in the late nineteenth century over military taxation (see Davis and Huttenback 1987).

[11]Another implication of the model is that aggregate revenues are actually slightly higher when the elite has near total control than when the fiscal system is in the king's hands, because the king cares less about the outcome of wars. But that result has limited implications for France since it was never in such an extreme case.

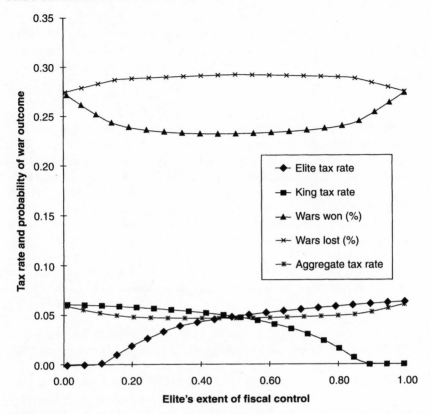

FIGURE 2.2. Political regimes, taxes, and warfare.

following the aggregate tax rate curve in figure 2.2, it is clear that aggregate revenue is high when either the elite or the Crown dominates the fiscal process, and it is lowest when taxation is most evenly divided. Indeed the case in which taxation is most evenly divided is that in which the free rider problem is most severe, whereas it is eliminated when taxation is consolidated. In the model, when either party controls the fiscal system, the tax rate is about 6.3 percent, whereas in the case in which the regime is evenly divided the tax rate falls below 5 percent, a drop in revenue of nearly one-fifth. This finding goes a long way toward explaining why per capita taxation was significantly lower in France or Spain than in England or the Low Countries.[12]

Finally, fiscal rates are skewed whenever fiscal control is unevenly divided. Whoever controls the smaller sector tends to tax at a lower rate than his

[12]The observed differences in rates between Great Britain and France are much larger than those found here, a finding that may well be driven by the fact that the elite was not a unified tax authority in France.

counterpart who controls the larger sector. The existence of such differences in tax rates was a hallmark of absolutist regimes, which were full of tax exemptions, as well as differences in intensity of taxation across provinces. The model is therefore consistent with much of the public finance of Early Modern France, yet for our purposes it is its implications for the process of war making that matter.

Fiscal regimes matter beyond their varying efficiencies because they affect the likelihood of war. Recall that in the model the Crown is more aggressive than the elite. To constrain the Crown, the elite would like to use the power of the purse to induce the king to be more selective about which wars are fought, but this is not always easy. To begin with, the elite would rather succeed than lose, so it would like to provide resources to increase the probability of winning if a war is to occur. Often, however, the elite prefers peace to war, so it has an incentive to deny resources to the Crown if it thinks that this approach will dissuade the Crown from launching its armies into battle. The Crown, in contrast, would like to go to war often; in fact it will always be willing to fight any war the elite wants to fight. The Crown, however, may be constrained because the elite can refuse to provide financial assistance. The model thus suggests that war was the source of tension in public finance, and that the Crown and the elite often found themselves at odds.

Furthermore the model argues that the decision as to which wars get fought depends on the resources that are raised and the willingness of Crown and elite to participate in wars (for empirical evidence see Kiser et al. 1995). Given a division of authority, some wars are so profitable that both the elite and the Crown want to fight. The region in which wars are popular is in the upper right-hand corner of figure 2.3 (region I). In this region wars are sufficiently socially profitable and the elite receive a sufficient share of the proceeds that they are happy to participate. That region grows in size as the elite increases its fiscal authority. Indeed as the elite gains control of taxation it also increases its share of the spoils of war. Therefore as its fiscal authority increases, the elite becomes more willing to go to war. Because it can spread the cost of draws over a greater share of the returns from winning. Similarly there are also some wars that are too unprofitable to fight; these are at the bottom of figure 2.3 (region II). In these cases, the returns from winning are sufficiently low that they do not offset the cost of losing, even for the Crown. Between these extremes we find two further regions. In one, the elite dislikes war, but the king will fight on his own (region III). Here wars occur because the king has sufficient resources to go to war alone. Wars are unpopular with the elite, though given that they occur the elite may provide some funding to the king. Finally, in the fourth region, the king wants to fight but needs the cooperation of the elite because he cannot fight alone (region IV). It is in this last region that the elite's control over taxation translates into control over foreign policy. By denying the Crown resources, the elite ensures that the Crown will not

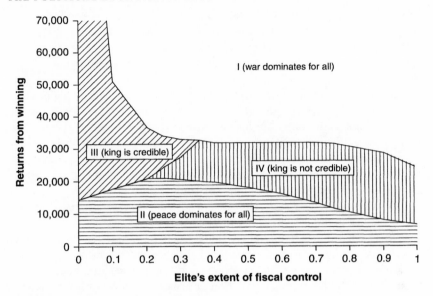

FIGURE 2.3. Warfare and political regimes.

fight. Thus the elite and the Crown care about the division of fiscal authority because it has implications for which wars are fought. More important, as long as fiscal authority is reasonably divided (no party controls more than 90 percent of taxation in the model), then small changes in authority affect which wars are fought. Indeed increases in royal authority free the king to fight more wars. In theory, therefore, the king would use every opportunity to increase his fiscal authority because such authority directly translated into greater policy autonomy.

In France, at least, monarchs used increases in political authority to increase their fiscal independence. Following a revolt in Normandy in 1624, Louis XIII rewrote the province's statutes so that its estates became irrelevant to the fiscal process and stopped meeting (Esmonin 1913; Mousnier 1974:1, 608–15). Estates were the key institutional constraint on the French Crown's fiscal cravings. In fact, during the latter phases of the Hundred Years War, a weak Crown had leaned on estates in nearly every region of France to decide and assess taxes. Over the next two hundred years French kings progressively disbanded most estates during periods when their thirst for funds had temporarily abated (Major 1994:3–56). By the early seventeenth century only some regions, *pays d'états,* had been able to retain their estates. Others, often known as *pays d'élections,* had no such legal guarantees. Their estates ceased to meet in the sixteenth century—and thereafter the Crown imposed some taxes at will. To be sure, significant reform in taxation implicitly required the convening of some form of estates, provincial or general.[13] Thus, although the Crown's power was never unchecked, in many provinces it had acquired the freedom of action that comes with discretion over tax revenues. To the extent that it could raise resources without consultation, it was more independent than if it had to use estates.

The link between domestic politics and fiscal evolution can be underscored by examining the fate of a *pays d'état* that ran afoul of royal power: Provence. Provençal nobles revolted during the Fronde (Pillorget 1975:601–800). Although the rebellious aristocrats were treated relatively lightly when Louis XIV reasserted his authority, the province's fiscal privileges were abrogated and its estates did not meet again until the late 1780s. To many the issue of estates may appear benign, since the Crown was closely involved in taxation decisions even in *pays d'états*. However, dispensing with estates removed very real obstacles to the growth of tax revenue (Beik 1985; Major 1994:342–45). Reforms such as those that Louis XIII and Louis XIV were able to impose on regions like Provence and Normandy effectively freed the Crown to set most tax rates there and represented clear reductions in the local elite's authority. At least until 1720, the political evolution of France was toward a Crown more and more powerful in fiscal matters.

This trend did not go unchallenged by the elite. Given the opportunity for a regency, the elite revolted in 1652 in the hope of securing royal political concessions. That revolt, known as the Fronde, was the last violent attempt by the elite to limit royal authority before the Revolution. After the Crown prevailed, Louis XIV was able to expand his fiscal authority with little challenge.[14] As a result, the elite's control over taxes was weaker during his reign than at any other time in French history. Conversely, after the bankruptcy of 1714–21, the elite was able to usher in a new regime that effectively reduced the Crown's fiscal autonomy (in the model, an expansion of elite control). That new regime was based not on the traditional privileges that had been the mainstay of the *pays d'états*, but on strict legalism interpreted by judicial bodies known as *parlements* (Norberg 1994).

Until 1789, France, unlike Britain, never converged on either autocracy (in which the Crown controls all taxation) or parliamentarism (in which the elite monopolizes fiscal decisions). Instead fiscal authority remained divided between the Crown and the elite. The equilibrium that was established by the end of the first half of the seventeenth century was broadly stable, and it featured

[13]The distinction between *pays d'élection* and *pays d'état* is less obvious than it appears. Dauphine's estates failed to meet after 1628 even though it was a *pays d'état,* whereas before 1620 Normandy had estates even though it was a *pays d'élection.* By 1660, however, being a *pays d'état* seems to have been a necessary condition for estates to meet.

[14]Yet Louis heeded the warning of the Fronde and did not significantly challenge the myriad of fiscal privileges that were the domain of the elite until nearly forty years into his reign. In 1695 the *capitation* was introduced. It was intended as a progressive tax that no one could evade.

divided fiscal authority. It was stable because French kings managed to rule and compete internationally for 160 years without calling the Estates General. The Crown was able to do so because it had considerable autonomy over some tax rates. Yet that equilibrium did not leave the Crown unconstrained, because there were clear limits on what and whom the king could tax.

The stasis that characterized the period between 1720 and 1789 was not associated with any major change in priorities by either party. In fact, at first neither side was prepared to accept this equilibrium. Given the chance, the French elite strove to reduce the fiscal independence of the king. In 1714, after the death of Louis XIV, the aristocracy persuaded the regent to eliminate some of his new taxes despite the desperate need for revenue (Marion 1927–31). As Jean Egret (1962) has detailed, the pre-Revolution (1787–88) was less a debate over administrative reform than a tug of war between the Crown and the aristocracy over how much fiscal autonomy the Crown would have to surrender to receive increased funding. After his reform efforts of 1787 and 1788 failed, Louis XVI was in a weakened position, and he was forced to call the Estates General. The Estates quickly seized budgetary control from the Crown (Sutherland 1988).

The model then offers some key revisions to the narrative of French political history—in particular to the key problem of why France did not evolve political and economic institutions similar to those of Britain. First, the political stasis that we observe was less likely to have been caused by mere stodginess than by a clear perception by the Crown of the dangers of political reform. Although the Bourbon monarchs may not have been tireless workers seeking to improve their nation, there is little evidence that they behaved significantly differently than their British counterparts. Louis XIV with Colbert and Vauban in the 1660s and 1670s; Louis XV with Maupou, Turgot, and Terray; and Louis XVI with Calonne and Brienne all made significant efforts to alter French institutions in the hope of spurring economic activity. In each case these efforts met with at best partial success. Louis XIV abruptly halted his reforms with the onset of wars that ended only with his death. Louis XV was spurred to change by the outcome of the Seven Years' War, and at his death most of his reforms were still in place. Louis XVI was moved to reform by the financial consequences of the War of American Independence. For French absolutist monarchs, war, institutional change, and the budget could not be separated. We shall return later in this chapter to the scope and impact of the reforms; let us simply note here that the monarchs were keenly aware of the importance of prosperity for their popularity and power. If they failed to address France's economic problems it was because they had international ambitions and these were ruinous; but that scarcely sets them apart from other kings and queens of Europe.

The model also addresses another proposed explanation for the lack of institutional change in France: the absence of representative institutions. Hilton Root has recently argued that the lack of representative organizations substantially raised the costs of reform because there was no forum in which socially improving bargains could be struck.[15] A "representative" institution existed in France, namely the Estates General, but it was not used. The Estates General failed to meet after 1629 because the Crown opted to dispense with representation. Since the king alone decided when to call the Estates, he was able to avoid them entirely. The Crown must, therefore, have felt it was not in its interest to call the Estates. In other words, from the Crown's point of view, the economic gains of the Estates were outweighed by the political costs. In particular, the king must have perceived that the Estates were likely to make decisions that he would not like. For instance, the Estates would probably try to limit further the Crown's fiscal autonomy—an undesirable outcome from the king's point of view.

The fact that the French Crown decided to forego the bargaining opportunities represented by regular callings of the Estates General in return for autonomy suggests that representative institutions are not simply mechanisms for resolving collective action problems and thus enhancing the welfare of all the participants. It may be that certain political institutions exist to alter property rights for socially improving reasons; but they can rarely do so without consequences for the distribution of wealth and power, and it is the latter as much as the former that concerns decisionmakers. One might presume that regular meetings of the Estates General would have allowed the Crown and the elite to negotiate a more efficient system of taxation that would have, in turn, created more economic growth and more resources for war. However, the Crown's interest in war and the elite's preference for peace created an insurmountable impasse. A more efficient fiscal system demanded a unified tax agency. If the elite controlled that agency it would surely have used it to dictate foreign policy. The fact that the Estates intended to use their fiscal authority to curtail the autonomy of the Crown in other matters was something no king was prepared to accept lightly.[16] Negotiations could not change this situation, so French kings were correct in perceiving no reason to call the Estates General. Indeed, as French monarchs discovered in the seventeenth century, they only controlled

[15]Root (1994:8–13, 182–83). For Root the crux of the problem for France is the institutional inability of the Crown to make binding promises (credible commitments). Root suggests that representative institutions could have solved that problem. The history of the developing world and some industrialized countries economic policies' offer at best mixed support for this thesis. Governments with representative institutions have experienced massive inflation, budget deficits and other poor economic policies when those have been popular or expedient. This is not to say that democracy offers worse economic policies than other political regimes rather it is that democracy is not a sufficient condition for growth.

[16]In the model the joint profit maximum occurs when the Crown is an autocrat. Theoretically it would be possible for the Crown to compensate the elite for what ever losses they might suffer from political change and move to autocracy. The fact that no such bargain has ever been made suggests that such a "welfare-improving" bargain is stymied by transaction costs—in particular the inability of the sovereign to commit to paying the compensation.

when representative institutions met, not what happened at those meetings. The proceedings easily turned to issues that the Crown was not willing to discuss. Indeed, these assemblies were golden moments for a usually scattered elite to communicate and therefore to oppose the Crown.[17]

We can now turn to the implications of the model for political and economic reform. Under absolutism, the Crown controlled the reform agenda: thus it would not carry out reforms it did not like. If the model's stress on taxation is correct, then the Crown would allow reforms that would increase fiscal receipts and disallow others. Thus we should expect the French Crown to have favored market development since this process stimulated growth and increased the king's revenues. Once again political institutions derail our economic intuition. The political structure of absolutism placed severe constraints on the Crown's ability to encourage economic growth because the division of the economy between the royal and elite sectors was fixed and hard to change. The only mechanism for reallocating the tax base was the Estates General. In the absence of calling the Estates, the Crown could not easily react to changes in the tax base. The model therefore predicts that economic processes that reduced the tax base (or encouraged investment in the elite sector of the economy) would be discouraged, whereas those that increased the tax base would be viewed more favorably. More generally, economic processes that increased royal autonomy would be warmly welcomed, whereas those that required tying the king's hands would be vetoed.

The alternative approaches to the one just outlined argue that privilege[18] and the past evolution of institutions limited reform in France. Furthermore, for many these problems worsened between 1660 and 1789 and were thus at least in part responsible for the Revolution (Root 1994). The alternatives fall by the wayside when we consider the findings of recent work in French economic history. Far from ossifying in a tangle of corporate and contractual constraints, the Old Regime was in fact quite capable of evolution. French

---

[17]If, however, one neglects (as Root does) the fact that domestic and fiscal reform would have curtailed the Crown's ability to wage war, then Bourbon monarchs appear somehow blinded, since in the domestic sphere everyone, including the Crown, favored the efficiency gains made possible by "representative" institutions. The issue of representative institutions has brought us straight back to fiscalism and foreign policy. Yet in *The Fountain of Privilege* there are but three references to war in the index—and they are all single references to specific wars. French kings failed to make credible commitments because they did not have enough revenue both to always keep their promises (to bondholders in particular) and to fight wars. More generally the inability to commit to policies that would be popular with the elite suggests that the elite and the Crown had divergent preferences (as I suggest they had over war). The institutional solution examined by Root (representative institutions) might have enabled the Crown to make credible commitments—but it would also have enabled the elite to dictate policy. It is likely that the Crown preferred to make its own policy in an imperfect world than carry out the elite's policy in a perfected one.

[18]By *privilege* I mean to take in the whole nexus of special rights whose beneficiaries encompassed, among other groups, corporations of royal officers, provincial institutions, and urban guilds.

absolutism had at least two distinct incarnations separated by the convulsion of the Regency (1715–23). Prior to 1715, the Crown used privilege to expand revenues. The Crown accomplished this by alternating between promoting and attacking privilege, but in most years new privileges were granted and new venal offices were sold (Mousnier 1971; Desert 1984; Bien 1987). One can understand this process by recalling that a Crown with incomplete fiscal control has serious incentives to have high tax rates on the sector of the economy it controls (as suggested in the model by the fiscal asymmetries in the absolutist range). During Louis XIV's gambit to control Europe from 1682 to 1713, the financial demands of war rose dramatically. Since revenues, as defined by the division of fiscal authority of the 1670s, were clearly insufficient for the war, the Crown faced two options. First, it could surrender fiscal autonomy in order to secure revenues at the moment. This involved calling the Estates General, and quite likely reducing the king's autonomy in international affairs in the long run.[19] Alternatively, Louis XIV could try to go it alone and raise tax rates wherever he could. He chose to follow the latter policy to financial bankruptcy and stalemate in international affairs.[20]

Louis's XIV's financial legacy was resolved in the massive default of the Regency. Yet during the 1730s, the Crown adopted different policies, which made privilege and officeholding a minor component of public finance relative to regular taxation and public borrowing.[21] Servicing the obligations incurred to officeholders under Louis XIV, however, remained an important item in the budget.[22] The Crown not only reduced its predation, but also invested some energy in encouraging economic growth. Efforts were made to increase the circulation of goods across the country. By one measure at least, the integration of markets increased significantly during the century— proof that the commercial economy was expanding (Weir 1988). Also testifying to the vitality of the economy was the migration of textile manufacturing to the countryside, following the British example of a few decades earlier. Although corporate guilds slowed that movement, they proved unable to halt this process; at best they were able to co-opt it by specializing in specific activities that

---

[19]The Estates would probably have questioned the king's international ambitions and refused to vote any meaningful tax increases. They might have also pressed political demands unpalatable to the king. So calling the Estates may well have been undesirable in the short as well as the long run.

[20]Louis XIV must have viewed the increased intensity of taxation as temporary—the new territories he expected to conquer would bring in new revenues and thus allow fiscal pressure to ease.

[21]The significant differences in the political economy of Old Regime France before and after 1720 have been overlooked by many authors—Skocpol (1979), Bien (1987), and Root (1994), for instance—in particular because they have neglected crucial quantitative information about financial markets, government debt, and tax receipts.

[22]According to Marion (1927–31:1:62, 2:131) the value of venal offices was nearly the same in 1715 and 1789.

complemented rural crafts (Clark 1987).[23] In any case, they did not find the royal
administration an effective support in their attempts to curtail rural production
(Bossenga 1991; Vardi 1992). Clearly the expanding economy was not the target
of a new round of taxation. Indeed tolls and other internal barriers to trade were
either reduced or left unchanged in the latter part of the century (Kaplan 1976).[24]
The general economic expansion depended on a stable currency and the growth
of the financial sector. In short, though there was no industrial revolution in
France prior to 1789, there was a good deal of economic change. Furthermore,
in many cases the Crown assisted market development because it stood to
reap fiscal rewards. For instance, the Crown stood to benefit directly from the
growth of rural manufacturing because it could tax the countryside much more
easily than urban dwellers. On the other hand, the grain trade was never fully
liberalized. Indeed the Crown had no mechanism to offset the loss of revenue
from internal tolls that would have been eliminated by the reforms.

The expansion of the economy took place only after the 1720s because it
depended on the end of government attacks on the financial sector. Such attacks
had been common under Louis XIV because the currency and the financial
sector were convenient sources of royal revenue (Hoffman et al. 1995). In
particular, monetary manipulations were very attractive sources of revenue for
the king. By reducing the metal value of the unit of account the Crown reduced
the real value of its debts and forced all coins to be reminted, thereby securing
seignorage revenue. Between 1688 and 1726 the livre's value fell by nearly
half (Goubert 1960). As a result, intertemporal trade was subject to uncertainty
because private contracts had to be drawn up in the unit of account. It seems
likely that investment was discouraged by the Crown's monetary practices under
Louis XIV. By contrast the silver value of the livre remained unchanged from
1726 to the Revolution, reducing the risks faced by parties in private contracts.
More generally during the 1720s, royal attitudes toward the economy seem to
have undergone a significant change from attack to neutrality.

The observation that the Old Regime changed direction after Louis XIV's
death is most accurate when considering credit markets. Recent research has
sharply redrawn our understanding of public and private credit markets in Old
Regime France, particularly in Paris (Hoffman et al. 1992, 1994, forthcoming).
Prior to 1720, private credit markets in the capital were largely stagnant and
government debt was closely held by members of the elite. The Crown used
both currency manipulations and defaults to reduce its obligations after military

---

[23]The fact that a spinning factory opened in France less than a decade after the first one had
opened in Britain is vivid illustration of the limited impact of the institutional differences between
countries. France was behind, but not by much.

[24]The attack on internal trade barriers failed to a large extent, but the point remains that the
situation did not worsen and that, at least in the Northeast, private institutional innovation in
commerce apparently continued apace.

defeats—and therefore it passed as much of the burden of wars on to the elite as it could. After 1726, by contrast, the Crown marketed its securities to the general public, with the result that they were broadly held by the richer segments of the French population as well as by some foreigners (Luthy 1961; Hoffman et al. 1992). Privileged corporations became less important providers of resources, both because few new offices were sold and because members of corporations now held a shrinking fraction of the debt. Thus general debts rather than obligations to corporations constituted the new financial frontier. Those general debts were issued in the Paris capital market under an apparently unusual set of rules. As I have argued elsewhere, this development was contingent on the development of the Parisian capital market (Hoffman et al. forthcoming). One might presume that such an evolution would have required the creation of a commitment mechanism to guard against default.

However, no such mechanism was ever put in place. Instead, the Crown innovated while preserving its ability to default. This evolution brought to the Crown a clientele of lenders who were largely disenfranchised. Defaults occurred periodically, but they targeted specific debt issues rather than specific bondholders. The characteristics of the bondholders and the nature of the risks they faced in their public debt holding had changed in tandem. All this is hardly consistent with a government ignoring the economy. Clearly the Bourbons promoted or allowed economic change when that change did not interfere with their policy autonomy.

The creation of a large capital market in Paris should be enough to disprove the notion that the Old Regime ossified, yet even in credit it evolved in other ways as well. A second component of innovation lay with the use of regional estates as financial intermediaries (Potter and Rosenthal 1997a). The estates afford an illuminating perspective on the Old Regime. Manned by the local elite, the estates carried out three tasks. First, they controlled taxation in their provinces; second, they shared control of local politics with the Crown's agents; finally, they acted as financial intermediaries for the Crown. The estates issued bonds in return for a royal agreement allowing them to keep a certain amount of royal tax revenues until interest and principal had been repaid. Unlike the debts issued directly by the Crown, estates bonds were repaid on schedule, interest was paid regularly, and if the bonds were involved in royal defaults, the estates minimized the effect on the pocketbooks of bondholders within the constraints of the law. So confident were the estates of their credit reputation that they announced with great fanfare in 1773 that they would serve as their own secondary market. They did so because they thought this step would make placing the bonds easier. They also gambled that few investors would want to resell them at any one time—and their expectations were realized [Archives Départementales de la Côte d'Or, series C4569 (délibération des élus), 18-2-1773].

Regional estates' bonds provide a wonderful natural model of what a more modern—more British—credit market might have looked like in France.

Furthermore, they provide suggestive clues to the reasons for its absence. Estates bonds from all provinces composed 15 percent of the debts of the Old Regime in 1790. They composed a good deal more of the debts issued between 1726 and 1789 because such bonds were paid off with greater regularity than other royal debts. The estates, however, could only bear a limited burden of debt because the penalties they could impose on the Crown were equally limited. As Potter and Rosenthal (1997a,b) argue, the estates were no more than provincial institutions, rendering strictly local services with the backing of the local elite. Had the estates supervised a large fraction of the debt, the Crown would no doubt have forced them to default more frequently because the fiscal savings would have exceeded the political costs of default. To extend the benefits of regional estates the king would have had to create more provincial estates or to call the Estates General regularly. Because such strategies would have reduced royal autonomy, the Crown passed on the opportunity.[25] As in the case of the Estates General, the regional estates alert us to the fact that France did not lack institutions that could increase fiscal or financial efficiency; instead the Bourbons deliberately chose not to use these institutions. Indeed the monarchs feared the consequences for royal autonomy of increased reliance on the estates.

The Old Regime, therefore, was quite capable of evolution, even if it was not an economic powerhouse like Britain, its closest competitor. The ability of the Bourbons to adapt to changing environments explains why they managed to avoid negotiating with the elite and yet endured so long. If they had been unable to access capital markets at all, French kings would no doubt have been forced to call on the Estates General in each major war after 1660. However, they had access to credit and they had information about the value of different institutional arrangements. Therefore, they allowed credit markets to evolve up to a point, to increase the number of investors that they could solicit. Yet the Crown also knew that creating a large anonymous credit market for a consolidated public debt was only worthwhile if it was going to honor its obligations. Indeed in a large consolidated market the Crown would have been forced to equate the risk on new bonds with the risk of default on the outstanding debt. In return the Crown would have reduced the cost of debt service because government bonds would have become much more liquid. Yet such a reform was worthwhile only if the Crown knew it would not default. Indeed in the case of a consolidated debt it would have to pay a default premium on the whole debt, whereas by marketing varied types of bonds the Crown could choose to pay that premium only at the margin. The fiscal constraints under which the French kings operated made it impossible to avoid defaults, and thus the French debt was never consolidated under the Old Regime.

[25]The estates' pool of bondholders also broadened dramatically at the same time as the estates increased the borrowing they undertook for the Crown, suggesting that the political independence of the estates had increased (Potter and Rosenthal 1997a).

Credit markets represent but a small fraction of the economic environment that mattered in royal decisions. However they are one of the rare areas for which we have sufficient evidence to assess the impact of the Old Regime on the economy. In particular, credit markets allow us to make the British comparison explicitly. In this case the comparison has an unambiguous outcome: capital markets were less well developed in France than in England, but they were thriving in both countries. The Old Regime might have limited growth in France, but it did not prevent it. Reform was halting and piecemeal because significant reforms would have also required a transfer of fiscal authority, and on that issue the elite and the Crown had irreconcilable differences.

Thus the burden on political analyses of the Old Regime is to explain this piecemeal or partial evolution. I argued earlier that such evolution is inconsistent with previous explanations stressing the Old Regime's increasing ossification. However, the important, if limited, evolution of the Old Regime is consistent with the view that after Louis XIV's reckless war making, the Crown had discovered that few wars were in fact worth fighting and that fiscal resources were important. Louis XV and Louis XVI then had every incentive to promote economic growth within the existing political framework. Because they were no more powerful than Louis XIV, they could not expect to acquire more fiscal authority. On the other hand they were unwilling to compromise with the elite over foreign policy. Thus to fund their international ambitions they had to depend on the fiscal windfalls provided by overall economic growth and the willingness of capital markets to redistribute taxation over time. Given that the Bourbon monarchs shared the general eighteenth-century view that the prospects for growth were rather limited, their ambitions were correspondingly limited. The elite perceived reform proposals from a slightly different perspective. Those reforms that would effectively increase the Crown's fiscal independence were not welcomed, and to the extent that the elite could impede or prevent the progress of such change it did. On the other hand, the elite was actively involved in every aspect of the French economy, from credit markets to trade and manufacturing (Forster 1960, 1980; Chaussinant-Nogaret 1976; Hoffman et al. forthcoming). Piecemeal evolution and economic growth were welcomed in Old Regime France as long as they did not upset the political equilibrium.

Whether the Crown was willing to sacrifice the economy in the pursuit of glory, or whether it shepherded the economy to increase royal resources, it had the same overriding concern: preserve its autonomy in international affairs. Given that overriding concern and the king's perception of gains from war, he chose whatever policy for the nation he preferred. In other words, in France the Crown opted for growth as long as it did not conflict with its broader political agenda. Because that agenda included fighting unpopular wars, turning over fiscal authority to representative institutions was a reform that no king would entertain. In France, therefore, the political regime evolved via conflict, not bargaining. The next section considers the same issue for England and arrives at much the same conclusions for the seventeenth century.

The Model Applied to England

Both Britain and France began the seventeenth century with fiscal authority divided between the elite and the Crown. The British king was a person of considerable wealth. Often the monarch was granted some revenues for life upon accession to the throne, and he could exercise considerable discretion in the collection of other revenues. On the elite side, England and Wales, Ireland, and Scotland each had a parliament, with England and Wales providing the bulk of government revenues. However, these separate parliaments were not unified in a single institution. In fact the only joint assembly occurred in 1653 (Coward 1994:359). It was not until 1707 that Britain was unified and not until 1801 that the United Kingdom fully coalesced. Thus, from a historical perspective, the unification of fiscal authority occurred at about the same time in France and Great Britain. However, parliaments, unlike French estates, maintained effective control over land taxes, and they never legally surrendered their authority over excises.

As in France, war consumed the bulk of the British Crown's revenues, and fiscal policy was the central source of conflict between Parliament and the king. Again as in France, the king's ordinary revenue was ample enough to allow him to pursue any domestic policy he chose; thus in the absence of war British kings were as absolute as their French cousins. This absolutism did not necessarily prejudice good relations with the elite. James I's relations with the elite were amicable enough, but one should bear in mind that at that time England remained at peace. By contrast his successor, Charles I, had both domestic and international disagreements with the elite. On the domestic side, his authoritarian church doctrine was at odds with both of the dominant elite persuasions: traditional Anglicanism and Puritanism (Coward 1992:119–84). His foreign policy, which was favorable to Spain, was also highly unpopular. Unable to secure subsidies from Parliament, Charles tried to dispense with elite consultation and expand his fiscal prerogative. As a result Parliament did not meet for twenty years. Thus, between 1621 and 1640, the division of authority seemed to tilt toward the Crown, mostly because large amounts of resources were not required. The situation, however, was abruptly reversed when a Scottish rebellion forced Charles to call Parliament in 1640.

The elite's power came from the inability of the king to fight any wars without parliamentary support. Here the contrast with France is quite telling, for the Bourbons were able to deal with internal violence without recourse to elite taxation. Hence England clearly corresponds in the model to a division of fiscal authority that was more favorable to Parliament from the outset. Henry VIII and Elizabeth I had to call upon Parliament regularly to fund their conflicts with either Spain or France. For Charles II, the Scottish revolt of 1640 was a brutal reminder of the limits to his fiscal independence. Parliament quickly moved to exercise the power of the purse, granting Charles some financial relief on the condition of religious reform and increased parliamentary authority. The civil war that followed was precipitated by Charles's refusal to accept this political realignment.

Tension over policy persisted under Cromwell but focused on domestic rather than international issues. The failure of the Protectorate led to the Restoration in 1660. Charles II was brought back to the throne under conditions that curtailed his fiscal autonomy compared with that of his father. Consistent with the model, Parliament attempted to avoid a repetition of the early seventeenth century by limiting the Crown's fiscal independence. Yet the resources granted to Charles were not ungenerous as long as the king limited his foreign policy objectives. At first, the Crown and the elite shared foreign policy objectives. These focused on the Dutch, whose commercial and maritime activities competed against those of British firms. Yet the rise of Louis XIV as a major force and the decline of the Dutch shifted the elite's position from antagonism toward the Low Countries to deep suspicion toward France. Throughout Charles II's reign the royal fiscal sector remained small enough that he accepted substantial French subsidies. Charles had a close connection to France because he had grown up there. The elite, however, viewed Louis XIV's government with a great deal more reserve. Yet despite Charles's favorable attitude toward France the Restoration was a stable settlement. Domestic tensions were limited because England remained at peace; Britain was not forced to choose sides in a significant conflict in part because Louis XIV was not yet bent on conquering the Spanish Netherlands.

The reign of James II was a period of great conflict, and I examine it in detail in the next section. It suffices to note here that under his rule the elite was unable to block the king's policies as long as they only concerned domestic questions. Historians have noted that when William and Mary were offered the Crown in 1688 the political bargain to ensure Parliament's existence was more implicit than explicit (North and Weingast 1989). Yet in one dimension the bargain was blatant: William and Mary were only voted subsidies for a few years and had to make annual requests for further funds from Parliament (Dickson 1967; Coward 1992:365–79). Their prerogative powers in revenue matters were curtailed, shrinking royal autonomy in taxation. In other dimensions, however, they were not given more stringent fiscal terms regarding ordinary revenue than the Stuarts. What is less clear is whether, in the absence of the wars that raged nearly uninterrupted from 1688 to 1713, William and his successor Anne would have been willing to adhere to this settlement. William and Anne clearly disliked parliamentary politics, even though they usually got what they wanted (Coward 1992:397–400).

In the short run the sovereigns of England were fighting a popular war, and this fact suppressed the underlying discord between the Crown and the elite.

In the long run, the institutional evolution that climaxed in 1688 would lead to a permanent shift whereby the Crown would accept the fiscal powers of Parliament (though it would take another forty years before Parliament would exercise significant executive authority). The budgets of William and Anne were always approved; so were their choices for prime minister, as well those of their Hanoverian successors (Langford 1992). Clearly after 1688 England and Wales had a fiscal regime in which decisionmaking was centralized in Parliament. The extent of centralization would increase even further after 1707, when Parliament extended its purview to Scotland. Yet that outcome was precisely what the Stuarts had attempted to avoid through the seventeenth century because of its implications for policy.

Once the equilibrium of 1688 was in place, William and his successors worked to create a more efficient financial system. The Bank of England, while representing creditors of the state, was an innovation heavily influenced by William's Dutch advisers. It was not so much a creation of Parliament set against the king as a creation of the king and Parliament to serve their common interests, given the fiscal equilibrium. It is unclear whether William would have engaged in the same institutional innovation if he had perceived a possibility of seizing direct control of British taxation. It is similarly unclear what James would have done had he perceived that any gambit to reduce Parliament's fiscal control would fail. Thus the evolution of financial institutions in England, as in France, was contingent on the evolution of fiscal institutions. William and Parliament showed little concern for the political consequences of financial changes because the entire economy was part of Parliament's tax base. Precisely because fiscal authority was unified after 1688, financial change was not relevant to the distribution of political power. Its impact on international politics, however, was profound, since it enabled England to become a dominant power.

The history of Britain highlights several aspects of the model in a more dramatic fashion than the history of France. First, the division of fiscal authority changed a great deal more in Britain than in France and that change allows us to ascertain the impact of fiscal authority on the political process. Prior to the Glorious Revolution, Parliament did exercise power through its control of taxation, but this power was relatively weak. Indeed Parliament again and again conceded significant long-term fiscal revenues to the king even though these revenues allowed him to act in ways of which Parliament disapproved. In the seventeenth century the king was regularly granted long-term revenues for reasons of ideology (the divine right of monarchs) and efficiency.[26] As long as

---

[26]Here the argument of Kiser et al. (1995) about the structure of tax farming becomes highly relevant. They show that the Crown centralized tax authority in response to improvements in transportation and information diffusion. The same argument applies to representative assemblies. Given the technology of transportation, it was simply too costly for the elite to have regular assemblies during most of the Early Modern period—but such monitoring was much cheaper in a small country such as England than in a large country such as France.

Parliament was willing to make such grants, British kings strove to gain fiscal independence, the first step toward absolutism.

Conversely as Parliament's fiscal authority grew the Crown's discretion in matters of policy shrank. Finally in 1688 Parliament monopolized fiscal authority, and royal challenges to its legislative powers ceased. Moreover, the Crown had to nurture parliamentary support for its policies in ways unimaginable in France. If the Bourbons were watching events unfold in England, it is not surprising that they did not call the Estates General. And they were watching. In fact the lessons of British history formed vivid tableaux for the French Crown. Indeed Charles II grew up at the French court during the Cromwellian protectorate, and James II was to spend the last decade of his life in France.

The key role of the power of the purse is easier to observe in England because its kings were always more constrained then their French counterparts. Nonetheless the two countries started the seventeenth century with fiscal authorities sufficiently divided that conflicts between the elite and the Crown were inevitable. Initial conditions did matter in that the elite's greater fiscal control in England than in France made it much more likely that a parliamentary system of government would emerge in London than in Paris. Finally in England tensions over international policy were more marked than in France because, beyond the Crown's war bias (in modern terms, internationalism), there were key ideological differences between the elite and the king. These differences made the Crown's policies unpalatable to the elite (increasing the fixed costs of war) and sharpened the tension between Crown and elite. Since the source of these differences lie beyond the scope of the model we examine them separately in the next section

Beyond the Model

The model specifies only two variables: the value of warfare and the fiscal structure of the economy. Therein lies its power, and therefore its weakness—it is by its very nature an incomplete account. It must be evaluated on the basis of its substantive power. Were critical variables missed? If so the preceding accounts of politics in France and England could be substantially improved by explicitly incorporating other factors. Two historically relevant factors were left out of the model: elite structure and religion. These omissions may appear at first glance damning, since in the case of England religion was a source of significant tensions in the seventeenth and eighteenth centuries. In France, it has been argued that the lack of cohesion of the elites was in large part responsible for the rise of absolutism. This section attempts to show how these omissions affect the narrative and that they are less onerous than they may at first appear. A better understanding of the internal structures of elites and the politics of religion would surely enrich our understanding of the evolution of French or English institutions, yet the brief examination that follows shows that the connections among taxes, warfare, and political conflicts remain unchanged.

The model and the narrative treat the elite as a unified entity. This approach ignores two well-known facts about Early Modern elites: they were quite heterogeneous, and in their dealings with the Crown they were rarely unified. It would appear that diverse and divided elites could not provide the kind of unified response to fiscal demand that the model suggests. The point can be made even more clearly by noting that the representative bodies of most European countries were often multiple and poorly organized to voice dissent from the king's will. Even Great Britain did not unify its Parliament until 1707—well after the Glorious Revolution. Yet although we can easily acknowledge the existence of these divisions, their impact on the substantive conclusions of the model is more ambiguous.

The structure of domestic politics affects the model in two ways. To begin with, it dictates the returns that the Crown will achieve in using bribes and threats to extract revenue from the elite: a more unified elite will be less easy to cajole or coerce. It also dictates the free riding incentives of each elite group: a more divided elite has less direct incentive to aid the Crown. These two forces therefore have opposite effects on the ability of the Crown to raise money in the sector of the economy where it does not have fiscal control. We would face a particularly damning problem if the political structure of the elite were directly related to the extent of its fiscal control. Variation in elite structure could offset changes in the extent of its fiscal control. To take a perverse case, we can imagine that the distribution of regimes would be such that as monarchs lost fiscal control the elite became more atomized. Then one could find that absolutist regimes raised more taxes than parliamentary ones. Fortunately that was not the case, at least as far as Britain and France were concerned: though there was a secular trend toward fiscal unification in both countries, it was overshadowed by the growth in Parliament's fiscal authority in Britain and the growth of royal fiscal independence in France. Given that the current model predicts the variation in tax rates properly, it may well be unnecessary to be concerned with elite politics, at least at this initial stage of the research.[27]

If the internal structure of the elite calls into question the level of institutional detail that the model should capture, religion forces us to confront the sources of conflict between Crown and elite. Between 1620 and 1688, British politics was

[27]The Crown in any case could affect the institutional fragmentation of the elite; it is therefore likely that the political structure of the elite reflected the perception by the Crown of the balance between the cost of fragmentation and its return. Had increasing or decreasing elite cohesion yielded more revenue for the Crown, it would have worked in that direction by using its institutional authority. One brake on such tinkering with the elite's political structure was the clearly perceived implications for the division of power between Crown and elite. Change in domestic institutional structure affected both the internal cohesion of the elite and the fiscal division of the economy between elite and Crown. For instance, in 1789 the calling of the Estates General in France resulted in the unification of taxation in a national assembly at the same time as it made elites cohesive (for a time at least) in their resistance to royal demands.

heavily charged with religious conflicts. At first it was Protestant dissenters who battled the king for control of the Church of England; later the conflict would be between a Catholic monarch and his largely Church of England opposition. This conflict leads to two sets of potential problems for the model. First, it may be that tension over warfare was fueled by divergent preferences about different wars owing to ethical rather than profitability concerns—countries of one religion, for instance, preferring to fight countries of another religion. Second, religion, rather than struggles over the power of the purse, may have been the engine for institutional evolution.

That preferences over warfare may have been shaped by concerns other than profitability does not raise a fundamental problem for the approach set forth here as long as the conflict between the Crown and the elite persists. Indeed the model focuses on how often a country should go to war, whereas when religion becomes the dominant factor, the concern will shift to which enemies should be engaged. This shift does not require a wholesale change in the model. As long as the Crown and the elite want to fight different wars, and the Crown controls foreign policy, the elite will be tempted to use its power of the purse to control war making. In this case it would want to withhold funds for wars of which it does not approve. The free rider problem that drives most of the model remains because the king and the elite, all other things being equal, would prefer to lower the tax burden on the sectors they each control. The accretion of fiscal authority by the Crown allows it to become involved in wars on its own—wars that the elite may support with resources if not prayers. Hence the broad relationships would still hold even though ethics rather than profits affected preferences about war.[28] Most important, the arguments about political evolution remain valid in this different context—in fact they may be reinforced because having a king of a different religion from the elite may be perceived as an irreconcilable difference. Thus the examination of an omitted variable shows that the model's insights may well extend beyond Early Modern Europe.

Religion, however, may still have been an important force in shaping elite behavior. Indeed changes in religious beliefs could imply changes in preferences about national policy that could either divide or unite the elite. Recall that in France by 1600 issues of religion had become relatively minor, because the monarch and the bulk of the population were all Catholics. Protestants simply did not control sufficient resources to challenge the Crown effectively. In England religion was always more important, but until the 1670s religious conflicts between the Crown and the elite had always turned to the advantage of the Crown, unless foreign policy intruded, as it did in 1640. It was the invasion

[28]One point should not be lost, however. In cases in which ethics matters, the policy space has two dimensions (profits and ethics), and this characteristic may complicate the political process greatly. Though the tension in policy would remain, equilibria could be difficult to attain within the model.

of the Scots that empowered Parliament; Charles's tinkering with Church of England doctrine neither unified the elite nor made it a unified force. Indeed the king had at his disposal sufficient resources to pursue religious policies independent of Parliament.[29] After the Restoration, conflicts over religion became institutionally relevant because the rift between the Anglican majority and the dissenting minorities appeared to give the Crown a chance to achieve political gains at the expense of Parliament. Yet again after 1670 it was the interaction between religion and foreign policy that drove the political process. Although the elite was deeply divided in religious affairs, it was relatively united in its foreign policy preferences: only the Catholic minority favored alliance with France, whereas Protestants favored alliance with Holland. Because both Charles II and James II were suspected of Francophilia, the true conflict was between the Crown and the elite, not among the elite.

Matters came to a head in 1673 when Parliament required that public officers—including James of York, the heir apparent—affirm their allegiance to the Church of England. James in turn revealed his Catholicism. As a result, tensions rose between Parliament and the Crown. The Protestant elite was now aware that Charles II, whom it did not trust, could be succeeded by a Catholic. But religion alone proved an insufficient force to alter the political equilibrium: attempts to remove James from the line of succession failed.[30] The elite therefore foresaw a bleak future. James, as a Catholic monarch, would likely pursue foreign and domestic policies that the elite deeply disliked. In particular, he was likely to continue favoring France over the Low Countries. James came to the throne in 1685 with his Catholic convictions intact, and he implemented policies that favored religious toleration at home and France on the international scene. Although the elite was rather divided on religious issues, it was united in its dislike of France. The elite could put pressure on James II to change his policies by decreasing its grants of revenue. It could also attempt to reduce the king's fiscal independence. Either James II could acquiesce to the elite's fiscal pressure and change his policies or he would have to attempt to increase his fiscal independence, in other words to seek absolutist powers. In the short run, James's favorable policy toward France had to be tolerated by the elite because the power of the purse was ineffective in peacetime. In the long run, his Francophilia posed a greater problem because when the next war occurred England would enter on the "wrong" side. Yet even the long-run tensions did not create an immediate rift between Parliament and the king. Indeed, when James

[29]Religion was very divisive among the elite, yet it was not divisive enough to allow Charles to prevail against Parliament in the civil war, nor were James II's overtures to dissenters sufficient to avert the Glorious Revolution.

[30]The exclusion crisis underscores the danger of calling Parliament representative. The Stuarts had such control over the election process that the elite was unable to prevent James from ascending to the throne.

inherited the throne, he did not immediately embark on a course leading toward absolutism, for his heirs, Mary and Ann, were both Protestant and thereby likely to reverse any pro-Catholic policies.[31] An increase in his authority would lead to short-term gains during his reign but in the long run would likely have little effect. The elite performed the same calculation: they had no reason to enter into a bitter conflict with the monarch because his influence could not be expected to last very long. Given his Protestant heirs, James II would be an unpopular but tolerated king. From Parliament's point of view, limiting the Crown's fiscal resources seemed sufficient to control James II's policies.

In 1687 James's wife became pregnant, and that event precipitated the Glorious Revolution. Indeed the expectation of the birth of a Catholic prince of Wales dramatically reduced the value of accommodation both for the King and for the elite. For James II absolutist power was now far more valuable. He did not attempt a coup or use violent means against the elite; instead he sought to massively increase his fiscal independence by packing Parliament. Armed with fiscal independence, he would be able to implement policies that he could now expect to persist through the reign of his Catholic descendant (Jones 1972:93). The birth of an heir who would be likely to follow policies similar to those of James led the elite to a simple conclusion: the longer they waited to act, the stronger James would be. The only possible response was a permanent limitation on the king's fiscal independence. Yet the elite had no institutional mechanism to change the country's fiscal balance, because the Crown controlled the agenda in choosing when to call Parliament. The elite thus had to act outside the normal political process. Within a few short months, the positions of the Crown and the elite had diverged completely, setting the stage for the Glorious Revolution.[32]

Religion therefore appears to be one of the important forces that upset the political equilibrium. Yet one should bear in mind that religion was not a force sufficient to cause change. Domestically James had built a coalition of Catholics and Protestant dissenters that parliamentary leaders could do little to stop. That coalition, however, was sundered by the coming war between Louis XIV and the Low Countries in two ways. First, Protestant dissenters could not accept alliance with France. Second, William of Orange intervened in British affairs to avoid England's joining ranks with the French. Thus religious conflicts were a mainstay of British politics and have received a great deal of attention, yet on their own they had little real impact on royal authority unless they were aided by events on the international scene.

The examination of issues of elite cohesion and religion—two factors that the model ignores—helps to delineate the limits and the power of the model.

---

[31]James was fifty-two in 1685. He would live until 1701.

[32]One proposal that circulated during the transition was to have William and Mary be succeeded by the prince of Wales (James II's son), provided he was raised an Anglican (Jones 1972:308).

Increasing the complexity of the model to better reflect the structure of domestic politics could well be the key to understanding differences in tax rates and national policy choices within broad classes of political regimes (absolutist or parliamentary), but it is unlikely to change the fundamental relationship between Crown and elite. The discussion of religion suggests that one should take a broad view of the factors that might shape a population's preferences. Yet such a broad view increases the importance of the relationships that this model highlights rather than weakens them. We can therefore return to the Early Modern period to examine the source of institutional change.

Political Evolution

Political change, in Early Modern Europe, had several potential sources. Regimes could evolve because elites became more unified as a result of organizational or ideological changes. They could also change because of changes in the technology of the state. As the British elite always feared, the rise of a standing army could enable the creation of a despotic government. Furthermore, change could arise from advances in warfare; magnifying the impact of differences in funding levels on the outcomes of wars would increase the level of pressure for the unification of taxation. Finally, evolution could come from strategic interactions between countries, so that fiscal or financial innovators would be imitated. Some of these possibilities were envisaged as early as the eighteenth century by Montesquieu:

> La plupart des gouvernements d'Europe sont monarchiques, ou plutôt sont ainsi appelés; car je ne sait pas s'il y en a jamais eu véritablement de tels; au moins est-il difficile qu'ils aient subsisté longtemps dans leur pureté. C'est un état violent, qui dégénère toujour en despotisme ou république: la puissance ne peut jamais être également partagée entre le Peuple et le Prince; l'équilibre est trop difficile à garder. Il faut que le pouvoir diminue d'un côté, pendant qu'il augmente de l'autre; mais l'avantage est ordinairement du côté côté du prince, qui est à la tête des armées. (1721, letter CII:281)[33]

From Montesquieu's point of view, monarchy was absolutism, a regime in which the Crown wielded considerable, though not unchecked, power. He considered monarchies to be unstable and believed that such regimes would converge on one of two extremes: despotism (in the model, complete royal control of

---

[33]"Most European governments are monarchies, or rather are called such; because I do not know if there ever were any such; in any case it is unlikely that they survive any real length of time in their pure state. It is a violent state, which always degenerates into despotism or republicanism: power can never be equally split between the people and the prince; the equilibrium is too hard to maintain. Power must decline on one side as it increases on the other; but the prince who leads the army usually has the advantage."

taxation) or republicanism (in the model, parliamentary control of taxation). Yet our model and the history of Europe suggest that Montesquieu may have been overly optimistic. Let us begin by considering the Crown's and the elite's preferences across regimes. Table 2.2 details the returns from warfare for the Crown and the elite under various political regimes. As suggested by the first row of the table, in the aggregate the Crown prefers to control the fiscal system by itself. In this case it receives the most it can ever receive. As previously discussed, the history of France up to 1789 and that of England well past 1688 suggest that monarchs cherished their fiscal independence. The model goes further to argue that monarchs would prefer fiscal despotism over any other form of government. The elite has exactly the opposite reaction, preferring to control taxation directly.

Montesquieu then turned to a consideration of what might be stable as an equilibrium outcome. His conclusion was that only extreme regimes were stable in the long run. Although monarchies might arise temporarily, sooner or later despotism or parliamentarism would arise. To relate Montesquieu's conclusion to the model, we can focus on which distributions of tax authority between the elite and the Crown are locally stable. Indeed dramatic movements in the distribution of authority were rare (even in Britain, Parliament had accumulated a very large fraction of the fiscal authority long before 1688). To be sure, without specifying exactly what forces acted upon the evolution of the fiscal system we cannot pinpoint the stable divisions of fiscal authority in a particular country or time period. Nonetheless the analysis allows us to formulate necessary conditions for stability, and these have clear implications. Fiscal institutions will be stable whenever both the Crown and the elite prefer the current division of fiscal authority to any proximate division of fiscal authority, or when they want to move in opposite directions.

Returning to table 2.2, we can examine how changes in fiscal authority affect the expected payoffs from war when war opportunities vary along a single dimension: the value of winning. In the model, the elite and the Crown only care about the spoils of war—they have no value for war or victory or fiscal authority per se. As a result they have diametrically opposed preferences about regime type, as suggested by columns 4 and 5 of table 2.2, which detail the expected returns from war for each group. The Crown always prefers to lower the elite's fiscal authority whereas the elite wants to increase it. Thus all distributions of fiscal control appear stable. Such stability points to a key limitation in the model: it fails to suggest how political change might come about. Indeed should the division of power shift to allow the elite to reapportion fiscal authority, it would immediately seize all authority. Thus without a model that translates domestic power into fiscal authority we appear to predict either rapid convergence on the extremes or no change at all. Yet the division of fiscal control changed regularly in both Britain and France between 1600 and 1730. Civil wars and other political processes that significantly shift power from Crown to elite or

TABLE 2.2
Selection of Wars, Returns from War, and Likelihood of Success

Regime type	Value of winning the war	Expected value of winning	Returns from war			Likelihood of a:		
			Elite	King	Joint	Win	Loss	War
0.01	11,000	30,500	−42	6,581	6,539	0.368	0.368	1.00
0.10	11,649	30,825	696	5,531	6,227	0.348	0.380	0.98
0.15	12,430	31,215	1,074	5,281	6,355	0.345	0.382	0.96
0.20	13,315	31,658	1,446	5,076	6,522	0.342	0.384	0.94
0.25	13,380	31,690	1,777	4,779	6,556	0.340	0.385	0.94
0.30	13,390	31,695	2,091	4,491	6,582	0.338	0.386	0.94
0.36	13,400	31,700	2,434	4,173	6,607	0.337	0.387	0.94
0.40	13,500	31,750	2,690	3,947	6,637	0.337	0.387	0.94
0.50	13,850	31,925	3,282	3,427	6,708	0.336	0.388	0.93
0.60	14,200	32,100	3,869	2,882	6,751	0.337	0.388	0.92
0.70	14,350	32,175	4,451	2,283	6,734	0.339	0.386	0.91
0.75	14,320	32,160	4,743	1,959	6,701	0.340	0.386	0.91
0.90	13,010	31,505	5,569	858	6,426	0.348	0.380	0.95
0.99	11,610	30,805	6,552	91	6,643	0.368	0.368	0.98

Note: The model analyzed to arrive at the values in the table has the following parameters: $Y = 10,000$, $L = -6,000$, $D = -500$, $d = 1,000$. For the functional forms see the appendix.

vice versa can be thought of as changes in the size of the sector in which the elite controls taxation. The model should reflect this possibility.

This failure suggests that the model is overly oriented toward describing the material impact of warfare and that a better model would take into account the ideological consequences of war. Indeed as we saw in the case of Britain, beyond the material rewards of war there were considerable ideological differences between the bulk of the elite and the Crown over foreign policy. For instance, after 1660, no matter how profitable a defeat of the Dutch might have been, British elites strictly preferred fighting the French. Since the ideological rewards of engaging one foe versus another are pure public rewards, they do not depend on the distribution of fiscal power; in other words, they are fixed rewards. One should not overstate the intensity of these ideological differences, since elites spent a large fraction of their time attempting to gain in a direct fashion from the pursuit of war or to shield themselves from its costs. In the French case, the ideological dimensions of warfare were more limited, though the elite is likely to have enjoyed victory per se.

Consider column 7, which details the probability of winning given that wars occur. As the elite increases its fiscal authority, the probabilities of war making and victory fall, then rise, while the chance of defeat has a symmetric shape. If the rewards from war for the elite and the Crown were independent of their control of taxation, then their preference about political regimes would be directly correlated with the probability of winning. At this point the preferences of both groups would be similar: they would both want to maximize the probability of winning. At first glance this different reward structure has appeal since it would allow for changes in the equilibrium. Furthermore, such fixed rewards were very real in the seventeenth and eighteenth centuries. Both monarch and elite gained prestige through victory and were shamed by defeat. Both of them derived part of the rationale for their existence from military service. More generally, these returns from victory or war making were partly noneconomic: gains came in the form of prestige or the utility of fighting (not unlike the utility that some derive from the exercise of power). The fixed returns may also have been partly economic to the extent that a portion of the returns from war was given to each group independent of its fiscal authority. The profit-sharing rules of the original model provided too little movement (every division is potentially stable) and too much contention (the Crown and the elite are always at odds). Fixed rewards offer too much movement (only the extremes are locally stable because they offer the highest probabilities of war and winning) and too little contention (the Crown and the elite nearly always agree). In the case of fixed rewards, the elite and the Crown each wants to move to the extreme closest to its current location.

The best specification for the returns from war for both parties is clearly a combination of fixed rewards and shares in the spoils. In this case, provided the fixed rewards from victory are sufficiently large, the king's returns from war will take on a U-shaped form as one changes the fiscal division of the country. If the king controls taxation in a sufficiently large fraction of the economy, then he desires to increase his fiscal authority, because that will increase the probability of winning and his share of the spoils. If, however, the king's fiscal sector is small enough, the effect of changes in fiscal authority on the share of spoils is negligible, and the king prefers to surrender his tax powers to the elite in order to increase the probability of winning and thus the likelihood that he will earn his fixed reward.

The converse will occur for the elite. In other words, once the division of fiscal power is heavily skewed the elite and the Crown will have the same objective: to unify taxation in the hands of the party that already controls most of it. The elite, however, will never encourage a move toward autocracy if it controls taxation in at least half of the economy, and the king will never agree to parliamentarism if he controls taxation in at least half of the economy. As a result, if fiscal authority is relatively evenly divided, elite and king will have opposite goals because each will seek to appropriate the other's fiscal powers. The mixed set of preferences thus described seems the one best suited to describe Old Regime Europe: individuals cared about the returns of war and those were divided in a political process in which fiscal authority mattered; however, they also cared about victory per se.

With a mix of fixed and variable rewards one can define three types of political regime, each of which is stable. First, if the king controls enough of the tax regime, the political system is likely to evolve smoothly toward autocracy. Indeed the elite will surrender its remaining fiscal power to increase the effectiveness of the tax regime and to increase the probability of winning. Similarly, if the elite controls enough of the tax regime, the political system is likely to evolve smoothly toward parliamentarism. Finally, there exists a third type of regime, absolutism, in which the elite would like to increase its fiscal authority while the Crown would like to decrease it. Consensual political change cannot occur, as was the case in France.

Over the range of absolutist regimes, the problems for political evolution are multiple. Indeed within this range changes in fiscal authority have complex effects. To trace these effects we can hypothetically consider increasing the elite's fiscal power further. This step will change the efficiency of the fiscal system and the probability of winning (although unless we can determine precisely where that range is located, we cannot predict whether taxation will be more or less efficient). If taxation becomes more efficient then the probability of winning will also increase. Furthermore, the growth in the elite's fiscal authority will increase its profits from war. Finally, the decline in the power of the king will reduce warmongering since it will reduce the Crown's ability to fight on its own. The effect on fiscal efficiency of changes in which sector has the power to tax should lead to consensual evolution. The effects on the distribution of profits as well as the effects on warmongering lead the Crown and the elite to have opposite objectives. This regime classification, along with inflection points for regime preferences, is displayed in figure 2.4.

Figure 2.4 contains key lessons for the analysis of France and England. To begin with, the evolution from absolutism to parliamentarism is not an equilibrium phenomenon—because the king prefers an opposite evolution. Furthermore, and more important, incremental bargains are rare. If the society is in an unstable situation it will converge toward either autocracy or parliamentarism. Alternatively it may find a stable equilibrium in the range of absolutism. Within absolutism the king will never find it in his interest to transfer authority to the elite or to promote the development of "representative" fiscal institutions.[34] Therefore, whenever taxation and spending are contentious issues, there are no bargains to be made between the king and the elite—because no change will leave them both better off. Montesquieu's insight therefore foreshadows many of the results of the present analysis. In this context, the creation of powerful

[34]Since absolutist regimes are such that the elite controls taxation in less than half of the economy, the convergence toward parliamentarism is in fact less likely than the convergence toward autocracy. Indeed on average the decrease in elite fiscal authority that would be necessary to move a regime from absolutism to autocracy would be smaller than the increase that would turn the same regime into a parliamentary one.

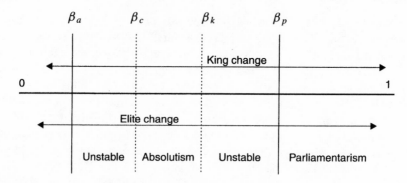

FIGURE 2.4. Taxation authority and political regimes.

representative institutions (increasing the share of the economy in which the elite controls taxation to the point that it dictates policy) represents not the creation of a bargaining nexus but a fundamental shift in the distribution of power with important consequences for policymaking and international politics.

The Crown's distaste for parliamentarism explains why the creation of a unified tax authority required revolutions in both countries. It also suggests that (in this case at least) there was a fundamental political schism that few contingencies could resolve. In particular, external events such as changes in the technology of war or strategic interactions among countries will play only a limited role in pushing absolutist states to evolve. Instead contention between the elite and the Crown will probably be the primary engine for change. To make this case I consider the impact of changes in the value of warfare on the potential for political evolution. An example of a change in the value of warfare would be the weakening of the Spanish Crown that made the Spanish Netherlands an easier target for Louis XIV. An alternative would involve the decline in the economic significance of the region that made it a less appealing goal. Finally, the increased investment of the British in combating the French reduced the Bourbon likelihood of success. Thus the rise of Britain as a major contender implied that the French would have to devote more resources to attaining each prize.

The model suggests that as the expected value of war falls, the political process is affected in two distinct ways. First, the Crown's credibility problem increases because there are more wars that it is unwilling to fight alone. Second, the elite is more likely to oppose war because there are more wars that it does not want to fight at all. To mitigate the first problem, the king would like to increase his fiscal autonomy; thus he may engage in domestic political actions designed to weaken the elite.[35] At the same time the elite wants to increase the

[35]For instance, creating a royal administration that is independent of the local aristocracy, as Louis XIV did with the intendants.

constraints on the Crown so as to reduce the fraction of wars that the Crown may start credibly. To do so it must increase its fiscal authority; that is, the elite comes to a conclusion exactly opposite to the Crown's about what the political process should yield. Thus massive changes in the value of war are likely to intensify the degree of domestic conflict.

It is important to bear in mind that although the cost of warfare clearly affected political evolution, what was critical was the expected cost of success. Given that different political equilibria gave rulers different levels of resources, it is no surprise that the historical record shows that changes in warfare were coincident with political changes. Indeed Louis XIV's expansion of taxation was in part underwritten by his early military successes. Yet his methods for raising revenue during the war of the League of Augsburg and the War of Spanish Succession were heavily resented by the elite, who seized upon the regency of 1713–23 to halt and partially overturn Louis's past fiscal expansion (Marion 1927–31:1:65). After the War of American Independence both the Crown and the elite realized that France needed fiscal reform if it was to engage in international competition. The Crown sought to bring about fiscal change without political change, whereas the elite seized upon this opportunity to demand political change.

A different scenario played out in England in 1687–88, as James II attempted to achieve fiscal independence by packing Parliament. It is unclear what role international objectives played in his attempt, though historians have usually focused on religious and domestic issues (Caruthers 1996). His successor, however, had clear foreign policy objectives. Intent on resisting Louis XIV's attempt to conquer the Spanish Netherlands, William realized that the funds available in the Low Countries were insufficient to oppose the French successfully. Indeed the French had done well in the previous engagements in 1682. Given that James would be at best an unreliable ally, William joined the conspiracy that would become the Glorious Revolution. William then accepted Parliament's fiscal supremacy because he was in no political position to secure revenues without Parliament's assistance. What is clear is that, had William not faced the prospect of a war with Louis XIV whose successful prosecution required British aid, he either would not have challenged James or would not have accepted the settlement of 1688.

In both France and England, the elite and the Crown appear to have favored opposite goals. The elite's victory in Britain is usually set in parallel with the Crown's victory in France. The British elite was able to gain an uncontested dominance in fiscal and financial affairs. Not only did Parliament approve all new taxes and loans, but it also chartered the major joint stock companies that provided funds to the Crown. After 1688 British monarchs had few if any avenues to seek funds beyond Parliament. In France, however, the Crown never achieved such dominance. Although it made significant gains in the early seventeenth century by eliminating some fiscal institutions, its advance was

stopped. Thus political evolution went further in England than in France—
although, as this section has suggested, not because of the pressures of any
international situation. Rather it was the differential outcomes of domestic
conflicts over foreign policy that mattered. Neither the French nor the British
came to a negotiated settlement. The British elite monopolized fiscal authority
despite their monarchs' opposition. The French by contrast settled into an
uneasy equilibrium, which was broken in 1789 when the Estates General
announced that they were the National Assembly and that all taxation not
approved by them was illegal (Sutherland 1988:45).

Some Broader Implications

Although this chapter focuses on two countries at a particular point it time,
it also has implication for the debate about how the state and ruling classes
interact (see Tilly 1994). If one wishes to understand how political structures
affect social evolution, one must deal with several methodological issues. First,
it is crucial to specify what independent actions the state will take and what
actions the elite will take. If there is no potential independence of action by these
parties then a model in which the state and the elite coincide is observationally
equivalent to one in which they are distinct. It is equally important to investigate
areas in which the state and the ruling class may have divergent preferences.
This is precisely what the model does theoretically and what the historical
setting achieves empirically. The research shows that there were periods in the
historical record when some actors enjoyed very limited independent action
(e.g., the elite in Britain prior to 1640, the elite in France from 1660 to 1715,
and British kings after 1688). In these cases, though the king and the elite have
different preferences, these differences have little substantive impact. There
were also key periods in which the elite and the Crown had similar goals (e.g.,
Britain under William and Mary). In all these cases a scholar who concludes
that the state controlled the ruling class or vice versa could not be proved
wrong simply on the basis of the evidence internal to the particular period under
study. In other words, thinking about rulers as independent actors is not useful
unless one steps into periods in which this independence becomes important.
Finally, in the case of the debate over the importance of fiscal versus financial
innovation in propelling Britain to the forefront of European politics (Brewer
1988; North and Weingast 1989; Caruthers 1996), the comparison with France
proves critical. Indeed the divergence of Britain and France was much greater
in the case of taxation than credit. The development of large financial markets
in both countries suggests that politics played a limited role in their rise. In the
case of taxation, however, politics proved to be a binding constraint. Thus the
causal structure should run from politics to taxation; developments in financial
markets were largely ancillary.

The substantive conclusion also has implications for the developing world. Many poor nations face problems with either securing adequate revenue or limiting expenditures. In many cases the individuals making expenditure decisions have little control over revenue. These problems can be quite devastating because their resolution is intimately bound up with the distribution of political power. The comparison must take into account a key variable, absent from the model, that distinguishes Old Regime France from many other despotic regimes: the security of the ruler. France had four kings between 1610 and 1789. French rulers were secure enough to take the future into account in making their decisions.[36] That long-term perspective had two effects. First, it made the Crown unwilling to negotiate politically in periods of peace because it knew that in the future a war would occur that it would want to fight despite the elite's objections. Second, it made economic growth and prosperity desirable prospects because they would raise the resources available for future wars. Up to 1715, English rulers faced more uncertainty, and they were alternatively more predatory than the French and more innovative. The implications for the developing world are twofold. First, some rulers may be willing to engage in reform to lengthen their tenures. Second, most rulers care more about their tenures than about the economic growth of their countries. The poor economic policies followed in many developing nations have their origins not in despotism but in political instability. The indictment of despotism as a political regime must be moral, not economic.

The history of France and England suggests more broadly that institutional change in the economic arena may well depend on the evolution of political power. Indeed the political institutions of preindustrial Europe induced a divergence in objectives between rulers and elite. As long as the king and the elite had substantially different preferences about policy outcomes the movement toward representative institutions would be difficult. Despite the clear connection between fiscal institutions and economic growth, the evolution of these institutions is constrained by the ruler's concern over the impact of fiscal reform on his or her autonomy in other arenas like foreign policy. The case of France provides a particularly stark example of these constraints, since that country had a "representative" institution that could have raised the efficiency of the fiscal system, yet the Crown chose not to exercise it for a century and a half. The Crown thus was willing to forego increases in fiscal efficiency and increases in economic activity in order to preserve its autonomy. To the extent that such constraints exist on the objectives of contemporary rulers, the lure of economic efficiency will not be sufficient to allow for reform to progress. Reform will occur only if it promises to offer the rulers a bundle of resources and policies that improve on the status quo.

---

[36]Levi (1988) similarly emphasizes the importance of discount rates for fiscal decisions. For a differing view see Olson (1993).

Appendix: The Model Specified

The Model

Let us focus on wars of aggression. All the public finance results of the model carry through in the case of a war of defense, but the political problems are diminished. Indeed when the country is attacked the occurrence of war is exogenous, so there can be no conflict about whether or not to fight, which is the key political question in our model. One should not overstate the difference between wars of aggression and wars of defense, since even in the latter the population might want to pressure the Crown to negotiate and avoid war by limiting its fiscal autonomy.

To fight a war the king must raise resources. Raising resources is itself a costly enterprise, so that funding a war effort of size E in an economy of size Y imposes a burden of $\tau(E, Y)$. $\tau(E, Y)$ thus includes both the resources raised for warfare and the cost of raising those resources. We require that (E, Y) be homogenous of degree 1, increasing and concave in E, and decreasing and convex in Y. For simplicity assume that $Y = 10,000$ and choose $(E, Y) = (EY/10)/[(Y/10) - E]$ for $0 \leq E < 1,000$.[37] Taxation is decided separately by the elite and the king. Assume that the elite controls taxation in a fraction β of the economy. Define the tax burden tau_e that the elite needs to raise in order to fund a war effort E_e as $\tau_e(E_e, \beta 10,000) = (E_e \beta 1,000)/(1,000 - E_e)$. The tax burden τ_k that the king needs to raise in order to fund an effort E_k is defined in an analogous way:

$$\tau_k(E_k, (1 - \beta)10,000) = [E_k(1 - \beta)1,000]/[(1 - \beta)1,000 - E_k)$$

Fiscal resources are only used in war. Winning, losing, or stalemate are uncertain outcomes. The effect of expenditures (E) by one country on the probability of winning or losing depends on the level of expenditures by its opponent (E_o). Specifically, I assume the probability of winning to be

$$p = E/(E + E_o + d)$$

The probability of losing q is symmetric in E and E_o. The role of d here is to create a likelihood that the conflict ends in a draw; $p + q = (E + E_o)/(E + E_o + d) < 1$. The more resources both sides invest in a conflict, the more likely is a victory for one party, and increasing d reduces the decisiveness of a conflict at all expenditure levels. The reason I include draws explicitly is that they were quite frequent outcomes of conflicts. It is also a convenient way of creating war bias because only elites bear a burden for draws, as I discuss later in this appendix. Increasing the likelihood of draws

[37] If $E = Y/10$ then $(E, Y) = \infty$.

has predictable effects on equilibria: it reduces the profitability of war and thus discourages participation in conflicts, and because it reduces the likelihood of winning it discourages investment in warfare.[38]

The outcome of wars can be defined as follows. For the elite, $W_e > 0$; $D_e < 0$; $L_e < 0$. For the king, $W_k > 0$; $D_k = 0$; $L_k < 0$. We assume that the elite and the Crown share the returns from winning and losing according to the extent of their fiscal control of the domestic economy. The elite's share in victory, W_e, is simply βW. Similarly its share in defeat is $L_e = \beta L$. In addition, the elite bears a cost of draws, D_e and $D_k = 0$.[39] Therefore W, L, and D_e are the returns from war that the elite and the Crown share ($W > 0$; $L < 0$; and $L < D < 0$). Most of the burden of wars is in fact passed on to the rest of the population so that these payoffs do not mirror the country's return from war. In the analysis that follows I will assume that wars vary only by the value of success ($W \in [W_l, W_h]$).

This structure requires us to specify a set of exogenous variables—Y, L, D, and d—that will be kept constant throughout. There is an additional set of variables that the king and the elite take as given but that we will vary: β, the division of fiscal authority in the country, and W, the aggregate value of winning. Furthermore, in the example described in the tables and figures, the country under study always meets a country in which the elite fully controls taxation ($\beta = 1$) with an economy of identical size. Hoffman and Rosenthal (1997) show that the choice of an opponent has some importance to the analysis in that some regimes fight harder than others. For the purposes of this chapter, however, we can hold the opponent's type constant since no further results are obtained by varying it. Because war efforts are nonseparable, E_o, the opponent's effort, is endogenously determined.[40]

Our scenario is that the king controls foreign policy and is presented with a conflict opportunity. He chooses a war making probability α, a random variable that is realized as $\alpha(\alpha = 0, 1)$.[41] If $\alpha = 0$, there is peace. If $\alpha = 1$, there is war, and the king, the elite, and the opposing country simultaneously select their levels of effort, E_k, E_e, and E_o. The war then occurs with an outcome that can be W, L, or D. The goal of each party is to maximize the returns from war. The king has the following objective function:

---

[38]Hoffman and Rosenthal (1997) also explore a specification of war returns in which separability is maintained and arrive at similar results.

[39]The remaining cost of draws, $(1 - \beta)D$, is borne by the rest of the population.

[40]The objective function of the opponent is the same as that of the elite when is set to 1. The strategic interaction concerns the elite and the king; the opposing country makes no decision about whether or not to go to war. It only fights the war if it occurs.

[41]One might assume that is realized later, in particular after expenditure decisions have been made. But that would create considerable inefficiencies, for resources would be raised to satisfy an expected war rather than a realized war, leading to a surplus of resources in peacetime and a dearth of resource in wartime.

$$V_k(E_k, \alpha) = (1 - \alpha)0 + \alpha\{-\tau(E_k, (1 - \beta)Y)$$
$$+ p(E_k + E_e, E_o)(1 - \beta)W + q(E_k + E_e, E_o)(1 - \beta)L\}$$

The elite chooses a level of effort E_e to provide to the king so as to maximize their objective function:

$$V_e(E_e) = -\tau(E_e, \beta Y) + p(E_k + E_e, E_o)\beta W + q(E_k + E_e, E_o)\beta L$$
$$+ [1 - p(E_k + E_e, E_o) - q(E_k + E_e, E_o)]D$$

Although it is possible to show that a unique equilibrium in war expenditures exists under a large set of tax and war technologies, the process of obtaining further general results is stymied by problems of third partial derivatives. In particular, the model must be further constrained to describe the evolution of the endogenous variables as political regimes change. It is therefore necessary to choose a specific example:

$$V_k(E_k, \alpha) = \alpha\{-(1 - \beta)E_k 1{,}000/((1 - \beta)1{,}000 - E_k)$$
$$+ (E/(E + E_o + d))(1 - \beta)W + (E_o/(E + E_o + d))(1 - \beta)L\}$$

$$V_e(E_e) = -\beta E_e 1{,}000/(100 - E_e) + (E/(E + E_o + d))\beta(W - D)$$
$$+ (E_o/(E + E_o + d))\beta(L - D)$$

Given β, W, L, and D, it is easy to show that the optimization of $V_k(E_k, \alpha)$ and $V_e(E_e)$ has well-behaved solutions. Figure 2.2 and table 2.1 illustrate the choices of effort level by the king and the elite over the range of β, with the following set of parameters: $W = 18{,}000$, $L = -6{,}000$, $D = -500$, and $d = 500$.

Credibility

To keep matters simple, we assume that there are no informational asymmetries between the king and the elite. War then breaks out whenever the king makes a credible announcement that hostilities are imminent.[42] His announcement is credible as long one of two conditions is satisfied. The first is that the elite wants to fight the war.[43] In other words, war must have a higher return than peace for the elite. The first condition thus becomes

---

[42]One alternative would be to write a model in which the king has the ability to commit to wars. There are several possible rationales for such a model: kings can create "border incidents" that automatically degenerate into wars, and they have an incentive to gain a reputation for fighting all wars. But such reasoning neglects the fact that the elite was itself also a long-run player with its own reputational motives. If the elite can commit to funding levels, then it can force the Crown to fight only those wars it wants.

[43]All wars that are profitable for the elite are profitable for the Crown.

$$- \tau(E_e^* | E_k^*) + p\beta W + q\beta L + (1 - p - q)D > 0$$

Here $\tau(E_e^* | E_k^*)$ is the tax to which the elite agrees, conditional upon what the king will furnish. The second condition that makes a declaration of war credible is that the king be willing to fight without help from the elite. In this case, we must have

$$- (E_k^* | E_e = 0) + p(1 - \beta)W + q(1 - \beta)L > 0$$

Here $(E_k^* | E_e = 0)$ is the tax that the king levies when the elite furnishes nothing. Clearly credible declarations of war are not always followed by positive contributions by the elite.

Define $W_e(\beta, E_k^*)$ to be the value of victory in war that makes the elite indifferent between war and peace, given that both it and the king contribute to the war effort and that the elite controls taxation in a fraction of the economy. $W_e(\beta, E_k^*)$ solves the following problem:

$$p\beta W + q\beta L + (1 - p - q)\beta D = \tau(E_e^*, \beta Y)$$

$W_k(\beta, E_e^*)$ is the value of victory that makes the king indifferent between war and peace, given that both parties contribute to the war effort and that the elite controls taxation in a fraction of the economy. $W_k(\beta, E_e^*)$ solves

$$p(1 - \beta)W + q(1 - \beta)L = \tau(E_k^*, (1 - \beta)Y)$$

Finally, $W_k(\beta, 0)$ is the value of victory required for the king to be indifferent between war and peace, given that he alone contributes to the war effort and that the elite controls taxation in a fraction of the economy. $W_k(\beta, 0)$ solves the following problem with E_e set equal to 0:

$$p(1 - \beta)W + q(1 - \beta)L = \tau(E_k^*, (1 - \beta)Y)^{44}$$

Figure 2.3 computes $W_e(\beta, E_k^*)$, $W_k(\beta, E_e^*)$, $W_k(\beta, 0)$ assuming that the value of winning wars is distributed between 0 and 70,000 and that D and L are fixed.

Furthermore, in the example β_a, the lowest value of β such that the Crown requires the assistance of the elite to fight at least some wars, is 0.15. β_p, the lowest value of β such that the Crown is unwilling to fight any war, is 0.357.

For table 2.2 we assume that the costs of wars are homogeneously distributed between 15,000 and 50,000 and determine which regimes initiate which wars, how the spoils are divided, and the probability of winning.

---

[44] In the most general case the derivatives of $W_e(\beta, E_k^*)$, $W_k(\beta, E_e^*)$, and $W_k(\beta, 0)$ need not be well behaved. That is what requires us to specify the example fully.

References

Archives Départementales de la Côte d'Or, series C, 4568–69.

Beik, William. 1985. *Absolutism and Society in Seventeenth-Century France.* New York: Cambridge University Press.

Bien, David. 1987. "Offices, Corps, and a System of State Credit: The Uses of Privilege under the Ancien Regime." In *The French Revolution and the Creation of Modern Political Culture,* edited by Keith Baker. Oxford: Pergamon Press.

Bossenga, Gail. 1991. *The Politics of Privilege: Old Regime and Revolution in Lille.* New York: Cambridge University Press.

Brewer, John. 1988. *The Sinews of Power.* New York: Knopf.

Caruthers, Bruce. 1996. *City of Capital.* Princeton, N.J.: Princeton University Press.

Chaussinant-Nogaret, Guy. 1976. *La Noblesse au XVIIIe Siècle de la Féodalité aux Lumières.* Paris: Hachette.

Clark, Gregory. 1987. "Why Is the Whole World Not Developed?" *Journal of Economic History* 42 (March): 141–74.

Collins, James. 1988. *Fiscal Limits of Absolutism: Direct Taxation in Early Seventeenth-Century France.* Berkeley: University of California Press.

Coward, Barry. 1992. *The Stuart Age: England 1603–1714,* 2nd ed. London: Longman.

Davis, Lance, and Robert Huttenback. 1987. *Mamon and the Pursuit of Empire.* New York: Cambridge University Press.

Desert, Gabriel. 1984. *Argent, Pouvoir et Société au Grand Siècle.* Paris: Fayard.

DeVries, Jan. 1976. *The Economy of Europe in an Age of Crises, 1600–1750.* Cambridge: Cambridge University Press.

Dickson, P. G. M. 1967. *The Financial Revolution in England; A Study in the Development of Public Finance 1688–1756.* London: St. Martin's Press.

Egret, Jean. 1962. *La Pré-Révolution Française.* Paris: Presses Universitaires de France.

Esmonin, Edmond. 1913. *La Taille en Normandie au Temps de Colbert 1660–1683.* Paris: Hachette.

Fearon, James. 1995. "Rationalist Explanations for War." *International Organization* 49 (Summer): 379–414.

Forster, Robert. 1960. *The Nobility of Toulouse in the Eighteenth Century.* Baltimore: Johns Hopkins University Press.

———. 1980. *Merchants, Landlords, Magistrates: The Depont Family in Eighteenth-Century France.* Baltimore: Johns Hopkins University Press.

Goubert, Pierre. 1960. *Beauvais et le Beauvaisis de 1600 à 1730.* Paris: SEVPEN.

Hirshleifer, Jack. 1995. "Anarchy and Its Breakdown." *Journal of Political Economy* 103 (January): 26–52.

Hoffman, Philip T. 1994. "Early Modern France 1450–1700." In *Fiscal Crises, Liberty, and Representative Government 1450–1789,* edited by Philip T. Hoffman and Kathryn Norberg. Stanford, Calif.: Stanford University Press.

Hoffman, Philip T., Gilles Postel-Vinay, and Jean-Laurent Rosenthal. 1992. "Credit Markets in Paris 1690–1840." *Journal of Economic History* 52 (June): 293–306.

———. 1994. "Economie et Politique: Les Marchés du Crédit à Paris 1750–1840." *Annales E.S.C.* 1 (January): 65–98.

———. 1995. "Redistribution and Long-Term Private Debt in Paris, 1660–1726." *Journal of Economic History* 55 (June): 256–84.

————. Forthcoming. *Priceless Markets: Credit and Institutional Change in Paris, 1660–1869.*

Hoffman, Philip T., and Jean-Laurent Rosenthal. 1997. "The Political Economy of Warfare and Taxation in Early Modern Europe: Historical Lessons for Economic Development." In *Frontiers of Research in Institutional Economics,* edited by John Nye and John Dorbak. San Diego, Calif.: Academic Press.

Jones, Eric Lionel. 1981. *The European Miracle: Environments, Economies, and Geopolitics in the History of Europe and Asia.* Cambridge: Cambridge University Press.

Kaplan, Steven. 1976. *Bread, Politics and Political Economy in the Reign of Louis XV.* 2 vols. The Hague: Martinus Nijhoff.

————. 1984. *Provisioning Paris.* Ithaca, N.Y.: Cornell University Press.

Kiser, Edgar, Kriss Drass, and William Brustein. 1995. "Ruler Autonomy and War in Early Modern Western Europe." *International Studies Quarterly* 39 (January): 109–38.

Levi, Margaret. 1988. *Of Rule and Revenue.* Berkeley: University of California Press.

Luthy, Herbert. 1961. *La Banque Protestante en France.* Paris: SEVPEN.

Major, Russell. 1994. *From Renaissance Monarchy to Absolute Monarchy: French Kings, Nobles, and Estates.* Baltimore: Johns Hopkins University Press.

Marion, Marcel. 1927–31. *Histoire Financière de la France,* vols. 1 and 2. Paris: Rousseau.

Michaud, Claude. 1994. *L'Eglise et l'Argent sous l'Ancien Régime.* Paris: Fayard.

Miller, John. 1987. *Bourbons and Stuarts: Kings and Kingship in France and England in the Seventeenth Century.* Basingstoke, U.K.: Macmillan.

Montesquieu, Charles-Louis de Secondat. *Lettres Persanes* (1721; reprint Paris: Gallimard, 1949).

Mousnier, Roland. 1971. *La Venalité des Offices sous Henri IV et Louis XIII.* Paris: Presses Universitaires de France.

————. 1974. *The Institutions of France under the Absolute Monarchy, 1598–1789.* Chicago: University of Chicago Press.

Norberg, Kathryn. 1994. "The French Fiscal Crisis of 1788 and the Financial Origins of the Revolution of 1789." *In Fiscal Crises, Liberty, and Representative Government 1450–1789,* edited by Philip T. Hoffman and Kathryn Norberg. Stanford, Calif.: Stanford University Press.

North, Douglass C. 1981. *Structure and Change in Economic History.* New York: Norton.

North, Douglass C., and Barry Weingast. 1989. "Constitutions and Commitment: Evolution of the Institutions Governing Public Choice in Seventeenth-Century England." *Journal of Economic History* 49 (December): 803–32.

Olson, Mancur. 1993. "Dictatorship, Democracy, and Development." *American Political Science Review* 87 (September): 567–76.

Pillorget, Rene. 1975. *Les Mouvements Insurrectionels en Provence.* Paris: A. Pedone.

Potter, Mark, and Jean-Laurent Rosenthal. 1997a. "Politics and Public Finance in France: The Estates of Burgundy, 1660–1790." *Journal of Interdisciplinary History* 27 (4): 577–612.

————. 1997b. "Politics and Entrepreneurship in France 1660–1790: The Making of the Burgundian Bond Market." In *Des Personnes aux Institutions Réseaux et Culture du Crédit du XVIe au XXe Siècle en Europe,* edited by Laurence Fontaine, Gilles

Postel-Vinay, Jean-Laurent Rosenthal, and Paul Servais. Louvain, Belgium: Bruylant-Academia.

Root, Hilton. 1994. *The Fountain of Privilege: Political Foundations of Markets in Old-Regime France and England.* Berkeley: University of California Press.

Skocpol, Theda. 1979. *States and Social Revolutions: A Comparative Analysis of France, Russia, and China.* Cambridge: Cambridge University Press.

Sutherland, Donald. 1988. *France 1789–1715: Revolution and Counterrevolution.* Oxford: Oxford University Press.

Tilly, Charles. 1990. *Coercion, Capital and European States,* A.D. *900–1990.* Cambridge, Mass.: Basil Blackwell.

Vardi, Liana. 1992. *The Land and the Loom.* Durham, N.C.: Duke University Press.

Weir, David. 1988. "Grain Prices and Mortality in France 1600–1789." In *Famine, Disease and the Social Order in Early Modern Europe,* edited by John Walter and Roger Schofield. New York: Cambridge University Press.

Three

Conscription: The Price of Citizenship

MARGARET LEVI

> We're coming, ancient Abraham, several hundred
>   strong
> We hadn't no 300 dollars and so we come along
> We hadn't no rich parents to pony up the tin
> So we went unto the provost and there were
>   mustered in.
> *Sandburg 1948:2:362*

THROUGHOUT the nineteenth century states enhanced the extent and depth of their administrative and coercive capacity while also expanding the privileges and numbers of their citizens. Rulers developed increasingly efficient and centralized administrative apparatuses to monitor and extract manpower from the countryside, but they had to appease citizens who were also voters and to ensure the cooperation (or at least avoid the resistance) of those whose services they sought, whether or not they were voters. Consequently, nearly all the European, North American, and antipodean states—democratic or autocratic—redefined the mutual obligations of citizens and government actors.

The substantive focus of this chapter is on the disappearance of various forms of buying one's way out of military service if conscripted: commutation (a fee paid to government) and substitution and replacement (payment to someone else to take one's place). "Buying out" had its origins in the feudal obligations of subjects to their lord; feudal subjects had the option of paying a fee in lieu of military service. The nineteenth-century defense of medieval practices led to a series of rationales, but all were based on distinctions among classes. Buying out, advocates claimed, protected the sons of the well-off from the greater suffering and costs military service would impose on them than on those more used to the rough life. Furthermore, they pointed to the benefits to society of a

This is a significantly different version of the piece that appears as chapter 4 in *Consent, Dissent, and Patriotism* (Levi 1997). Special thanks go to Jean-Laurent Rosenthal, whose conversations and encouragement (and pictures) made this a much stronger chapter than it would otherwise have been. Robert Bates, Gary Cox, Avner Greif, Ira Katznelson, Edgar Kiser, David Laitin, Ron Rogowski, and Barry Weingast also offered helpful comments on draft versions. Steve Miller provided invaluable research assistance.

system in which those who could serve the country better in other occupations were permitted to do so while also contributing to the government's coffers or to a poorer person's pocketbook.

These rationales generally prevailed at the beginning of the nineteenth century. There was some, but relatively little, outcry against either the practices or their justifications. By the end of the nineteenth century, however, the practice of buying out was disappearing everywhere. During the debates over military organization in the decade prior to World War I, buying out was no longer among the possible policy options.

This analytic narrative of institutional change in nineteenth-century France and the United States explores how and why the practices of commutation, substitution, and replacement disappeared from the public agenda. It speculates on the role that the move toward a more democratic regime played in this transformation. Was the effect of democratization the voice it gave to the previously disenfranchised, or was its effect to transform popular ideas about what constitutes a fair policy? Prussia, a nondemocratic state that eliminated buying out, provides a case that is both out-of-sample and seemingly anomalous. The Prussian case was not part of the research for *Consent, Dissent, and Patriotism* (Levi 1997), but Prussian experience provides a means for evaluating the arguments developed in light of the French and American material.

Modeling Military Service

Nineteenth-century governments had available four basic military formats: (1) professional armies, usually composed of an officer corps drawn from the traditional elite and of enlisted men drawn from long-service volunteers, mercenaries,[1] and the impressed; (2) universal conscription with exemptions only for those who failed to meet the medical standards or who worked in occupations deemed essential for the society; (3) conscription with provision for substitutes or replacements for those who were drafted; and (4) conscription with provision for commutation, payment by the draftee of a fee to the government in exchange for exemption. Conscription generally implied some form of universal registration and selection by lottery or other objective criteria.

Several kinds of explanations are offered in the literature for the elimination of purchased exemptions. The first is the antagonism between the practice of buying one's way out and increasing democratization. Sales de Bohigas (1968:262) makes the strong claim that "Commutation and censitary systems,[2]

---

[1]For one interesting account of how the European states eliminated mercenarism, piracy, and other arrangements that inhibited the development of "modern" sovereignty and international relations, see Thomson (1995).

[2]I have been unable to find the term *censitary* in the dictionary, and I believe it may be Sales de Bohigas's creation. As noted in the quotation itself, it refers to property qualifications for voting.

i.e., electoral systems in which voting is restricted to the propertied classes, are commonly twin institutions." Thus the extension of the franchise and the growth of political parties representing the interests of workers and peasants increased the pressure to change a military system that was the product of unrestricted bourgeois and landed power.[3] When the bourgeoisie constituted the bulk of the electorate, their consent was bought by the state; when the franchise was extended, policies changed. However, in France universal male suffrage did not become a reality until 1875; in the United States, both blacks and illiterate whites, generally Irish, were denied the vote until after the Civil War (Therborn 1977:13–16). Nor was Prussia exactly a democracy in 1814, the year it forever eliminated commutation and substitution.

Another line of argument is military efficiency. Challener (1955), for example, argues that France and other countries sought to emulate the extraordinary success of the Prussian military in the late 1860s and early 1870s by reorganizing their militaries along Prussian lines (see also Skowronek 1982:85). Since 1813, Prussia had relied on universal military service that permitted no replacements, substitutes, commutation, or free exemptions. Large-scale warfare and the advent of changing military theory that required mass mobilization, rather than a small professional army run by an elite corps of officers, reinforced acceptance of reform.

There are two problems with this line of argument. First, it assumes that the voice of the military hierarchy was determinative in the construction of military service policy, but it was demonstrably not. Second, it is far from clear that the elimination of buying out makes for greater efficiency. Throughout most of the nineteenth century, even during the extraordinary mass mobilization of the Revolutionary and Napoleonic periods, the supporters of replacements and commutations claimed that those who chose to pay their way out were precisely those whose value to the state lay in running the economy or continuing their training in the liberal professions. By setting the price high enough, government could ensure the loss of only the marginal soldier.

The analysis offered in this chapter subsumes the arguments based on the extension of the franchise and on military efficiency. Moreover, it grounds these arguments in the micromotives of four sets of key actors: government policymakers, the army, legislators, and constituents. Which military format becomes the equilibrium policy in a particular place and at a particular point in time is a function of the interaction among these actors. Government policymakers, influenced by the army hierarchy's portrayal of its costs and needs, recommend a policy. However, the decision on policy generally takes place within the legislature, with the legislators acting as the representatives of constituents in the bargaining with government. The government proposes, the army and other interest groups lobby, and the pivotal legislator determines the outcome.

[3]Challener makes a similar argument, as does Schnapper (1968).

Under standard rational choice assumptions, government policymakers prefer the military service policy that most efficiently allocates labor to its best
use as producers or soldiers and in the proportions dictated by military needs.
The concern of government policymakers is the costs to government of various
military formats and the quality of the army that results. Government costs
include direct costs of paying recruits, housing and feeding them, and providing
benefits to them and their families, and the indirect costs of implementing
a particular military format. Two factors significantly affect these indirect
costs: the administrative capacity of government and popular acceptance of
government and its policy. The process of state-building includes the creation of
means for measuring, monitoring, and enforcing compliance with government
demands. Governments without bureaucracies capable of registering eligible
men, examining them, and ensuring their compliance face very high indirect
costs in raising armies through any means except relying on volunteers and
mercenaries. However, governments cannot afford to rely only on compulsion;
they must also promote contingent consent: behavioral compliance that is
contingent upon citizen perceptions that government is trustworthy and that
it will ensure that others in the polity are also contributing their share (Levi
1997). At the least, governments avoid acting in ways that will evoke electoral
opposition, riots, or other forms of active opposition. Citizens who do not accept
the right of government to conscript them, who object to a particular regime, or
who object to a particular war can significantly raise indirect costs by increasing
the level of noncompliance and other forms of resistance.

The costs to government of a particular recruiting scheme also depend in
part on the demand for troops. Ceteris paribus, the more men that are needed,
the higher the marginal cost to government of each additional recruit. Only
universal conscription has a relatively constant marginal cost curve.[4] Achieving
a high-quality army requires men who are healthy and who are also either
well trained or highly motivated, or both. A market mechanism, such as a
mercenary army or an all-volunteer force, may be efficient in sorting out
individuals who prefer military service to other employment, but it is not
necessarily the best mechanism for selecting and retaining recruits of the highest
quality or physical standards.[5] To locate good soldiers requires additional
government investments in reviewing applicants and in training them. Although
it might be argued that appeals to motivations such as patriotism and civic
virtue may reduce adverse selection,[6] there is considerable evidence (Levi

---

[4]Although this curve, too, will rise at the end, given the excessive costs of securing those last
recruits.

[5]There has been considerable demographic research on nineteenth- and early-twentieth-century
armies, and one of the problems they often faced was unhealthy soldiers (see, e.g., Floud et al.
1990 and Winter 1985).

[6]Barzel (1989:100–102) claims that relying on donations rather than purchase of blood tends to
screen out those most likely to carry disease and to select those whose motivations are to help others.

1997) that the cost of volunteers goes up exponentially in the same way as does the cost of mercenaries. Once government has tapped the initial pool of professional soldiers, unemployed young men, or highly committed patriots, it becomes increasingly difficult to locate and increasingly expensive to attract each additional volunteer.

Government policymakers, once they possess sufficient administrative capacity, generally prefer professional armies in times of peace and conscript armies in times of war. However, their preferences change with the administrative and political costs of various options. Given significant indirect costs, commutation (a device that brings income to the government with only small losses in manpower) is, ceteris paribus, government's most preferred alternative, and substitution or replacement are attractive as long as they significantly reduce the costs to government of implementing conscription.

The army shares the government's concern with efficiency, but whereas government policymakers have an interest in the allocation of men to their most productive use, be it civil or military, the military hierarchy wants the best men it can get for the army, whatever their potential uses elsewhere.[7] The army will tend to object to replacement and substitution as systems that increase the administrative and informational costs associated with locating and screening men, costs that tend to be born by the army without sufficient budget compensation for the allocation of resources away from training, fighting, and defense. The army is likely to be indifferent to or tolerant of high-priced commutation. Its objection to cheap commutation, as well as to substitution, will increase with the numbers required to serve, for these devices can significantly alter the available pool of eligibles.

Legislators have an interest in securing enough votes to retain office. Thus legislators have an interest in demonstrating that they are serving constituent interests. This means the position of the pivotal legislator, who holds the determinative vote, will vary with the constellation of interests represented in the legislature or otherwise possessing effective bargaining clout. In this very stylized model, legislators have no autonomous policy positions, nor is there an institutional arrangement that permits a veto over military policy in the way that the South had a veto over new states in the antebellum United States (see Weingast, this volume). Legislators merely array themselves over the range of policy positions for which there is effective constituent pressure.

In principle, patriotism, religion, or some other nonmonetary and ideological basis for volunteering could have a similar effect by encouraging the enlistment of soldiers with strong commitments to serve the nation.

[7]This argument refers only to enlisted men. The army, throughout the nineteenth century, also had a set of interests associated with the class base of its officers. The officer corps was an elite institution. Initially, this meant that the criteria for officers had as much to do with social class as with their qualities as soldiers. Educational and merit requirements, first instituted in Prussia, screened out egregiously unqualified men but had little effect on the class composition of the officer corps.

The pivot nonetheless possesses an effective veto, for it can block policies by withdrawing from the coalition necessary for passage.

Constituents generally have an interest in the collective good of an army capable of defending them but one in which they and their relatives do not have to serve unless adequately compensated for that service. In the case of the traditional elites and wealthy, it is unlikely that the benefits of being a common soldier would ever exceed the costs. Thus their interests lie in a two-tiered army with the elite monopolizing the officer positions. They would prefer a professional army and, second, a system in which they could buy their way out through commutation since, in principle, price is no object. Their third choice would be a system of substitutes or replacements, which would require them to incur some search costs as well as pay a fee. Urban bourgeoisie, farmers, and propertied peasants would prefer substitutes and replacements over high-priced commutation. Either system would require them to pay to protect their valued sons from service, but the range of means for finding and paying for replacements would offer more alternatives for a wider range of incomes. Members of the highest economic and social strata would all put universal conscription at the bottom of their preference scale, unless they could be assured that the exemptions offered would protect their sons.

The preference ordering of unemployed and low-skilled workers and landless peasants should be, first, a volunteer army, then substitution, then universal conscription, and, last, commutation. Professional armies offer them an employment opportunity, and a system of replacements would not make them worse off if they were drafted and could make them better off if they were not, by enabling them to get a signing bonus should they choose to become a substitute. Commutation, on the other hand, should give them no such option.

All constituents, whatever their class, must always balance the tax implications of a policy against the costs imposed by military service. This means that constituents, like government actors, have different budget constraints and preferences in wartime versus peacetime conditions. When government requires a large army, taxes are likely to increase and so is the price of commutation or substitution. The individual who buys an exemption always pays a double tax, one to evade service and one to support the army, but the size of this tax bill will grow significantly when a large proportion of men are under arms.

On purely economic grounds, substitution and replacement tend to dominate universal conscription for everyone, and a professional army dominates both. A system of substitutes and replacements provides the rich with a way to evade military service, and it makes the poor potentially better off than under conscription by giving them the possibility of additional income.

If this is the case, why does so much of the population begin to object to directly purchased exemptions? It may be that, in fact, commutation, substitution, and replacement are not Pareto optimal. As government requires more men to serve, substitution and commutation may increase the probability of having to serve for those who can afford neither of those options. The more people who buy themselves out of the pool of eligibles, the deeper into the pool the army reaches. Thus it may not, after all, be an efficient system.

It may also begin to be perceived as an inequitable system. Those who cannot afford to purchase substitutes face the possibility of having to become soldiers when they would rather not; they compare themselves unfavorably both with those who have purchased exemptions and with those who become substitutes instead of draftees and thus receive additional money. Alternatively, the norm of fairness itself might change. In either scenario significant interest groups begin to argue that the policy is unfair, inequitable, and undemocratic. They demand equality of sacrifice. If such groups begin to dominate the electorate numerically or resist with riots, then policy change will result.

The most parsimonious explanation of any specific policy equilibrium would be that supply and demand determine the price of recruits, which in turn constrains the choice of format. One of the initial puzzles posed by the narrative is the failure of price to be a simple function of supply and demand. The price of substitutes and replacements goes up with the proportion of men the government puts under arms, and an increased government demand for troops often compels governments to contract or eliminate exemptions significantly. However, the rules changed in France even in the absence of the need for total mobilization. Post-Napoleonic conscription was instituted in peacetime, and the elimination of various forms of commutation often occurred postwar. In the United States, during the Civil War there was total mobilization, and yet substitution was retained.

Understanding the indirect costs salvages the supply and demand model by expanding the notion of cost. Also influencing the outcome are the probability of political acquiescence and the measurement, monitoring, and enforcement costs entailed in implementing a particular policy. These transaction costs are in turn influenced by, first, the level of state-building, which determines the capacity of the government to register young men and to implement its policies; second, the degree of industrialization and urbanization, which alters both the economic and the political resources of constituents; and, third, democratization, which affects the political clout and, perhaps, the ideological viewpoints of various interest groups. Thus the regime type itself, as distinct from the level of bureau-cratization and administrative penetration or the wealth-based organizational capacity of constituents, may influence indirect costs. In particular, an increase in the suffrage of working class and poor people is likely to increase effective opposition against a practice from which these groups believe they do not benefit and by which they believe—or come to believe—they are harmed. Thus it is not surprising that the administrative costs of implementing conscription decline by the end of the nineteenth century, ceteris paribus, and that the political costs of substitution and of commutation rise.

The comparative statics of a game between government policymakers and legislators suggest the following hypothesized causes of a shift in the preferences of a government policymaker toward a more universal military service policy:

1. Increased government demand for troops (as measured by proportion of men put under arms).

2. Variation in the price of recruits (as measured by the pay and bounty offered recruits and the costs of housing, feeding, and providing benefits to recruits and their families) at different times and under different recruitment schemes.

3. The indirect costs of establishing and maintaining a particular military format (as measured by the costs of establishing an adequate administrative capacity).

Figures 3.1 and 3.2 illustrate these shifts. In period 1, modern state-building is just beginning, and the lack of penetration and legitimacy of state administration significantly raises the costs of conscription. Although the costs of a professional army, commutation, and substitution are initially the same as each other and all lower than conscription, they soon diverge. The cost of commutation, which brings income to the government without a significant loss of manpower and

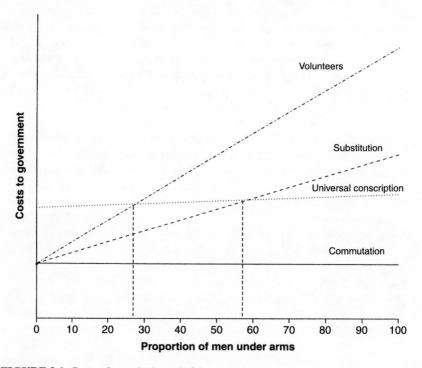

FIGURE 3.1. Costs of recruits in period 1.

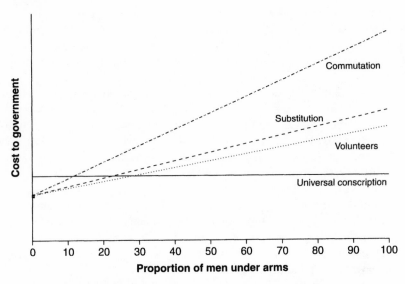

FIGURE 3.2. Costs of recruits in period 2.

which implies a concession to the most powerful constituents in the society, is always less than that of conscription. Substitution has costs associated with screening the replacements, but it too reduces political costs of administration by means of an affordable concession to powerful interests without major welfare losses to the army. The costs of professionals are ultimately the highest, given the difficulties of attracting sufficient numbers of sufficient quality.

With enhanced state administrative capacity, the administrative costs of conscription decline. With increased democratization and an expanded electorate, the political costs of commutation and substitution go up. Urbanization and industrialization further contribute to these costs by facilitating organization and protest by the workers, the disenfranchised, and the poor.[8] The indirect costs of commutation go up the most sharply, for it is clearly a device that benefits the rich with no corresponding benefits to those who cannot afford the fee. Substitution is likely to survive longer owing to its continued support among the rural landholders. A professional army becomes more appealing but will still be more economically costly than conscription if a significant proportion of men is under arms.

This depiction of the problem accounts fairly well for the timing of the shifts in the preferences of government policymakers among military formats,

[8]This is, of course, the insight of Marx and Engels in *The Communist Manifesto* (1978 [1948]:480). Bates (1981) makes use of this insight in his more contemporary political economic account of the effect of urban worker organization on national policy in sub-Saharan African cities.

but it is still necessary to account for the shifts in the response of the pivotal legislator. What factors explain why and when the key coalition of small rural landholders and the urban bourgeoisie, the coalition the pivotal legislator represents, changes its position from support of commutation and substitution to opposition?

The rest of this chapter explores hypotheses concerning the shift in position of the pivotal legislator. The key coalition in the legislature captures the pivot's position, and the composition of this coalition is constrained by the franchise. Thus when only the traditional elite have the vote, they control the pivotal legislator. Once land-owning farmers and urban bourgeoisie obtain the franchise, the position of the pivotal legislator will shift. In either case, the pivotal legislator will seek class-based exemptions for his constituents. Thus it should not be surprising that substitution was the stable policy throughout most of the nineteenth century (figure 3.3). One interesting revelation of this picture is that the preferences of the government policymakers and the low-wealth population are the same, thus helping to account for the policies that emerge when the franchise is significantly extended.

The question remains, however, of why the policy shifted when and where it did. One possibility is a change in the composition of the interest groups the pivot represents. Political institutions that determine the franchise and other

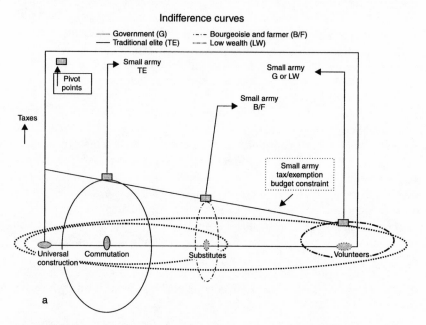

FIGURE 3.3. Preferences, indifference curves, and pivotal positions of key actors. (a) Small-army case; (b) large-army case; (c) pivot points for both small and large armies.

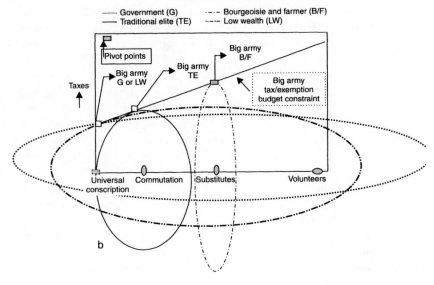

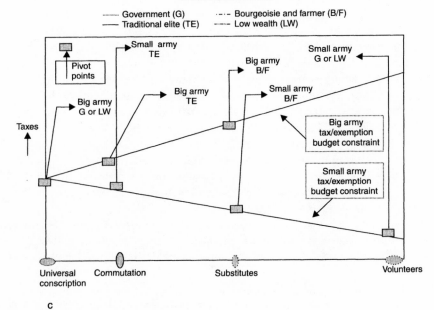

FIGURE 3.3. (*continued*)

means of access to the decisionmaking process can alter who has relative bargaining power and, therefore, which policies become politically viable. The enlargement of the franchise gives the workers and landless peasants direct influence on the pivot. However, this is not the case in France, the United States, or Prussia, where the introduction of universal conscription precedes the introduction of universal manhood suffrage.

A second possible explanation is a shift in the preference ordering of the pivot. The members of the key coalition may alter their perception of the costs and benefits of the alternatives and, therefore, their preferences, in light of actual experience with commutation and substitution. They may discover that they are positively harmed by the prevailing practice. What once seemed advantageous or simply neutral is now a positive bad.

A preference shift could also be the consequence of a shift in political costs. Certainly, government costs go up in the face of threats of considerable noncompliance, and the pivot is aware of this fact. Rural landholders and urban bourgeoisie may fear the political and economic destabilization that draft riots or a rebellious army might precipitate. Thus they perceive a reduction in the net benefits of retaining the practice of buying out and an increase in the net costs of maintaining it. Riots are the off-the-path behavior that both government actors and pivotal legislators seek to avoid.

These reestimations of the costs do seem to take place in France and the United States, but still the key coalition sought to retain substitution. The model of contingent consent (Levi 1997) generates some additional hypotheses about how to specify the factors that transform the position of the pivotal legislator. Contingent consent[9] is compliance with government demands based on a norm that compliance is the right thing to do as long as government is trustworthy. In nineteenth-century France and the United States this means that government's commitments of side payments are credible and that it can ensure that other citizens are also doing their share. Thus a third possible explanation of change in the position of the pivot is the creation of institutions that make credible government commitments to protect the sons of rural landholders and urban bourgeoisie from the worst effects of the draft. Unless the coalition members find government trustworthy, that is, unless they find credible its commitments to either exempt their sons or provide sufficient compensatory benefits, they will continue to support the devil they know.

There is another aspect of trustworthiness, also generated from the model of contingent consent but seldom embodied in political economic analyses: the role of norms and ideology.[10] The creation of institutions that ensure government

---

[9]For a fuller description of this concept, see Levi (1997).

[10]The most important exception to this rule is, of course, North (1981, 1990; Denzau and North 1994). However, others in the political economy tradition are currently taking up the challenge of incorporating culture, norms, and ideology into analysis (see especially Engerman 1997 and Ensminger and Knight 1997).

will maintain relative impartiality and evenhandedness in its treatment of citizens is necessary for citizens whose consent is contingent upon government fairness. In the case of military service, this implies relative equality of sacrifice. Democratization may actually transform ideas about what constitutes fairness and equity. Buying out, once considered fair, is no longer considered an equitable policy. The development of a democratic ideology may produce ideas and arguments that actually change preferences. The democrats introduce a new standard of fairness against which buying out is compared and fails.

The support for universal conscription during wars is difficult to explain, given the preferences of the key enfranchised actors, unless either ideology or credible government commitments, components of government trustworthiness, enter the calculation. If the pivot does not trust the government actors, it will not agree to a policy change. If government actors suggest a policy change but fail to convince the pivot of their trustworthiness, the actors will be worse off than if they had proposed no change at all. They have expended resources and triggered opposition. Given the political importance of military issues, especially if governments tend toward instability (as they did in France), the costs to government of a misstep can be quite high.

The position of the pivot accounts for why changes in military service policy are later than changes in government demand and government capacity would suggest but earlier than changes in suffrage would suggest. Fear of being disadvantaged by universal conscription may cause the key coalition to block the policy when government initiates it; on the other hand, the establishment of a basis for trusting government's commitments that they will be net gainers leads them to support universal conscription even before there is universal manhood suffrage. The model of contingent consent implies that institutional change toward more inclusive governmental decisionmaking processes or ideological change regarding what is fair will alter the location and preferences of the pivotal legislator and, therefore, the equilibrium policy. What was once on the equilibrium path is now off it, and what was once off the equilibrium path is now on it. The result will be universal conscription.

Delineating the preferences in this way and modeling the position of the pivot under different conditions permits derivation of testable implications. The most obvious ones are as follows:

1. As government administrative capacity increases, its preference orderings over different military formats change.

2. As the franchise is extended, the position of the pivot shifts.

3. The size of the demand for troops will affect the position of the pivot, depending on the extent of the franchise.

There are also some less obvious implications:

4. Credible government commitments about alternative criteria for exemptions are necessary to induce constituents with wealth and power to forego buying out and accept universal conscription.

5. Without significant extension of the franchise, universal conscription will not be stable.

The analytic narrative that follows explores two cases of nineteenth-century governments, France and the United States, that are simultaneously experimenting with military formats and developing democratic institutions. Relying on detailed accounts of substitution, replacement, and commutation, the chapter recounts the history of buying out, the political debate on the issues, and the response by affected publics to changes in conscription. The investigation of these cases was motivated by a set of deductively derived intuitions concerning contingent consent, but the research was concurrent with the refinement of the analytics. The chapter also considers Prussia, where buying out was eliminated and universal conscription introduced well before the development of democracy. The application of the model developed in *Consent, Dissent, and Patriotism* (Levi 1997) to Prussia poses a challenge to the explanation derived from the investigation of the French and U.S. cases.

The folk theorem teaches us that there are multiple equilibria, and simple observation teaches that citizen policy preferences can vary considerably across individuals and over time. Detailed historical research enables the analyst to specify who the influential actors are and what preferences and bargaining power they possess. The comparison of cases across countries and time further enables the analyst to clarify the mechanisms of variation and change. Comparison eliminates certain hypotheses and forces the reconsideration of others.

France

The French government introduced conscription in 1793 and has been experimenting with its form ever since. Until 1872 replacement or some other form of purchased exemption was almost always available as a legal means to avoid obligatory military service. The percentages of conscripts using replacement fluctuated (figure 3.4) and so did the price (figure 3.5). The practice of replacement began during the French Revolution and ended soon after the Franco-Prussian War and the Commune of Paris.

History

The French Revolution mobilized large numbers of men[11] and initially permitted replacement. However, the use of replacements contradicted the universalistic

---

[11] For more detailed accounts of conscription during the Napoleonic era, see especially Forrest (1989), Van Holde (1993), and Woloch (1994).

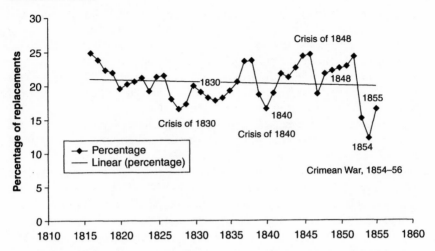

FIGURE 3.4. Percentage of replacements in the French military. *Source:* Schnapper (1968:291–92).

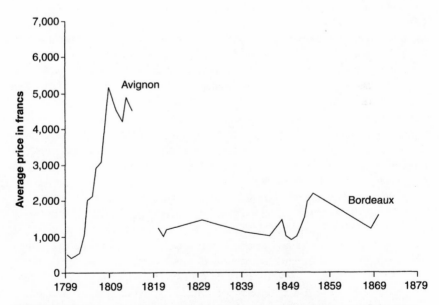

FIGURE 3.5. Price of replacements in Avignon and Bordeaux. *Sources:* Schnapper (1968:296), Forrest (1989:59), and Woloch (1994:42, table XIII-2).

ideology of the Revolution and appeared to be one source of resistance to military enlistment by the central state. Consequently, the *levée en masse* of 1793 and the 1798 *loi Jourdan de 19 fructidor VI* prohibited replacement. Napoleon reintroduced the practice with his first conscription law of 1800 for those "who cannot sustain the fatigues of war or who are more useful to the state in continuing their work and their studies rather than in becoming part of the army" (Schnapper 1968:21, my translation).

Replacements had to meet the physical qualifications of conscripts but could come from any part of the country and be under age. The overall rate of replacements was 16 percent among the 70,000 men incorporated into the service, with a rate as high as 30 percent in some districts, even among districts that usually could be relied on for recruits. In 1802 the government sharply restricted replacement but permitted substitution, a practice that permitted men from the same communes to exchange numbers. The laws of 1803, 1804, and 1806 permitted replacements for those in certain occupations of particular value to the state, for those in training in valued professions, and for those who were in the second and third classes and had drawn a bad number (Schnapper 1968:20). However, replacement was initially a privilege, not a right, and it was closely administered. The replacement had to meet all the qualifying conditions and be among the previously uninducted from the same department as the person who hired him. The purchaser paid an indemnity of at least 100 francs to the state and stayed on the list until his replacement was discharged or died. If the replacement deserted, the purchaser was responsible for filling his shoes. Given the numbers of men called up, the prohibition against intermediaries, and the numerous legal requirements, replacements were relatively expensive (see figure 3.7) and rare. Schnapper (1968:26–28) estimates that replacements never accounted for more than 4.3 percent of those drafted. He also notes considerable regional variation in price, with the highest at about 9,400 francs in 1813 (see also Woloch 1994:401–3, especially table XIII-2 on p. 402). Given the cost, contracts developed between the replacement and the purchaser of his service so that the sum could be paid out over time. The abolition of conscription in 1814, therefore, provoked a series of lawsuits by those who had contracts to receive ongoing payments as replacements against those who were now unwilling to honor those contracts (Schnapper 1968:33–34).

The use of replacements was not restricted to those of great wealth. Peasant proprietors commonly relied on replacements as a means to retain their sons for work on the family farm even though they had to make large commitments of assets and money, particularly when payments were made over time and subject to interest. The advantage to government of this system was that it maintained the complement of soldiers while providing an alternative to propertied citizens who might otherwise resist conscription politically, avoid the draft altogether, or desert. Moreover, the average replacement tended to be more enthusiastic, or at least more resigned, about being in the military than the coerced and reluctant conscript (Forrest 1989:61). The disadvantage was its potential divisiveness to the extent the relatively poor perceived replacement as a means for the rich to escape military service.

Those who became replacements tended to reflect a relatively wide cross section of French society, both occupationally and geographically (Forrest 1989:60–61). Veterans were particularly numerous among the replacements. For at least some of the replacements, the law permitted them to receive a bonus for doing what they preferred to do anyway, that is, join up. The fact that the wealthier bore this cost alleviated some of the sense of injustice that might otherwise have arisen. Woloch (1994:403), for one, considers Revolutionary replacement a form of redistribution from the rich to the poor.

Between 1814 and 1818 young French men were not subject to a draft. The law of Saint-Cyr in 1818 reintroduced both conscription and buying out. Replacements had to meet the physical standards of the military and be free of susceptibility to the lottery. In other words, they were veterans, those with good numbers, or those already excused owing to the completion of the cantonal allotment. They could come from any region in France (Schnapper 1968:40–41). Substitutes, on the other hand, were from the same canton; they were those with a good number who were willing to change places with someone with a bad number. Substitutes represented less than 1.8 percent of the military, and the process of substitution seldom involved a middleman even when money was involved (Schnapper 1968:70). The regulations affecting substitutes remained constant until 1855, but the regulation of replacements, for which a market arose, underwent numerous readjustments over time, until the temporary suppression of all replacement in 1855. The regulations were most liberal in 1818 (Schnapper 1968:41).

Between 1819 and 1826, statistics on military recruitment (Ladurie and Dumont 1972) reveal significant regional variations in percentages of conscripts meeting the physical standards and percentages finding means to evade the draft, often going so far as cutting off fingers or toes. Of particular interest is the large number of evaders from the Midi, the *pays basque*, and linguistic minorities, suggesting a lack of national integration of these groups (Ladurie and Dumont 1972:25–26).

Those who complied with the law, particularly those with money, resorted to other means to escape from military service. By 1820, a market in replacements had developed, and widespread insurance schemes evolved to cover the price of a replacement in case a son was chosen in the lottery. The price of replacements varied principally with the size of the contingent of those called to arms, the geographical area and its success in meeting its allotment, the call-up of the reserves, and, most markedly, war. The state of the economy seemed to matter less than the numbers demanded, which were largely a function of international crises. During most crises (that of 1848 being the exception), replacements decreased as a percentage of the French military (see figure 3.4). The supply went down relative to the demand, in part because of the increased demand and in part because of the increased danger, and the price went up, often quite significantly (see figure 3.5). However, there were certain occupations, particularly leather and textile workers, who seemed particularly affected by economic crises (Schnapper 1968:124–26); indeed artisans of various sorts disproportionately supplied the ranks of the replacing and were only clearly outnumbered by peasants in the mid-1840s and after (figure 3.6). Moreover, throughout this period the major demand for replacements was rural, largely by proprietors of family farms wishing to keep their sons on the land.

Always prone to fraud and corruption, the insurance schemes and the actions of agents who offered the insurance and located replacements became even more suspect over time. The regime crisis of 1830, in which the monarchy of Louis Philippe replaced the Restoration, did not seem to have much effect on the price or practice of replacement, but the commercial and international crises of 1840 did. In this year France was in conflict with England over Egypt and Syria and faced problems in Turkey while the economy slowed. More reserves were called up. Several insurance companies failed. Families discovered their payments had not purchased a replacement after all, and replacements had difficulties securing pay they were owed by contract. Thus it is not surprising that there were 11,000 draft resisters in 1840, a high number for this period. The median price of a replacement did not change, but the price fluctuated significantly throughout the country, and increasingly replacements began to demand cash and refuse to serve on credit (Schnapper 1968:157–59).

The crisis of 1848 and the institution of the Second Republic intensified the fears of the propertied voters that they would be unable to secure exemptions for their sons. The coup of 1851 and the rule of Louis Bonaparte under the Second Empire led to a major reconsideration of the military system, propelled further by the Crimean War and the surge in the price of replacements across France. Consequently, replacement was suppressed in favor of a form of commutation, *exonération*, in which a payment to the government secured a discharge. There were to be no intermediaries or need for them. One aim of *exonération* was to cut intermediaries and insurance companies out of the system.[12] The payment went into a central fund controlled by the Ministry of War and used to pay premiums to reenlistees and veterans' pensions. The conscript had to pay up within ten days, and there was no credit. Since there were more *exonérations* than reenlistments and since the price of a discharge was higher than the premium for reenlistment, the army soon had a surplus. In return it bore the administrative burden of finding reenlistees (Schnapper 1968:225–29).

The real beneficiaries of the system were the very rich, who could afford to buy replacements. The real losers were those with middle and lower incomes,

---

[12]In fact a new kind of insurance company, the *mutuelles,* emerged to establish funds to buy *exonération*s for those who received a bad number (Schnapper 1968:229–43).

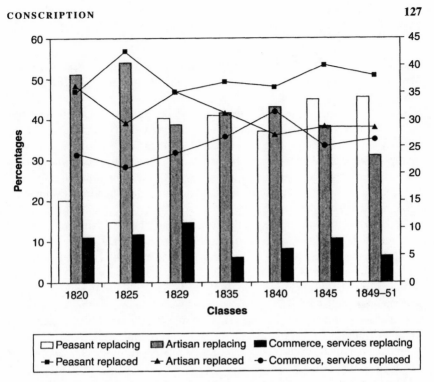

FIGURE 3.6. Occupations of replaced and replacing in Gironde. *Source:* Schnapper (1968:143).

especially peasants, whose chances of being chosen by lottery may have increased and whose opportunities for receiving a premium by becoming a replacement certainly decreased. The price no longer fluctuated with the regional market, and regional inequalities intensified (Schnapper 1968:245–49). An increasing number of peasant proprietors who had benefited from the replacement system found it harder to come up with the lump sum required for *exonération*, and even the new insurance was out of the reach of many. The combination of resistance to *exonération*, the enhanced power of the military provided by its surplus funds, and the demands for more men caused by the military disasters of 1866 led to the brief reintroduction of replacement and the consequent reinvigoration of the agents. The temporary suppression of replacement after 1855 and its brief reappearance after 1866 were a response to the needs and complaints of the military. There may have also been an attempt by Thiers to manage the political responses of both the well-off and the rural population who opposed conscription and relied on buying their sons out of the service (Jauffret 1984:46).

Legislative Debate

The relative lack of debate over replacement even during the Revolutionary period is indicative of its widespread acceptance at that time. In 1818 only a few ultraroyalists opposed substitution and replacement (Schnapper 1968:39–42). Well into the 1830s, only the army hierarchy was opposed, for they believed substitution and replacement represented civil interference in the military and tended to produce poor-quality soldiers. They also were offended by the existence and behavior of the intermediaries (Schnapper 1968:47–48). Replacement, believes Schnapper, fit nicely with the economic liberalism of the era and with an electorate defined by property qualifications (Schnapper 1968:57; see also Sales de Bohigas 1968).

By the 1840s, however, there began to be debate about whether replacement represented a labor market or a form of white slavery, *la traite de blancs*. Louis Bonaparte was among those who wrote a pamphlet condemning the practice, but he shared the contradictory attitudes of others of his day when he voted to uphold replacement in 1848 (Sales de Bohigas 1968:266). In the parliamentary debates of 1841, 1843, and 1844–46, there were other expressions of concern about inequities. However, even most of the republicans seemed to support exemptions and other forms of discharge that released the citizen from obligatory personal service, still regarded as a remnant of the *Ancien Régime* (Schnapper 1968:46–47).

The first real debate occurred in 1848–49 (Schnapper 1968:186–201), and there was actually a chance replacement might be abolished on democratic principles. It was not. However, the discussion did clarify three distinct ideological positions on the question of replacement and the nature of the army. The first was the Jacobin vision of a nation in arms, in which every male citizen was a soldier sworn to the defense of France. The second position was the democratic and, in some instances, socialist view that advocated equality of sacrifice and was generally antimilitarist. The third was the bourgeois view of social order, in which an armed proletariat was a threat to be permitted only in times of defense; a professional military and provisions for exemption were the best means to build an army that would protect boundaries and property and that could fight foreign wars.

The left was, in fact, badly divided on the military question. All leftists decried the injustices of the current system and the advantages given the rich over the poor. However, some envisioned an army as a means of social reform while others worried about the army as a repressive force. Nonetheless, the members of the *Assemblée constituante* did overwhelmingly declare support of abolition of replacement.

The replacement agents and the right engaged in a formidable public campaign. The arguments of Thiers, in particular a speech he made in parliament in 1848, were widely cited. Thiers argued eloquently against the concept of a nation in arms on the grounds that it would promote "barbarism" and "communism." He objected to the personal service it implied and appealed to French nationalism in his hostility to the adoption of the Prussian system. He and others echoed a common sentiment that equality of service is not true equality; the poor are better able to bear the conditions of the camps and sacrifice less in their work lives than do the well-off. The vote of the *Assemblée nationale* was 663 against and 140 in favor of his position.

Between 1848 and 1870, legislators hotly debated the best form of buying out, and republican support increased for a more universalistic system. In the meantime, urban protesters took to the streets. In Toulouse in 1868, for example, demonstrators expressed republican sentiments and slogans such as "Down with the rich!" (Aminzade 1993:106, 133).

The military defeats of 1870 and the Commune of Paris were to sound the death knell for replacement. The first inspired a desire to emulate the Prussian system of universal military service and the second, a spirit of reform. In 1872, a new law passed that took a step toward making the military obligation universal and personal for all young men. There was still to be a lottery to divide those who had to serve three years in uniform from those who had to serve but six to twelve months, but replacement and substitution were never again to be acceptable practices.

Analysis

The narrative as presented so far provides evidence for all of the factors initially hypothesized to influence the shift in preference by the government policymaker: increased demands for troops; military and market problems that revealed previously hidden costs of the replacement system; and a greater likelihood of citizen compliance with a policy of standardized exemptions and of noncompliance with buying out. However, the question of why the pivotal legislator also shifted position can only partially be explained by these factors.

Increased requirements for troops did raise the price of replacements and fuel citizen dissatisfaction with the prevailing system. The costs to government of implementing and using replacement decreased in some ways over time, as central government enlarged its bureaucratic and coercive reach and as private markets did much of the work of finding and allocating replacements. However, increasingly government was called upon to regulate a market quite difficult to regulate and to deal with serious objections by the military hierarchy.[13]

---

[13]The military argued that replacement and substitution increased civil interference in determinations of eligibility and tended to produce poor-quality soldiers (Schnapper 1968:47–54, 149, 186–201, 207–8, 226–27, 260). They encouraged reenlistment but perceived that the market in replacements complicated the decision to reenlist and introduced into the process contemptible

The analytics suggest that a major reason for the shift away from replacement should be a change in the preference ordering of the pivotal legislator. The experiences of the propertied classes with the military inefficiencies and market failures of the replacement system ultimately reduced their support for buying out. Until 1855, the propertied supported and benefited from substitution and replacement. Commercial crises and rises in the price of replacements caused by wars of mass mobilization led to a political demand for change. The solution, the institution of *exonération*, served only those with sufficient ready capital to pay the commutation fee. The peasant proprietors could not afford *exonération* and perceived that it enhanced the chances that they or their sons would have to serve by permitting some to buy their way out. They expressed their dissatisfaction politically, and they had clout.

Although extremely dissatisfied with replacement, the pivot fought for and won the reintroduction of the practice, if only briefly. This outcome suggests that the propertied peasants and their urban allies did not yet have confidence that universal conscription would be better; they did not yet trust the government's capacity to protect or adequately compensate their sons. There is no direct evidence on this issue, but there is evidence that the norm of equality of sacrifice became an effective standard by which to judge government actions and a violation of this standard a trigger for political sanctions. The norm of equality of sacrifice implied exemptions for medical reasons and for essential occupations; the first could be manipulated with money, and the second was a direct effect of economic opportunities.

The primary explanation for reform appears to be the increasing costs to the key coalition of purchased exemptions. The shift in the pivot's position largely reflected a change in the interests of the electors, but it was a sticky shift that also required sufficient confidence in the stability of the political system and the credibility of promises by government actors.

There is also evidence, however, of ideological shifts. Over time more and more legislators began to question the fairness of buying out even when it was arguably advantageous to their constituents. One possible cause, of course, might have been electoral pressure from nonpropertied citizens who perceived their interests as being harmed by replacement and substitution. Yet this argument does not seem to have much support given evidence of insufficient popular electoral clout to affect the median legislator with votes. Since full male democracy was not achieved until 1884, direct political pressure by those who had come to believe themselves most harmed by the inequities of the system cannot explain the change in governmental norms about military service. However, the objections of the nonpropertied could nonetheless have political consequences in the costs of achieving compliance with the draft.

---

intermediaries and agents who trafficked in men. They further believed that anything short of a professional army reduced military efficiency.

Increasing expressions of popular disaffection, as evidenced by working class riots in Toulouse in March 1868 against the revisions of the draft law (Aminzade 1993:106, 133), revealed the strong preferences of large numbers of people for a more universalistic system.

This analysis raises the question of why there was such a significant shift in citizen responses. There is little evidence that the nonpropertied opposed replacement until the late 1860s, when riots occurred and when there seems to have been a strong class bias in evasion and delinquency (Ladurie et al. 1969; Ladurie and Bernageau 1971). Why should there have been objections? Substitution and replacement contracts were win-win, permitting those who preferred to avoid military service to pay a supplement to someone else who perceived it as a reasonable alternative. In principle, the parties to the contract were better off, and no third party was harmed. The way the system worked meant that few faced increased chances of serving[14] *en principe*. However, strong regional variations in enlistment and evasion suggest that there was always disaffection with the system. The increased opposition over time suggests that experience with the system increased the perception of class bias. Moreover, figure 3.6 suggests that increasingly both the replacements and those being replaced were rural; urban and commercial populations seemed to have little to gain from the continuation of the system. Indeed, it was from their ranks that public disaffection found expression, and some of them were electors.

The political power of the propertied goes a long way toward explaining the persistence of replacement, and experience with a variety of its forms is part of the explanation for the change. So, too, is the desire to emulate the success of Prussia. However, at least part of the explanation must be a combination of increased state capacity and trustworthiness. In 1793, the French state lacked an effective centralized administrative capacity for enforcing conscription, and it faced a mobilized populace very self-conscious of its rights and very fearful of central state incursions. By 1870, the French state had the necessary administrative capacity and a citizenry accepting of the principle of the obligation to serve, but it was a citizenry whose behavioral consent was contingent upon their confidence that government would enforce universalistic standards of recruitment and relative equality of sacrifice. By the end of the eighteenth century, the costs of achieving compliance to a policy that produced anything less were too high. Replacement and substitution, which had become symbols of unfairness, were abolished.

The United States

Substitution was a common and traditional practice in the militias of colonial times and the early national period. According to Mahon (1983:37–38), even

---

[14] Avner Greif and David Laitin both raised this as a possible source of endogenous norm change.

during the American Revolution, "Masters of indentured servants and owners of slaves could send their laborers as substitutes, and fathers could send their minor sons. In Northampton County, Pennsylvania, 54 percent of the enlisted men were substitutes for actual draftees." There was not always straightforward commutation, but a series of fines amounted to the same thing. Those willing to pay the fines effectively paid a fee in lieu of participating in the required training. These practices continued throughout the nineteenth century. Commutation was not abolished until after the second draft in the Civil War, and substitution did not disappear until sometime at the end of the century.

History

The Civil War was the first war since the Revolution that required full-scale mobilization.[15] It also was the first time during which the issue of buying out was a subject of political debate. The Confederacy relied on national conscription from 1862 until the end of the war. Initially, its conscription law permitted substitutes, but when the price soared to $600 in gold, making this option unavailable except to the very rich, the Confederacy abolished substitution in favor of occupational exemptions (Chambers 1987:45–47). The North maintained the practice of substitution throughout the war but eliminated commutation.

For the Union the introduction of conscription was more important in inducing volunteerism by citizens and states than in its direct production of men. Only about 2 percent of the Union Army were conscripts; another 6 percent were substitutes furnished by those who had been drafted (Chambers 1987:44; see also Bensel 1990:138–39). Of those who actually were subjected to the draft, the totals were not much greater: 6 percent were actually conscripted, 9 percent furnished substitutes, 11 percent commuted, and a considerable 41 percent were exempted (figure 3.7). If one considers only the two drafts in which commutation was permitted, those actually drafted composed but 3 percent of the total eligible.

Only a tiny percentage of soldiers were obtained through the national draft. Most came through local and state drafts, and most of those by means of small towns furnishing their allotment of men. Perhaps the most common form of escaping the national draft (but not necessarily military service) was by living in a community that provided sufficient volunteers to meet the centrally established enlistment quotas. Local and state drafts persisted, and communities paid high premiums, called bounties, to attract volunteers they could count on

[15]However, as Katznelson (forthcoming) points out, there was a considerable American military apparatus well before the Civil War. In making his case, he is arguing for a more developed American state than that acknowledged by Skowronek (1982), Bensel (1990), and others.

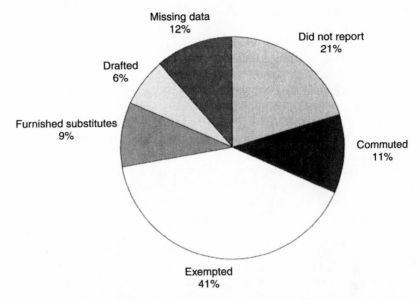

FIGURE 3.7. Total percentages for all Civil War drafts. *Sources:* United States War Department (1966:184–85, 199–200, 211–12) and Murdock (1971:356).

their rolls. Murdock (1971:281) estimates that the combined expenditure on bounties by federal, state, and local governments was over $700,000,000, of which approximately $300,000,000 was federal (about half of which was for direct volunteers and the rest for other categories of recruits) and $300,000,000 local. Government maintained the bounty system throughout the war, although the price varied with the need for volunteers. The price was a largely a function of the incentives needed to obtain sufficient manpower. The local price thus went up with the introduction of the draft and the desire to avoid it.

Substitution was a practice available only to draftees, and it too was maintained throughout the war. Local communities used both bounties and substitution contracts as means to attract volunteers to fill their quotas or replace their own men. However, the supply of substitutes was fairly limited, since substitutes had to be found among those not otherwise eligible for the draft: minors between 18 and 20, alien residents, honorably discharged veterans who had already served at least two years, and, eventually, blacks (Murdock 1971:179–80). The transaction costs of accepting substitutes were high for the enrollment boards, who had to ensure that the substitute was ineligible for the draft and was not a bounty jumper and that the contract was understood by and acceptable to both parties involved (Murdock 1971:181–84). A burgeoning market in substitutes and the role played by intermediaries in arranging substitution contracts (as well as finding bounty volunteers) contributed to fraudulent practices and official distrust of those who enrolled for the money (see especially Murdock 1971:178–96).

There were also problems with substitutes who failed to fulfill their contracts—who took the money and ran. This was equally a problem among those who volunteered only to obtain the bounty and among another kind of substitutes, not covered by the legislation: those whose services had been purchased by a community in order to meet its quota.[16] This situation led to various localized devices for withholding full payment until the substitute's term of service was complete and, in December 1864, a general order from Provost Marshall General James B. Fry that required monies paid to both substitutes and volunteers to be taken from them at the rendezvous and banked until they arrived at the front (Murdock 1971:184–85). As the war progressed punitive measures also became more severe, up to and including the death penalty (Murdock 1971:237–54). The aim was to make bounty jumping of any sort far more difficult.

Commutation was another legal device for getting out of the draft (Murdock 1971:197–217; Chambers 1987:57–61). A man could commute his or another's service for a fee of $300. This practice had the advantages of (1) permitting those who did not want to serve (for religious, economic, or other reasons) to buy their way out—albeit at a very high price; (2) providing industrialists a way to pay for the retention of their employees; (3) providing additional funds for the administration of the draft; and (4) keeping the price of substitutes low, since no one would pay more to a substitute than what it would cost him to commute. In many cases, it was not the draftee who supplied the $300 but his religious community, his town, or his employer.

Political Debate

The debate over conscription commenced with the start of the Civil War, but it significantly heated up as a consequence of the experiences of the actual draft. Interestingly, it was commutation that provoked serious opposition; substitution came under relatively little attack and was, in fact, the subject of a campaign to protect it.

By some accounts commutation stimulated the 1863 Draft Riots in New York, the largest riots the United States has ever experienced. Commutation reduced confidence in government's commitment to ensure equality of sacrifice. Servicemen objected to shirkers, and the Midwestern Congressional delegation was particularly vocal in objecting to its inequitably high contribution of men to the war effort and to the proclivity of other sections of the country to

---

[16]See Murdock (1971:218–36) for a more detailed discussion of bounty jumpers.

purchase substitutes or pay commutation fees (Chambers 1987:56–57). Nor was commutation particularly advantageous to the military, for it produced more money than men. Especially in the aftermath of the 1863 draft riots, numerous municipalities chose to raise money to cover commutation fees so as to head off the kinds of resistance that might produce a riot in their localities (Murdock 1971:199).

The combined power of the New England industrialists and the Peace Democrats, who used commutation as a way to escape military service, kept the practice alive for the second draft—although permitting exemption only for the life of a particular draft. However, by the third draft in 1864, the office of the provost marshall general, the administration, and more of the Congressional delegation advocated and succeeded in achieving its abolition—although their reasons varied. At the same time, they retained substitution and increased the bounty for volunteers to $400.

The puzzle in the United States is why commutation was abolished and substitution was not. In fact, the abolition of commutation increased rather than reduced inequities. In private correspondence, Lincoln noted that

> Without the money provision, competition among the more wealthy might, and probably would, raise the price of substitutes above three hundred dollars, thus leaving the man who could raise only three hundred dollars no escape from personal service. . . . The money provision enlarges the class of exempts from actual service simply by admitting poorer men into it. How then can the money provision be wrong to the poor man? The inequality complained of pertains in greater degree to the substitution of men and is really modified and lessened by the money provision. The inequality could be perfectly cured by sweeping both provisions away. (Cited in Murdock 1971:202–3)

Figure 3.8 suggests that Lincoln was right. Indeed, with the abolition of commutation, the price of substitution soared to $1,000 in some locales (Murdock 1971:190, 266). Moreover, the public debt of many state and local governments increased as they furnished stipends to help purchase substitutes in order to avoid a backlash from an electorate to which all draftees and their adult male relatives belonged (Chambers 1987:61).

The answer to the puzzle is largely one of class and politics. Commutation was visible and offensive to urban, industrial populations, whereas substitution was more of a rural and small-town phenomenon, highly integrated with local militia traditions. The urban opponents mobilized and rioted against commutation, making the practice sufficiently costly that government acceded to their demands even though many of the rioters, immigrants and the nonpropertied, lacked the vote. They were indifferent to substitution, which did not affect them.

Substitution, on the other hand, was implicated in the history and local prerogatives of rural America, but it was also a means for a rural community to

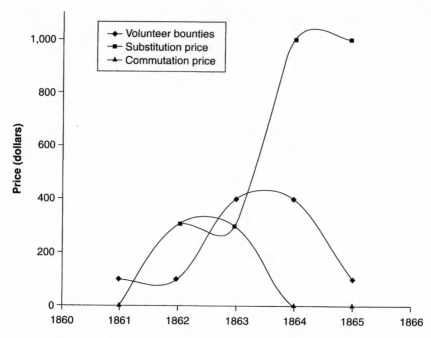

FIGURE 3.8. Civil War payments to soldiers. *Source:* United States War Department (1866:213).

protect its own men and economy against the demands of centralized government. In fact, the rural and small-town proponents of substitution rallied in its behalf. Substitution, particularly if subsidized by local and state governments (as it often was), was a means to legally avoid conscription. As long as they relied on their own forms of draft to provide their quota to the army, substitution provided a safety valve for those who wished to avoid service and, at the same time, ensured that there would be someone else to do the job. Commutation was only a means of buying one's way out of service; it did not require finding another body in one's place.

Thus substitution more than commutation served the interests of the urban bourgeoisie and rural landholders, whose representatives dominated Congress. The defense by the *New York Times* (June 22, 1864, cited by Chambers 1987:61) of substitution exemplifies the rationale for its maintenance as "the only means of sparing the class of the community whose labors are of most value to the nation, and who, once lost, cannot readily be replaced; namely those who work with their brains—who do the planning and directing of the national industry." This sounds remarkably like the early nineteenth-century French defense of replacement and substitutes.

Analysis

The analytic model presented earlier helps explain the abolition of commutation. Increased government demand for troops goes a long way in explaining the policy change. Total mobilization required men, and commutation produced money instead. The costs to the government, bureaucratically and politically, of administering the draft were high enough without the added costs created by commutation. The refusal of a large proportion of the citizens to consent to commutation and their expression of their disapproval through riots and draft resistance made the change inevitable.

The U.S. story is clearly one of political clout. The legislative pivot represented a coalition of rural bourgeoisie, farmers, and urban bourgeoisie. Those who did not have the franchise produced other sorts of political pressure to influence the pivot.

Over the next decades, an ideological shift did take place, however. Despite its maintenance during the Civil War, substitution was in its death throes. Following the war, the discussion of what constituted an equitable and democratic draft began to take shape. The arguments for increased democracy and universalism that led to extensions of the franchise and political reform arguably created a new norm of fairness in which equality of treatment, irrespective of class (and, eventually, of race) became the standard. The discussions of military service, at both the state and the national level, increasingly rejected substitution. By the start of World War I it had not been in use for years, was not raised in the discussions of the selective service system, and appears not even to have been thinkable. The administrative costs of achieving compliance to a military system that so blatantly exempted the rich were no longer feasible. The prevailing ideology of fairness made such a transaction unacceptable.

Prussia

At first glance, the abolition of buying out seems to be an effect of the development of the ideology of democratic egalitarianism and of constituencies supportive of such an ideology. As more people were enfranchised and as the norms of democracy took hold, policies that so clearly advantaged the wealthy and privileged became less acceptable. However, a second glance suggests a major problem with this argument: the United States, a democratic country, retained substitution throughout the Civil War. Even more tellingly, Prussia, a nondemocratic state, was the first to eliminate substitution and commutation.[17]

---

[17]This discussion draws largely from Shanahan (1945), Simon (1971), Kitchen (1975), Meinecke (1977), and Sheehan (1969).

History

After disastrous defeats by Napoleon in 1806 and 1807, a remarkable group of intellectual, humanist reformers became King Frederick William's advisors and policymakers and the masterminds of Prussian military reform. National and universal conscription was one of their dreams and was ultimately brought about through the combined efforts of Gerhard von Scharnhorst, Neithardt Gneisenau, and Hermann von Boyen. Having reorganized the army, improved training, reduced the incidence of corporal punishment, and raised the educational standard of officers and indeed the general standard of command, they proposed universal and universalistic service.

In the view of Meinecke (1977:99), "the reformers recognized that they could raise the army's effectiveness still further if they mobilized not only bodies but convictions." In the words of Scharnhorst himself (quoted in Meinecke 1977:100), "In implementing a universal principle, the principle must be preserved in all its noble purity if we wish to affect the mind of the citizen." And in the words of the conscription commission of 1809 (quoted in Meinecke 1977:100), "if the peasant and poor burgher sees that he is forced to take up arms while members of another class are exempt from this duty, then he cannot regard war for king and fatherland as a holy necessity that supersedes everything else."

The goal of the reformers was a free and activated citizenry, involved in political life and enthusiastic about its military obligations. The source of the latter quality was to be a militia, the *Landwehr*, which was both a reserve and a people's army and which depended upon the institution of universal conscription. Such a prospect provoked opposition from traditional elites and concern by a king who needed to retain the support of the noble and the well heeled, especially during the war with France.

Scharnhorst failed to convince Frederick William of the benefits of universal military service in 1809, but von Boyen succeeded only a few years later. On September 3, 1814, legislation made permanent the wartime conscription established in 1813. The Prussian state introduced universal, personal, and obligatory military service into its standing, professional army. All eligible men had to spend three years in active service and two in the reserve, and then they joined the *Landwehr*. As part and parcel of a universalistic conscription program, the government abolished commutation and substitution.

Analysis

Reform in this case appears to result primarily from the demand for soldiers created by the wars with France, but the form of the policy reflected the preferences of a small and powerful set of officials concerned with creating compliance with their policies at the least possible cost. They wanted universal conscription and a meritorious, if still elite, officer corps. The fact that the regime was autocratic permitted a small coalition to prevail, but the fact that the regime was not democratic meant that the policy equilibrium they achieved was unstable over time.[18] Totally missing from this account is the acquiescence of the citizens in, let alone their active demand for, reform. Nor is there any evidence that the population shared the preferences of the ministers. Thus it is not surprising that there is a postscript to this story. Later in the nineteenth century, Prussia reverts from the commitment to universal service toward exemptions clearly privileging the aristocracy and the wealthy. Although in France, too, there is some seesawing over the century between an egalitarian and a class-biased conscription system, the trend lines in the two countries are quite divergent. The commitment to universalism and the recognition of the importance of contingent consent that motivated the Prussian reformers could not be sustained without democratic institutions. First, the democratic institutions necessary to support such a norm of fairness were repressed, and the voice of the propertied peasants and urban bourgeoisie reduced. Second, the effective political clout of the aristocracy allowed the traditional elite to reinstate some of the special privileges that had been lost.

Conclusion

The French were the first to link mass conscription and citizen obligations with the extensive use of replacement as a means to assuage the discontent that accompanied the transformation of military service. Replacement eventually became a common solution to similar needs in Belgium, Holland, Spain, Sweden, and other countries in Europe. The excesses of intermediaries were a problem everywhere, and over time most European countries abolished private brokerage (Sales de Bohigas 1968). After 1848, purchased exemptions, previously identified with feudalism, were once again on the political agenda. Proponents seemed to view them less as noble privilege than as effective market mechanisms for funding the administration of the draft and determining who should be in the military. Widely adopted, they were not abolished until 1904 in Sweden[19] and 1920 in Spain. In Britain, recruits who had accepted the

[18]I thank Daniel Verdier for helping me to see this point.

[19]Bo Rothstein informs me that, commencing in the late nineteenth century, there was a campaign around the slogan "One man, one gun, one vote." Its participants demanded both the vote and an equitable, universal conscription system. Once again, the abolition of commutation preceded the extension of the franchise but followed a democratizing campaign. Voting rights were extended to all males in 1907, but the vote was proportional to property ownership. In 1917 property qualifications were removed, and in 1921 Sweden granted suffrage to women. Conscription based on individuals was also introduced in this era; prior to that a local community supported and provided soldiers to the nation.

king's shilling could pay "smart money" to avoid the service for which they presumably had contracted. By 1882, this practice no longer existed.[20]

Commutation, a fee paid to the government in lieu of military service, can be, ceteris paribus, a gain in trade both for those who pay the supplementary tax and for the government that receives a supplementary tax in its coffers. Substitution and replacement are mechanisms by which someone else serves instead of a young man who is drafted. Under conditions in which the exemption of one does not increase the chances of another of serving, substitution and replacement are Pareto optimal. Those who purchase and those who sell receive positive benefits, and those who are drafted suffer no harm. Even so, a market in purchase, commutation, substitution, and replacement is unacceptable today. The trade of money for position or in lieu of service is what Tetlock et al. (1996) label a nonfungible value and Walzer (1983:98–103) calls a blocked exchange. Payment for soldiering is, of course, thinkable; mercenaries still exist, and paid voluntary armies are common in twentieth-century democracies. Exemptions are also thinkable and quite common, only if they can be rationalized on universalistic criteria. Although educational and occupational exemptions tend to be class biased, they are nonetheless grounded in principles of equality of opportunity, on the one hand, and of objectively determined national need, on the other. What is now a blocked exchange, at least in democracies, is for a young man to contract with someone else to take his place in the military or to pay the state directly for an exemption.

What does the analytic narrative reveal about the causes of this change? It is clear that where change occurred and was sustained, there was an increase in both government demand for troops and citizen willingness to comply with government demands. The exigencies of war combined with experience with past policies to shape the nature of the military format sought by government actors. To the extent there were wars, there was a need to mobilize men. To the extent a country was successful in warfare, it had little impetus for organizational change. Moreover, government administrative capacity increased over the century, and governments were increasingly able to enforce regulations and thus ensure the compliance of more of their citizens.

Without exception, the high commands opposed substitution, replacement, and commutation. In large part, this was because they opposed universal military service and preferred a professional army. Even when they recognized the usefulness of conscription, they tended to consider buying out as creating problems of adverse selection and as a form of civilian interference in military administration of recruitment. However, the fact that abolition was consistent with military preferences does not necessarily make military pressure the cause of policy shift. It demonstrably was not in any of the countries under examination. In France and the United States throughout this period and in

---

[20]The most thorough account of the development of the British army is in Spiers (1980).

Prussia particularly at the time of its reforms, the influence of the military on policy was fairly minimal, and often its policy proposals went unheeded.

Government policymakers also preferred universal conscription when they needed to recruit a large army, and they shared this preference with the mass of the population, those with little wealth (see figure 3.3). Thus it is not surprising that democratization, particularly the extension of the franchise, facilitates and sustains the adoption of universal conscription during wartime.

However, this is not the whole story; also important is the distribution of class power. Figure 3.9 attempts to capture the effects of the required size of the army and the extent of suffrage on the probability of support for universal conscription. When government policymakers have to worry very little about the electorate and face a large-scale war, as in Prussia in 1813, they are able to introduce conscription. Alternatively, when suffrage is relatively widespread and the requirement for troops is also high, as in the American Civil War, then too will there be support for universal conscription. Support is lowest when the demand for troops is relatively low and the franchise is restricted.

This is the macrostory, but there is also a story of strategic interactions that provides a more finely tuned explanation of the timing and forms of military format. The model presented here emphasizes that the change in policy reflects a change in the position of the pivotal legislator. When the pivot represents the farmers and the urban bourgeoisie rather than the traditional elite and wealthy, commutation begins to lose ground to substitution and replacement, as figure 3.3 suggests. However, the more interesting question is what transforms the

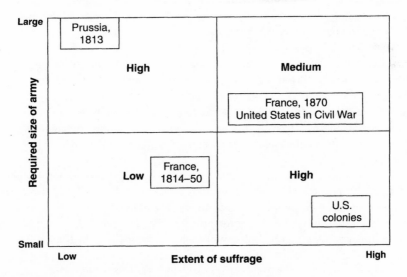

FIGURE 3.9. Probability of introduction of universal conscription.

preference ordering of the rural landholders and urban bourgeoisie. In part this is a story of a shift in the direct personal benefits of a particular military format. It is at least equally a story of changes in political costs that opponents could impose, of the construction of institutions to ensure credible government commitments, and of a transformation in ideas concerning individual rights and a fair conscription policy.

The experience of conscription itself, particularly when it made individuals aware of invidious differences in available arrangements and bargains, revised individual assessments of given policies. The market failures associated with replacement and substitution led to disenchantment with the system. So did consequent introduction of *exonération* in France and of commutation in the northern United States during the Civil War. In France the high cost of *exonération* provoked not only riots in Toulouse but also objections among many peasant proprietors who could not afford the price. Commutation had little effect on rural landholders in the United States, but it did generate opposition and draft riots in the cities, especially New York. Urban workers in both France and the United States expressed with riots their resentment of their increased probability of being drafted. Their actions significantly raised the political costs of maintaining this policy and transformed the game between policymakers and citizens by making a reality of riots as a probable off-the-path behavior.

Equally important to the shift in the policy choice of the pivot were assurances that government would provide exemptions for or adequately compensate the draft-age sons of the key coalition. This was most problematic in France, where political regimes were unstable and promises made by one regime were not always kept by another. However, the ideology of equality of sacrifice may have helped achieve this goal. As the population accepted this norm as the criterion for military service policy, it became harder for a government to devise policy inconsistent with it. The rural landholders and urban bourgeoisie had the votes to punish governments that reneged, and the threat of popular resistance, made plausible by the draft riots in both France and the United States, provided a further sanction. Also crucial were credible commitments by government actors. Institutions that ensured nondiscriminatory implementation of policy promoted citizen compliance while also providing means for special privilege, veiled as medical and occupational exemptions that in principle were available universally.

It should be noted, however, that purchased exemptions did not disappear completely until the franchise was extended to the working class, a norm of equality of sacrifice took root, or both. Buying out may have survived as an accompaniment to censitary democracy, as Sales de Bohigas (1968) argued, but it appears to be incompatible with popular democracy. In France and the United States, elimination of most of the practices associated with purchased exemptions preceded universal suffrage, but the extension of the franchise made it difficult, if not impossible, to go back to the old equilibrium policy. In Prussia there was no universal franchise when buying out was eliminated. However, the lack of institutionally based political enforcement allowed the postreform generation to reintroduce special privilege without fear of adverse political consequences.

Interests do not capture the whole story, however. No one raises substitution as a possible policy today although it may still be Pareto optimal. The importance of democratic ideas seems to leap out from the study of the legislative debates and the historical conflicts. Norms of fairness, particularly the norm of equality of sacrifice, have taken root in the minds of the citizens. Over the course of the nineteenth century, opposition arose to commutation, replacement, and substitution even among many who would seem to have a class or personal material interest in their maintenance. One reason was the growth of democratic and republican parties, reflecting the changing ideology of democracy over the course of the nineteenth century. Democratic rights were no longer the exclusive privilege of the propertied; they were to be the privilege of all adult males. This notion of a more universalistic polity extended to the institutions of government. Equality before the law and equality of sacrifice increasingly became the standard by which citizens evaluated government. This ideology took hold even in those whose sons might benefit from some form of commutation, as evidenced by the relative class similarities of proponents and opponents in the French Second and Third Republics. The evolution of democratic and republican parties was a critical factor in this development, but hardly conclusive. The narrative of the United States, particularly its local governments, suggests a view of democracy that extended only to immediate neighbors and friends.

Throughout the nineteenth century in France and the United States, the incidence of evasion and desertion seemed to increase with regional and class inequities in military service obligations. Consequently, government policymakers and legislators had to revise their expectations about citizen responses and devise policies that were more likely to promote contingent consent. In Prussia, the reformers, anticipating the off-the-path-behavior of endemic evasion and desertions and even riots in response to inequitable requirements, chose universal conscription. Their successors chose to bear some of these costs, in part because they did not need so large an army and in part because they preferred some efficiency losses to the political, social, and economic losses to their class coalition.

The combination of experiences that provoked resentment, the strengthening of democratic institutions, and the growth of democratic parties and ideologies seems to account for much of the shift in the position of the pivotal legislator. Increasingly, the contingent consent of the potential rank-and-file was necessary before a military policy could be enacted or successfully implemented.[21] The

---

[21]Finer (1975) makes a somewhat similar point in a very wide-ranging essay.

arguments of Sales de Bohigas (1968) concerning censitary democracy and of Challener (1955) concerning military efficiency suggest partial explanations but are subsumed in the account offered here. One additional alternative interpretation that, at least initially, appears equally consistent with many of the facts was the desire of government actors, both policymakers and legislators, to create nations, not just states.[22] Policies that privileged certain groups pitted people against each other within the nation rather than against the enemy. The ideologies of nation-building and of democratization shared a commitment to equality of sacrifice. However, Prussia, self-consciously nation-building, reintroduced special privilege, whereas the more democratic countries did not.

Although substitution was practiced throughout the Civil War and replacement was not finally abolished in France until 1872, the new equilibrium policy bargain on democratic conscription was beginning to emerge. Once a universalistic conscription policy was in place, it became the equilibrium policy, at least as long as there was democratic government. Although there were pressures in all countries to return to practices that benefited the economically advantaged and although governments gave in to these pressures to some degree by creating exemptions and loopholes, there was nowhere a return to commutation, substitution, or replacement. At the commencement of World War I, even before governments recognized the need for total mobilization, the possibility of commutation, purchase, and the like did not arise. The direct exchange of money as a means to escape military obligations had become a blocked exchange.

This analytic narrative of military service offers a tale of a specific institutional change, but it also offers several methodological lessons. The first is the usefulness of a model derived from rational choice and relying on the logic of game theory. These tools helped produce a more nuanced understanding of policy change than is provided by alternative explanations. At the same time, they also encouraged historical explorations of the legislative debate, the market in substitutes, the extension of the suffrage, and recognition of links among them that might otherwise not have occurred.

The second lesson is that the process of constructing an analytic narrative may reveal a rational choice account that does not involve a game among the key actors. Such is the case here. Bits of this narrative might be modeled in game form, most evidently the off-the-path threat of riots or the invidious comparison between those who benefit from substitution and those who experience an increase in the probability of being drafted. However, the explanatory focus, the changing position of the pivot, is a straightforward rational choice story. On the other hand, the search for a game disciplined the narrative by motivating a search for the conflicts, beliefs, and strategies that would need to be elements of a game theoretic but which, in any case, enrich the analytic.

[22]Avner Greif suggested this possibility.

Third, it is necessary to consider indirect costs, factors not adequately captured in the personal costs and benefits of each actor. This is, of course, the great contribution of the new institutional economics with its emphasis on transaction costs and credible commitments. By attending to the effects of noncompliance and to the administrative costs of achieving behavioral consent, it is possible to understand shifts in preference orderings that the personal returns from a particular military format would not predict.

Finally, there are certain problems that require an understanding of culture and ideology, phenomena that rational choice analysts normally eschew. Consequently, the tools for analyzing the role of ideas are still in their relative infancy, at least in comparison with the techniques for studying more material motivations. However, to understand how certain exchanges become blocked, we must begin to develop theories that incorporate norms of fairness and equity and that capture the cultural and historical variation in ideas about individual rights. This chapter is one modest step in that direction.

References

Aminzade, Ronald. 1993. *Ballots and Barricades: Class Formation and Republic Politics in France, 1830–1871*. Princeton, N.J.: Princeton University Press.

Barzel, Yoram. 1989. *Economic Analysis of Property Rights*. New York: Cambridge University Press.

Bates, Robert H. 1981. *Markets and States in Tropical Africa*. Berkeley: University of California Press.

Bensel, Richard. 1990. *Yankee Leviathan*. New York: Cambridge University Press.

Challener, Richard. 1955. *The French Theory of the Nation in Arms, 1866–1939*. New York: Columbia University Press.

Chambers, John Whiteclay, II. 1987. *To Raise an Army: The Draft Comes to Modern America*. New York: Free Press.

Denzau, Arthur T., and Douglass C. North. 1994. "Shared Mental Models: Ideologies and Institutions." *Kyklos* 47: 3–31.

Engerman, Stanley L. 1997. "Cultural Values, Ideological Beliefs, and Changing Labor Institutions: Notes on Their Interactions." In *The Frontiers of the New Institutional Economics,* edited by John N. Drobak and John V. C. Nye, 95–119. New York: Academic Press.

Ensminger, Jean, and Jack Knight. 1997. "Changing Social Norms: Common Property, Bridewealth, and Clan Exogamy." *Current Anthropology* 38 (February): 1–24.

Finer, Samuel. 1975. "State and Nation-Building in Europe: The Role of the Military." In *The Formation of National States in Western Europe,* edited by Charles Tilly, 84–163. Princeton, N.J.: Princeton University Press.

Floud, Roderick, Annabel Gregory, and Kenneth Wachter. 1990. *Height, Health, and History: Nutritional Status in the United Kingdom, 1750–1980*. Cambridge: Cambridge University Press.

Forrest, Alan. 1989. *Conscripts and Deserters: The Army and French Society During the Revolution and Empire*. New York: Oxford University Press.

Jauffret, Jean-Charles. 1984. "Typologie de l'Engagement sous la IIIe République." In *L'Engagement et les Engagés*, edited by Renée Remond, 42–89. Paris: Centre d'Histoire Militaire et d'Etudes de Défense Nationale and Centre de Sociologie de la Défense Nationale.

Katznelson, Ira. Forthcoming. "Garrisons and Fleets: The Military in Antebellum America." In *International Influences on American Political Development*, edited by Ira Katznelson and Martin Shefter.

Kitchen, Martin. 1975. *A Military History of Germany: From the Eighteenth Century to the Present Day*. Bloomington: Indiana University Press.

Ladurie, Emmanuel Le Roy, and Nicole Bernageau. 1971. "Etude sur un Contingent Militaire (1868): Mobilité Géographique Délinquance et Stature, Mises en Rapport Avec d'Autres Aspects de la Situation des Conscrits." *Annales de Démographie Historique* 1971: 311–37. Revised and translated in Ladurie, Emmanuel Le Roy. 1979 (1973). *The Territory of the Historian*. Hassocks, Sussex, England: Harvester Press.

Ladurie, Emmanuel Le Roy, Nicole Bernageau, and Yves Pasquet. 1969. "Le Conscrit et l'Ordinateur: Perspectives du Recherches sur les Archives Militaires du XIXe Siècle Français." *Studi Storici* 10 (April-June).

Ladurie, Emmanuel Le Roy, and Paul Dumont. 1972. "Exploitation Quantitative et Cartographique des Comptes Numériques et Sommaires (1819–1826)." In *Anthropologie du Conscrit Français: d'Après les Comptes Numériques et Sommaires du Recrutement de l'Armée (1819–1826)*, edited by Jean-Paul Aron, Paul Dumont, and Emmanuel Le Roy Ladurie, 7–190. Paris: Mouton.

Levi, Margaret. 1997. *Consent, Dissent, and Patriotism*. New York: Cambridge University Press.

Mahon, John K. 1983. *History of the Militia and the National Guard*. New York: Macmillan.

Marx, Karl, and Friedrich Engels. 1978. "Manifesto of the Communist Party." In *The Marx-Engels Reader*, 2nd ed., edited by Robert C. Tucker. New York: Norton.

Meinecke, Friedrich. 1977. *The Age of German Liberation, 1795–1815*. Edited and with an introduction by Peter Paret. Translated by Peter Paret and Helmuth Fischer from the 1957 German edition. Berkeley: University of California Press.

Murdock, Eugene. 1971. *One Million Men: The Civil War Draft in the North*. Madison: State Historical Society of Wisconsin.

North, Douglass C. 1981. *Structure and Change in Economic History*. New York: Norton.

———. 1990. *Institutions, Institutional Change, and Economic Performance*. New York: Cambridge University Press.

Sales de Bohigas, Nuria. 1968. "Some Opinons on Exemption from Military Service in Nineteenth-Century Europe." *Comparative Studies in Society and History* 10 (3): 261–89.

Sandburg, Carl. 1948. *Abraham Lincoln*. New York: Charles Scribner's Sons.

Schnapper, Bernard. 1968. *Le Remplacement Militaire en France: Quelques Aspects Politiques, Economiques et Sociaux du Recrutement au XIXe Siècle*. Paris: SEVPEN.

Shanahan, William. 1945. *Prussian Military Reforms*. New York: Columbia University Press.

Sheehan, James. 1969. *German History, 1770–1866*. Oxford: Clarendon Press.

Simon, Walter. 1971. *The Failure of the Prussian Reform Movement, 1807–1819*. New York: Howard Fertig.

Skowronek, Stephen. 1982. *Building a New American State*. New York: Cambridge University Press.

Spiers, Edward M. 1980. *The Army and Society, 1815–1914*. London: Longman.

Tetlock, Philip E., Randall Peterson, and Jennifer Lerner. 1996. "Revising the Pluralism Model: Incorporating Social Content and Context Postulates." In *The Psychology of Values*, edited by Clive Seligman, James D. Olson, and Mark P. Zanna, 25–51. Hillsdale, N.J.: Lawrence Erlbaum Associates.

Therborn, Goran. 1977. "Mass Democracy." *New Left Review* 103 (May-June): 3–41.

Thomson, Janice E. 1995. *Mercenaries, Pirates, and State Sovereignty*. Princeton, N.J.: Princeton University Press.

United States War Department. 1866. *Report of the Provost Marshall General*, 39th Congress, 1st Session, House Executive Document No. 1, vol. 4, part 2, serial 1251.

Van Holde, Stephen. 1993. "State Building and the Limits of State Power: The Politics of Conscription in Napoleonic France." Ph.D. diss., Department of Government, Cornell University, Ithaca, New York.

Walzer, Michael. 1983. *Spheres of Justice: A Defense of Pluralism and Inequality*. Oxford: Basil Blackwell.

Winter, J. M. 1985. *The Great War and the British People*. London: Macmillan.

Woloch, Isser. 1994. *The New Regime: Transformations of the French Civic Order, 1789–1820s*. New York: Norton.

Four

Political Stability and Civil War:
Institutions, Commitment, and American Democracy

BARRY R. WEINGAST

ALTHOUGH the stability of modern American democracy is rarely questioned today, it remained problematic throughout the first century of the republic.[1] In the late 1790s, the Federalist Alien and Sedition Acts explicitly denied the political rights of the Jeffersonian opposition in a manner associated more with the troubled democracies of modern Latin America than with modern America. In the early nineteenth century, several sectional crises threatened to disrupt the Union: in 1819 over the attempt to admit Missouri as a slave state, in the mid-1840s over the territory gained in the war with Mexico, and again in the 1850s following the Kansas-Nebraska Act's repeal of the Missouri Compromise. This last crisis culminated in the Civil War, the most striking failure of American democracy.

The literature relevant to antebellum American democratic stability and its breakdown in the Civil War is one of the largest in English. Although the literature covers every imaginable aspect of the problem, no consensus exists about the sources of antebellum American political stability and its breakdown. To address this lack of consensus, this chapter asks the following questions: What accounts for relative democratic stability in the United States for the first five decades of the nineteenth century? What accounts for its dramatic failure over the 1850s?

Traditional historians, focusing on national politics, emphasize the central role of slavery as a national political issue that undermined the stable second-party system (from roughly the election of Jackson in 1828 to the early 1850s), generating increasing sectional hostility that resulted in secession

I gratefully acknowledge Stephen Haber, Jeffrey Hummel, David Laitin, William Sewell, Sid Tarrow, Sean Theriault, and Gavin Wright for helpful comments and Lisa McIntosh-Sundstrom for editorial assistance. This chapter was begun while I was a fellow at the Center for Advanced Study in the Behavioral Sciences, Stanford, California. I thank the National Science Foundation (grant SES-9022192) for financial support.

[1]This is not a new topic for students of democracy, as Lipset (1960, 1963), Almond and Verba (1963), and Dahl (1966) attest; in recent years, however, students of democratic stability have tended not to study the United States.

and war (Craven 1957; Nevins 1947, 1950; Foner 1970; Potter 1976; see also Fogel 1989).

Historians of the "new political history" (NPH) challenge the traditional view, arguing that the focus on national politics is misleading. They argue that many if not most Americans cared more about local than national politics. Furthermore, under the second-party system, political parties suppressed sectional issues and sectional tension. Issues, such as nativism and anti-immigrant sentiment, were more central than slavery to the demise of the second-party system. These issues dislodged the "shrine of party" (Silbey 1967) that had suppressed sectional tension under the second-party system, allowing hostilities to rise and ultimately resulting in secession (Swierenga 1975; Holt 1978; Silbey 1985).

Although a few scholars (notably McPherson 1988 and Fogel 1989) have recently attempted to reconcile the traditional and NPH findings, no consensus has emerged about how to integrate the two approaches or whether one dominates the other. Were national concerns, such as slavery, a secondary factor in the demise of the second-party system? Did the existence of slavery make secession—and hence disruption of American democracy—inevitable?

This chapter explores the elements underpinning democratic stability during the antebellum years. It provides an explanation for the central phenomena of the era: the general stability of the party system prior to 1850, the punctuation of political stability by episodic crises, and the emergence of a sustained crisis in the 1850s, leading to democratic failure and civil war. Although an explanation of Southern secession and war is not my purpose, I provide new insights into the growing sectional hostility.

My approach rests on two components: the theory of political institutions and the problems of political commitment, and the relationship between political and economic policymaking. Using these theoretical components, I show how the traditional and NPH approaches fit together. The insights of both are needed to understand the antebellum era.

I begin with three of the NPH's central findings about the second-party system: First, economic issues, such as internal improvements, tariffs, land policy, and banking—not sectional issues—dominated the national political agenda. Second, many and perhaps most people most of the time cared more about local politics than about national politics. Third, both parties sought to suppress sectional measures that would pull the system apart. Any explanation of the coming of the Civil War must account for these phenomena. However, these were not abiding characteristics of the antebellum era that would have held under any circumstances. Instead, we must treat these characteristics as part of the phenomena to be explained.

My approach also integrates the traditional historians' focus on slavery. I argue that slavery was never far below the surface of national politics, and that it always held the potential to disrupt intersectional partisan cooperation, as demonstrated in the episodic crises. Although slavery as a political issue was largely suppressed under the second-party system, as the NPH emphasizes, the mechanisms for this suppression went beyond the party system. Political institutions were also necessary to suppress slavery and other potentially disruptive national issues. Specific institutions were carefully and explicitly designed to serve this role, and throughout most of the antebellum era they did so. In contrast to exponents of the NPH, I argue that parties alone could not have suppressed slavery from the national agenda under the second-party system.

Also in contrast to new political historians, I argue that there was always a sense in which most Americans cared about national politics. Citizens' focus on local politics was in part based on the contingency of strict limits on the national government. Throughout the antebellum era, most citizens exhibited a latent potential to turn their attention to national politics, and this latent potential erupted into actual attention during periods when the institutions limiting national government threatened to fall apart. This view provides an explanation for both the NPH finding about citizens' focus on local politics during normal times and the recurring national crises, for which the NPH provides no explanation.

In spite of the party politics emphasized by the NPH, antislavery proposals appeared on the national agenda with some frequency. With some regularity, these measures passed the House of Representatives, where Northerners held a majority for most of the antebellum years. For example, antislavery measures passed the House regarding the Louisiana territory in 1804, the admission of Missouri as a slavery state in 1819, the Mexican cession from 1846 to the Compromise of 1850, and the attempt to admit Kansas as a slave state in 1858. In addition, Northerners long delayed the annexation of Texas. The failure of most antislavery measures cannot be taken for granted, however, and the NPH provides no explanation for why these threatening measures arose in the first place and why they typically failed. New political historians have ignored the fact that, regardless of whether most people cared more about local than national politics, antislavery measures posed a dangerous threat that Southerners could not ignore. The periodic crises concerned the future not only of slavery but of the institutions helping to suppress antislavery measures and maintain a limited national government.

My argument is summarized as follows. Following scholars such as Hartz (1955) and Dahl (1966), I argue that most Americans believed in limited government, especially a limited *national* government.[2] Although this belief was widely held, it was not self-implementing, as Hartz seems to suggest. Hartz's logic seems to hold that, because most Americans believed in limited

---

[2]The Hartzian thesis has been amended in recent years, e.g., with an emphasis on the importance of civic republicanism. This belief parallels the NPH's emphasis on the importance of local politics over national politics in the minds of most Americans.

government, representative democracy would naturally produce it. This is false, as shown in this chapter. Although most Americans shared these general beliefs in limited government, they disagreed about a wide range of specific policies: Did limited national government prohibit legislation about slavery? About internal improvements? Should the national government foster economic development? These disagreements reflected an absence of consensus about the actual limits on the national government. Because citizen beliefs were not self-implementing, many interests had an incentive to use the national government for their own purposes.

A system of states' rights federalism with limited national government required institutional protections to prevent either section from dominating the national government. Of course, these institutions could not have been created and maintained had not the values discussed by Hartz been present.

Many institutional devices helped sustain federalism and a limited national government, but the most important one was the *balance rule in the Senate* (Weingast 1996). Made explicit during the Missouri Compromise, the balance rule had two components. It held, first, that the North and the South would have an equal number of states, and, second, that slave and free states would be admitted in pairs. Sectional balance afforded each section a veto in the Senate, allowing each to prevent the adoption of national policies they deemed onerous (see Potter 1972, 1976; Ransom 1989; Meinig 1993; Roback 1991; Weingast 1996). As shown later in this chapter, all of the major political features of the second-party system rest on this institutional convention; most important, the survival of federalism with a national government strongly limited in scope. The balance rule protected Northerners against the dominance of national policymaking by the South, and it protected Southerners against the antislavery initiatives of the North.

The balance rule also underpins many of the central findings of the NPH. These historians take the American federal system for granted, including a national government strongly limited in scope. As new governments around the world today struggle to implement and maintain limited government, we see that this feature of antebellum America cannot be taken for granted. Instead it must be explained.

American federalism with a strongly limited national government resulted from the deliberate construction of institutions to produce that result. Although parties under the second-party system helped suppress sectional issues, and antislavery measures in particular, this suppression cannot be taken for granted. Parties suppressed slavery issues because they had incentives to do so. These included the incentives provided by national elections, as the NPH emphasizes. Because winning national elections required electoral support in both sections, a purely sectional program would cause the party to lose its support in the other section. But electoral incentives alone were insufficient to prevent antislavery measures. The more populous North held the possibility for a purely sectional party. The relative frequency of antislavery measures during the sectional crises demonstrates that party alone could not suppress these measures.

The Southern veto afforded by the balance rule was necessary to prevent antislavery measures from becoming law. The much faster rate of growth in the North, especially in the late antebellum era, could have easily resulted in more Northern states, thus allowing Northern majorities in the House, Senate, and presidential electorate. Because parties alone could not suppress antislavery initiatives, the balance rule proved essential to protecting Southern interests.

An understanding of the incentives created by the balance rule helps to explain two fundamental features of the antebellum era: the seeming central importance of local politics for most Americans and the periodic crises over slavery. The importance of local politics depended on maintaining the system of federalism with limited national government. And limited national government required institutions designed to maintain it. As contemporaries understood, the balance rule along with other institutions prevented antislavery measures (see, e.g., Carpenter 1930).[3]

This view has a further implication. Whenever something threatened to destroy or dismantle the system providing for limited national government, public attention turned to national politics. Maintaining balanced delegations to the Senate required not only careful control over the policies concerning national expansion but also control over the designation of territories as free or slave. The design of territories and the admission of states could not be considered on the basis of the inhabitants' wishes alone. Balance required that neither section grow too fast relative to the other. Agreements about the structure of the territories were therefore central to the future of American democracy. Adverse decisions about the territories would affect both the Northern and Southern economies.

This perspective helps explain the period crises over national politics of the antebellum era. When agreements about balance remained in effect and unambiguous, limits on national government were self-enforcing. This situation allowed most Americans to focus on local politics without fear of intrusion by the national government. Crises emerged when these agreements reached their geographic limits—as in the 1850s—or when one section sought to outgrow the other—as many Northerners believed the South was attempting to do in 1819 and 1846. In each crisis, intersectional partisan coalitions gave way to sectional

---

[3]Another critical institution is the Democratic party's rule requiring a two-thirds majority to nominate a candidate for president (see Potter 1972, 1976; Aldrich 1995). This implied that a candidate with a national policy agenda was unlikely to become president, unless that agenda were very popular among Democrats. (Recall that the Democrats dominated national elections during this era.)

coalitions, antislavery measures typically passed the House of Representatives, and nearly all Americans turned their attention to national politics.

The argument in this chapter restores slavery to a central position in the crisis leading to the Civil War. It does not endorse the traditional view, however, but reflects a synthesis of that perspective with the NPH findings. As new political historians suggest, the traditional approach fails to account for phenomena central to the antebellum era, notably by neglecting to provide an explanation of the relationship between national and local politics. My approach also affords political institutions a more central role than historians, traditional or NPH, have accorded them.

This chapter provides a brief narrative of the antebellum events. It also provides two integrated models explaining the major phenomena of the era. The first model focuses on partisan stability under the second-party system (roughly 1828–50). The second shows how the balance rule was critical to this result.

As an analytical narrative focused on a unique event, my theory is developed in the specific context of antebellum America. It does not afford general tests on a series of other cases. Yet it does afford two types of empirical tests. The first are based on the model's characterizations of antebellum politics leading to particular results. Elsewhere, I demonstrate considerable empirical veracity between these characterizations and antebellum politics (Weingast 1996). The second concerns predictions from the model about what might have been observed had circumstances differed. Using data from the 1850s, I provide strong evidence for one of the model's central assertions concerning the breaking of sectional balance in the Compromise of 1850.

I develop my argument as follows. The next two sections provide a short narrative of the era and background on the second-party system, respectively. The following section develops a model of national politics with and without the balance rule, showing the danger to the South posed by the federal government and Northern antislavery sentiment. The next section translates this model into a sequential game, and an empirical test of one of the model's central assertions is then provided. The concluding discussion provides a synthesis between traditional historians and exponents of the NPH and then turns to the demise of sectional balance and the coming of the Civil War.

A Narrative of Events

During the first two decades of the nineteenth century, many Northerners, particularly traders in the Northeast, were highly dissatisfied with national policy. The War of 1812, for example, had cut off trade with a favored partner. Throughout this period, the North either retained parity with the South—i.e., there were an equal number of Northern and Southern states—or had a one-state advantage (table 4.1). The attempt to admit Missouri as a slave state in 1819 without admitting a free state for balance would have granted Southerners a one-state advantage. The threat of Southern dominance mobilized large numbers of Northerners against the South.

Northerners felt threatened by potential Southern dominance of the Union, and they met this threat with an attack on slavery. In the House of Representatives, where population advantage gave them a majority, Northerners amended the statehood bill to prohibit slaves from entering Missouri and to provide

TABLE 4.1

Free versus Slave State Representation in Congress, 1791–1861

Year	House balance (percent slave)	Senate balance (free:slave)	Free	Slave
1791	46	8:6	New Hampshire, Massachusetts, Rhode Island, Connecticut, New York, Pennsylvania, New Jersey, Vermont	Maryland, Delaware, Virginia, North Carolina, South Carolina, Georgia
1792		8:7		Kentucky
1796		8:8		Tennessee
1803	46	9:8	Ohio	
1812	45	9:9		Louisiana
1816		10:9	Indiana	
1817		10:10		Mississippi
1818		11:10	Illinois	
1819		11:11		Alabama
1820–21	42	12:12	Maine	Missouri
1836	41	12:13		Arkansas
1837		13:13	Michigan	
1845	39	13:15		Florida, Texas
1846		14:15	Iowa	
1848		15:15	Wisconsin	
1850	38	16:15	California	
1858		17:15	Minnesota	
1859		18:15	Oregon	
1861	35[a]	19:15	Kansas[b]	

Sources: Senate: U.S. Department of Commerce, Bureau of the Census (1975:210–63). House: Austin (1986, table 3.8).

a. This figure represents the slave state representation following the census of 1860 had secession not occurred.

b. Admitted during the Secession Crisis after the resignation of those congressmen from the seceding states of the lower South.

for a gradual emancipation of slaves already residing there (Moore 1953). Southerners, with their veto in the Senate, prevented the bill as amended from becoming law, and a crisis ensued.

Because a national antislavery initiative struck at the heart of Southern society, the crisis had a larger implication: the problem of sectional dominance was no longer one sided; it had become reciprocal. Reciprocal vulnerability, in turn, drove the two sections to resolve the problem (paralleling Rustow's 1970 observations). The Missouri Compromise did so through three components: it brought in Maine as a free state, balancing Missouri; it divided the remaining territory of the United States between free and slave; and it made the balance rule explicit. As revealed by table 4.1, for the next thirty years, states entered the Union as pairs (Potter 1976; Meinig 1993).

Balance and sectional veto had a profound effect on American national political behavior. First, the veto allowed each section to protect itself from onerous measures, for example, to prevent the other from growing at its expense. Second, over the long run, balance provided the basis for sectional cooperation. Because it meant that radical measures could not succeed, sectional balance induced moderates in each section to cooperate with one another. Although moderates might be tempted to support a sectional measure if it could succeed, knowing it would fail—implying sure costs without any compensating benefits—helped turn most moderates away from such temptations. Sectional balance thus complemented the electoral incentives noted by the NPH to produce political parties that helped suppress sectional issues.

Historians date the creation of the second-party system to the election of Jackson in 1828; the system fell apart in the early 1850s. Part of Jackson's legacy was the creation of the Democratic Party, which not only carried the hero's vision of states' rights beyond his own presidency but also dominated politics for the next thirty years. Between the election of Jackson in 1828 and the election of Lincoln in 1860, Democrats held united government— the House, the Senate and the presidency—in eight of the sixteen congresses. Their political opponents, the Whigs, held united government in only one. Divided government characterized the remaining Congresses. This pattern of electoral success allowed Democrats to implement and adjust their policies during periods of united government and protect them from encroachment by the Whigs during periods of divided government. National policymaking during this era therefore had a decidedly Democratic cast.

Part of Jackson's success rested on sectional veto. His party sought an alliance between Southern planters and the plain farmers of the North (Remini 1972:6). It emphasized states' rights, implying a national government strongly limited in scope with considerable freedom for state and local government in the management of social and economic matters. For the South, states' rights ensured that slavery remained the purview of the states and thus safe from interference by the national government. States' rights also implied the absence of any precedent for national intervention in the economy that might be used to rationalize national legislation on slavery in the states. Many Northerners supported this vision of states' rights because it provided local political freedom and a limited national government.

Another part of the Democrats' success rested on the institutions created by Jackson and his allies, notably Martin Van Buren (e.g., Remini 1957, 1981; Cole 1984; Aldrich 1995). One of the central Democratic Party institutions was the creation of the convention system for nominating a presidential candidate. Democrats used a two-thirds rule, requiring that party presidential nominees obtain the support of two-thirds of the delegates to the convention, not just a bare majority. This rule served several purposes. First, it prevented the nomination of candidates supported by only a minority of the party (for example, those whose support came from states with relatively few Democrats). Second, it provided the South with a veto, ensuring that only Democrats sympathetic to slavery would be nominated. Third, it prevented candidates with an agenda for national policymaking from gaining nomination unless that agenda was popular throughout the party. This requirement constituted part of the party's credible commitment to states' rights: because few policies could meet this test, this hurdle kept most new policy initiatives off the Democrats' national agenda.

The Democratic Party's credible commitment to states' rights gave it an electoral edge over the Whigs. Their promotion of national economic development allowed the Whigs to out-compete the Democrats in the Northeast, but elsewhere the Democrats dominated elections. Electoral dominance, in turn, allowed the Democrats to put their program into effect, and, through control over appointments to the Supreme Court, to adjust constitutional interpretations to make them consistent with their own views. This combination was especially attractive to Southerners, who feared for the future of their peculiar institutions.

Yet the system was not without its problems. Given a range of economic, geographic, and political constraints, national expansion created a dynamic that raised sectional tensions. To be sustained over a long period, sectional balance required that the two sections expand in tandem. Prior to 1850, balanced opportunities either existed or were created (as with the annexation of Texas) without too much political turmoil. By 1850, however, Southerners had no legally permissible and economically viable opportunities for expansion. The Compromise of 1850 resolved the crisis over the Mexican cession (what is now New Mexico, Arizona, and California), granting slavery access to the New Mexico territory. Yet, at the then-current slave prices, slaveholders did not find it profitable to move slaves into this territory. And without slaves, states derived from these territories were unlikely to be reliably proslavery.

The initial advantages of the Missouri Compromise's split of the Louisiana territory went to the South. Although the North got the lion's share of the remaining Louisiana territory, this land was of little initial value in 1820: few settlers sought to move there. Not one state was admitted from this area in the twenty-six years following the compromise. Although Iowa was admitted in 1846, a second free state was not carved out of this region (Kansas in 1861) until the secession crisis.

By the mid-1840s, it appeared that the North had substantial territories into which to expand, while the South had few. Democrats therefore adopted their stand of manifest destiny, admitting the then-independent Texas Republic in 1845 and initiating the Mexican War in 1846.[4]

The lack of economically viable, legally permissible opportunities for Southern expansion combined with the dynamic, expanding Northern economy to spread fear among Southerners that they would lose sectional parity in the nation. Many Southerners feared slipping into a permanent minority status without any influence in the national government (Carpenter 1930; Potter 1976). This prospect put Southern property, institutions, and the slave economy at risk.

At the same time, the fast rise of immigration had profound economic and political effects. The economic consequence was a triple crisis for native workers (Fogel 1989:354–69). Politically, the crisis dislodged large numbers of native workers from the Democratic Party in Northern cities (Holt 1978; Silbey 1985).

A major crisis resulted over the Mexican cession, which many Northerners felt would grant Southerners an edge in national policymaking (Potter 1976:19–20, 63–89; McPherson 1988:47–77). Northerners reacted in precisely the same way they had in 1820: with an antislavery initiative, this time called the Wilmot Proviso. The proviso held that none of the territory gained by the ongoing war could become slave territory, and it passed the House on a purely sectional vote. As Potter (1976:93) suggests:

> During the prolonged and angry territorial deadlock, Southerners had grown increasingly to believe that the issue raised by the Wilmot Proviso was merely a symptom of a far more serious danger to them. The long-standing sectional equilibrium within the Union was disappearing and the South was declining into a minority status, outnumbered in population, long since outnumbered and outvoted in the House, and protected only by the balance in the Senate. But there was not one slave territory waiting to be converted into another slave state, while all of the upper part of the Louisiana Purchase, all of the Oregon country, and now all of the Mexican Cession stood ready to spawn free states in profusion.

The crisis was resolved, for a time (Potter 1976), with the Compromise of 1850. Among other things, the compromise broke sectional balance with the

---

[4]This same spirit in the 1850s led to numerous proposals to expand the United States into the Caribbean and Latin America (May 1973). In the course of discussing the Southern perspective on expansion, Potter (1976:467) mentions a proposal for the United States to acquire Mexico and then concludes that "This annexation would solve the difficulties of the South as a minority section by bringing twenty-five new slave states into the Union."

admission of California as a free state without any balancing slave state. But this outcome did not reflect the Democrats' jettisoning of the balance rule: Democrats made a credible commitment to attempt to reinstate balance at the first available opportunity.

The compromise proved an immense political success for the Democrats. Democrats regained majorities in Congress in the 1850 election and the presidency in 1852; they also enlarged their congressional majorities in the 1852 election. Although a nascent Southern secessionist movement sought to oppose the compromise, unionists defeated it by wide margins in nearly every Southern state. In the short run, the compromise placated the South; over the long run, its failure to resolve the sectional crisis would feed sectional tensions (Potter 1976:90–120).

The huge Northern expansion, without any parallel Southern expansion, led many Southerners to stop cooperating with their Northern coalition partners. They began to obstruct policies they had supported under the Democrats for the previous two decades, such as territorial expansion. Southern withdrawal of cooperation ultimately harmed the Northern coalition partners.

The South's inability to expand led Northern democratic leaders to react as they had in the 1840s, namely to devise a new means for Southern expansion. In the mid-1850s, the strategy chosen was to overturn the hallowed 36°30' line of the Missouri Compromise. Led by Stephen A. Douglas, Democrats sought in the Kansas-Nebraska Act of 1854 to repeal this provision of the compromise, allowing Southern slaveholders to settle lands previously designated as free, namely Kansas and Nebraska.

Although Democratic leaders anticipated a negative reaction in the North, they believed their position sufficiently strong to weather it. Their judgment proved monumentally wrong: the Northern reaction was swift and permanent (Brady 1988:171–76), losing the Democrats their majority status in the North. With the loss of support, Democrats lost the ability to reinstate the sectional balance.

Nonetheless, the Democratic Party's credible commitment to reinstate balance, despite the costs, pushed it to the disastrous repeal of the Missouri Compromise in the Kansas-Nebraska Act. The result was a further disaster for the Democrats in the North, fostering the rise of the antislavery Republicans. But even this disaster did not undo the Democrats' commitment to reestablishing sectional balance. In 1858, the Democrats sought to admit Kansas as the sixteenth slave state to balance California. The status of the territory's constitution, especially concerning slavery, was steeped in controversy and fraud. Many Northerners considered the entire program part of a Slave Power conspiracy designed to control the national government for the benefit of slaveholders. Democratic leaders pushing Kansas as a slave state—in spite of the obvious problems with its constitution, organization, and legitimacy—contributed to this view. The result was greater distrust of the Democrats among Northerners, and hence greater support for the Republicans, culminating in Lincoln's election in 1860. That election unleashed the secession crisis, resulting in war.

The absence of sectional balance implied that the national government no longer faced a credible commitment to protecting slavery. The rise of a purely Northern party was therefore profoundly threatening to the South. In the prior history of the republic, Southerners had never faced such a threat.

National Politics under the Second-Party System

Following the "transportation revolution" of the early nineteenth century (Taylor 1951; North 1961; Fogel 1989), the U.S. economy grew, not only in absolute terms but also in terms of regional specialization and interregional trade. The South produced export crops, principally cotton but also rice, sugar, and other commodities. The Northeast specialized in transportation and financial services, carrying the South's crops to European markets and providing loans, insurance, and marketing services. This region was also the home of nascent manufacturing, which, toward the end of the antebellum era, became increasingly important. The Northwest, largely self-sufficient in the beginning, grew under the second-party system to specialize in food production, shipping its crops south along the river networks and east along the canals and later the railroad.[5]

The formation and stability of a pair of national political parties known as the second-party system paralleled this pattern of economic development and specialization. Two parties, the Jacksonian Democrats and the Whigs, competed for voters at both the local and national levels. New political historians emphasize the importance of local issues. National parties during this period are best considered as federations of local organizations formed to attempt to capture control of the federal government.

These parties offered competing visions of the future. At the national level, the principal issues fell into two categories. The first concerned economic issues, and specific policy questions included the following: (1) Should tariff rates be set solely to raise revenue for the national government or should they be set higher to protect domestic industries? (2) Should the federal government finance internal improvements such as roads, canals, and, later, railroads? (3) Should the federal government provide centralized control over banking? (4) Finally, how should the public lands be distributed? Should the price be set high to raise revenue for the federal government for other purposes or low to subsidize migration and growth? The second set of issues concerned the future of slavery

---

[5]This thesis, originally expounded among the new economic historians by North (1961), has been amended by several important studies, in ways that do not matter here. In every region, there were interests who specialized in production or services for that region alone, e.g., farmers producing food for local markets in the Northeast (see also Lindstrom 1970).

TABLE 4.2
Regional Preferences Regarding Economic Policy, 1832–50

Region	Public land	Tariffs	Banks	Internal improvements	Slavery
Northeast	Expensive	High	Favored	High subsidies	Opposed
South	Cheap	Low	Opposed	No subsidies	Favored
Northwest	Cheap	Low	Opposed	Some subsidies	Opposed

(and, to a lesser extent, states' rights). Although direct confrontations over slavery were episodic, the issue of slavery was never far below the surface. The critical policy questions concerned whether new territories would be free or slave and the role of the federal government in regulating and protecting slavery.

This description of the economy provides considerable insight into the second-party system. The pattern of economic specialization implied that each region had different preferences over the major political issues. Most Southerners opposed high tariffs and internal improvements, both of which primarily benefited Northerners or subsets of Northerners at their expense (table 4.2). Southerners were also hostile to the idea of a national bank. With respect to land policy, they had mixed motives, as will be discussed later in this chapter. Finally, Southerners advocated the expansion of slavery into new territories. They also favored strong limits on federal government, allowing them the local political freedom to maintain their peculiar institutions.

The Northeast contained a relatively high concentration of individuals with preferences nearly opposite to those of the South. These individuals favored high tariffs to protect their commercial and manufacturing interests. They advocated the federal promotion of internal improvements for two reasons: to enhance communication and commercial links with the other regions (notably to open up east-west trade routes) and to increase the demand for their capital. Because cheap land encouraged migration that raised labor prices, the Northeast also opposed this policy (Passell and Schmundt 1971). Interests in this region also favored a strong national bank. By and large, they opposed slavery.

In between these two opposed interests stood the Northwest, the pivotal player in the political system. As Kohlmeier (1938) observed, after the mid-1820s the Northwest became the "keystone of the arch of the Union," allowing it to mediate the political conflict between the Northeast and the South. This region favored low tariffs. Moreover, it voiced strong support for internal improvements, which not only lowered transportation costs to eastern markets but also increased the western flow of migration. The Northwest was largely hostile to a national bank, and it favored cheap land policies. These Northerners also opposed slavery and, increasingly over time, its expansion.

Undoubtedly this picture is too simple. Parties, for example, played important roles in organizing the political life of most individuals, and they had considerable impact on the political demands expressed, both locally and before the national government. Southern Whigs such as Henry Clay favored a strong federal presence and, with the exception of slavery, had preferences on many issues close to those of the Whigs in New England. Similarly the Democrats had a strong presence in the Northeast, and the Whigs, in the Northwest.

In spite of its overly sharp distinctions, however, this picture captures something of the essence of national politics under the second-party system. Elsewhere I provide empirical support for these propositions, showing, for example, that most representatives from each region voted on measures in accord with the preceding descriptions (Weingast 1996:7-1–7-15).

The Divisive Politics of Slavery

To understand national politics under the second-party system, I employ a simple spatial model of politics.[6] The model is extremely simple and is not intended to capture the full richness of the antebellum political environment. Instead it is intended to convey one of the central political principles underlying antebellum politics, one easily missed by other approaches. The model characterizes each region as a single individual with distinct economic and political interests: the Northeast (NE), the Northwest (NW), and the South (S). Elsewhere I demonstrate that the basic principles developed here generalize to include variations of preferences within regions, many more individuals, and political parties (Weingast 1996:3-23–3-24, 4-1–4-35).

For most of the second-party system, the major national political issues were economic. As noted previously, policy questions concerned the degree to which the government should promote agrarian expansionism or commercial development. The preferences of each region were correlated across these policy dimensions. Those opposing the tariff, for example, typically also opposed a national bank while supporting cheap land policy. For this reason, and for simplicity, the model depicts this set of economic issues as a single dimension. Both the South and the Northwest preferred agrarian expansionism and low tariffs and were against a national bank. Their differences concerned

---

[6]A brief summary of spatial models: (1) The *spatial model* (Hinich and Munger 1997; Shepsle and Bonchek 1997) used here involves the choice of national policy from along a one- or two-dimensional continuum. Each dimension represents a particular policy issue, in this case economic issues and slavery. (2) Each individual is assumed to have an *ideal policy,* one he or she prefers to all other policies. The spatial model in one dimension characterizes individuals by their ideal point with symmetric preferences (the further a policy is from the ideal point, the less it is preferred). In two dimensions, it represents preferences by an ideal point plus a set of *indifference curves* representing the set of points equally preferred to one another by the individual. These may be circular, indicating that the individual weighs each dimension equally, or elliptical, indicating that the individual weighs one dimension as more important than the other. (3) Finally, we often distinguish a particular policy as the *status quo,* that outcome which prevails if no alternative is chosen by the players.

FIGURE 4.1. Economic preferences by region.

the issue of internal improvements, with the South opposing and the Northwest favoring. In contrast, the Northeast favored commercial development, high tariffs, internal improvements, and a national bank.

This characterization is translated into the spatial model depicted in figure 4.1. By and large, the country was governed by a majority coalition favoring agrarian expansionism with strength in the Northwest and South (the basis for the Jacksonian Democrats). In opposition stood the minority favoring commercial development, with a major stronghold in the Northeast (the Whigs). Figure 4.1 portrays the essence of this situation by placing the ideal points of S and NW much closer to each other and to the left end of the policy issue, with NE on the right.

Were this the only relevant political issue, the median voter theorem implies that the politics of this era would have been straightforward and political stability would not have been an issue. The median voter theorem holds that, given a condition about voter preferences, when voters must decide among policy alternatives along a single issue dimension, the resulting choice is that of the median voter's ideal policy. This policy alternative can beat all others in a two-way majority rule contest (Hinich and Munger 1997:31–37; Shepsle and Bonchek 1997:82–91). In the present context, the median voter theorem implies that the Northwest's ideal point is the unique and stable policy choice of national politics.

However, it is unlikely that this issue alone would remain the basis of electoral conflict. As Riker (1982:213–32) argues, the losers in this system, the Whigs, were unlikely to remain satisfied with losing consistently. Riker contends that, in a setting in which political forces support a particular majority coalition, the losers have an incentive to search for a new political issue that splits the majority coalition apart in such a way that some of its members find action on the new issue offensive while others find it attractive. Riker further argues that slavery was such an issue. He suggests that the Whigs opportunistically raised this issue on a number of occasions to split the Democrats and win elections: "The 'precipitating force' to raise the issue of slavery was political; and political it was, rooted in an effort by the losers to manipulate the agenda to their advantage." Furthermore, "slavery was always an evil but not always a political issue. What made it a political issue was that, by reason of the structure

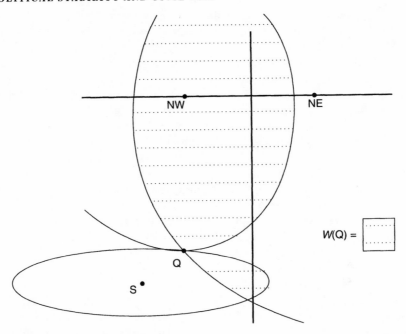

FIGURE 4.2. The Riker thesis.

of politics in the mid-1830s [and again later], it was to some people's advantage to place abolition on the political agenda (Riker 1982:216, 221).

To demonstrate the potential for political instability raised by the issue of slavery, figure 4.2 expands the issue space represented in figure 4.1 by adding the slavery dimension, placing the three players with ideals in two dimensions. All three players retain the same position along the horizontal economic dimension. The vertical dimension represents slavery, with proslavery views at the bottom, antislavery views at the top. As the most proslavery player, S is placed in the lower left-hand corner of the diagram. Both NW and NE, on the other hand, are shown as roughly indifferent about slavery, neither positive nor negative. Although the placement of NE and NW along the slavery dimension is somewhat arbitrary, what is central to the model is the enormous difference in commitment to slavery between the North and the South.[7]

Also depicted on the diagram is the status quo, Q, representing strong federal protection of rights in slaves and placed in figure 4.2 at the NW ideal along the economic dimension. Finally, the figure displays the indifference curves of the

---

[7]Most Northerners were probably somewhat negative, and increasingly so over the antebellum period. In order not to bias the outcome in favor of opposition to slavery, however, I depict them as indifferent. This placement does not affect the results.

players through the status quo. Southern indifference curves are represented as ellipses, with the short axis along the slavery dimension. This reflects the fact that the South cared far more about slavery than the other economic issues. Specifically, a small change on the slavery dimension would have had a larger effect on Southerners than a small change along the economic dimension. A complete reversal in, say, tariff policy would not have had as large an effect on the South as a major restriction on rights in slaves. The indifference curves of the two Northern players are drawn as circles.

I next turn to the construction of *winsets*. A winset is the set of policy alternatives that command a majority against a particular policy, such as the status quo. The first implication of the model is the existence of a nonempty winset of policies that command a majority against Q, clearly revealing why the issue of slavery was so dangerous to S. With two dimensions of policy at stake, it became possible for NW and NE to form a coalition against S, changing policy radically along the slavery dimension and moderately along the economic one. This result demonstrates the veracity of Riker's claims. I therefore call the political use of slavery to break up the intersectional coalition of NW and S the *Riker thesis*.

This insight led Riker to conclude that it was simply a matter of time before opponents of the Democratic Party used the issue of slavery to become the majority party. Moreover, as he observed, it was this possibility that Jefferson noted following the Missouri Compromise: "But this momentous question, like a fire bell in the night, awakened and filled me with terror. I considered it at once as the Knell of the Union. It is hushed, indeed for the moment. But this is a reprieve only, not a final sentence" (quoted in Ransom 1989:40).

The model's second implication is that, were policy to be made solely on the basis of majority rule, the greater number of Northern voters implies that a purely sectional majority party was a viable possibility. Having little direct concern for rights in slaves, a purely Northern coalition might well have altered these rights if it suited their purposes.

This analysis demonstrates that, on the basis of public opinion alone, nothing inherent in the antebellum era inevitably preserved rights in slaves. Nor did public opinion dictate a stable set of intersectional coalitions suppressing sectional issues. The model shows that the formation of a purely Northern coalition remained a possibility throughout this period, and such a coalition would have had minimal commitment to preserving Southern values, property, and institutions.

The model's third implication is that the South had good reason to be concerned about the North's tenuous commitment to rights in slaves. The natural variation in preferences along the slave dimension between Northerners and Southerners combined with different economic interests to create the potential for a coalition to form against the South from which it could not protect itself. Were the North to capture the presidency and a majority in both houses of Congress, Northerners would have had the clear means to alter rights in slaves. Moreover, some Northerners had the motive to do so. As the minority party, Whigs were typically prevented from implementing the economic policy changes they favored. In order to gain control of the government, Northern Whigs had substantial incentives to create a rift between Northern and Southern Democrats. Raising the issue of slavery would have precisely that effect.

This model provides a fundamental insight into the stability and fall of the second-party system. Yet, tempting as it is to take it as a model of the fall of the second-party system and the rise of regional political conflict in the 1850s, it fails to answer a series of fundamental questions. To begin with, it fails to explain the obvious stability of the second-party system. Although slavery was raised on a number of occasions (as Riker notes), it failed to break apart the ruling Democratic Party during this period. Equally important, the model provides no explanation for why, in the 1850s, this issue helped destroy the Democrats' longstanding national majority.

The theoretical instability of slavery that has been derived from the model just developed presents a striking contrast with the actual operation of the second-party system. From the founding of the Republic until the decline of the second-party system, slavery was widely accepted and no Northern, sectional party emerged to promote its demise. Though slavery was always a factor in national politics, direct conflicts were limited to specific episodes over its extension to the territories.

This contrast demands an explanation. The stability of rights in slaves along with a party system sustaining intersectional coalitions cannot be accepted as a set of "facts," however. These phenomena did not hold simply by virtue of overwhelming public support. Nor can scholars assume they were inevitable properties of antebellum politics. Rather they are part of the phenomena to be explained.

Although antebellum politicians appeared to accept slavery, creating the appearance of a "consensus" that it be kept off the national agenda, this apparent consensus was not the result of a nearly uniform preference or belief across the nation that slavery was acceptable. Instead, a set of institutions protected slavery from sustained contentiousness by impeding those with an interest in attacking slavery. These institutions left Northerners with a choice: they could ignore slavery in order to cooperate with the South on other policy issues, or they could challenge the South along this dimension, paralyzing the government and possibly leading to armed conflict. My argument is that until the 1850s, a sufficient portion of Northerners preferred the former option, and that this exchange was one of the principal factors underpinning the Jacksonian Democratic Party's dominance under the second-party system. If there were few sustained attacks on slavery—despite its constant presence below the surface as a source of discord—it was because institutions restrained those with the motives to launch such attacks.

In light of the potential risk of changes in slavery rights, the South sought to institutionalize some form of *credible commitment* from the North not to change rights in slaves. The specific form of credible commitment was the convention of equal representation or regional balance in the Senate, giving both regions veto power and, in particular, the South a veto over any policy affecting slavery. Though many historians have appreciated equal representation, its profound political consequences are not widely recognized. As we will see, these include the major features of the politics of this period, such as the stability of the second-party system and later that system's decline.

The logic of sectional equilibrium's equal representation in the Senate can be understood using a variant of the foregoing analysis. The results previously developed can be thought of as predictions about behavior when politics reflects public opinion. Although this approach provides a good characterization of politics in the House of Representatives, it affords an incomplete understanding of national political decisions, for policymaking requires the approval of both houses of Congress and the president. As the discussion of equal representation in the Senate suggests, politics in that body was likely to diverge considerably from that of the presidency and the House, both of which were more responsive to the larger and more rapidly growing population in the North.

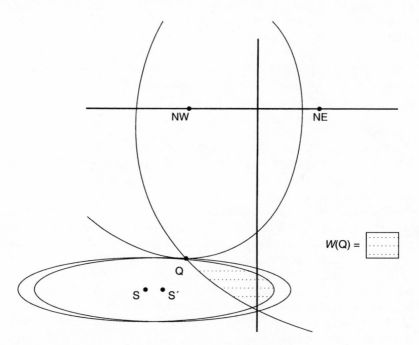

FIGURE 4.3. The effect of equal representation in the Senate.

The politics in the Senate is portrayed in figure 4.3, a slight modification of figure 4.2. The balance rule implies that the configuration of preferences based on population and public opinion—as in the House—did not hold for the Senate. Whereas figure 4.2 denotes each region with a single representative, figure 4.3 adds a second Southerner to provide the balance between the regions. Figure 4.3 also shows the status quo and the associated winset reflecting the Senate's regional balance.

The contrast between the winsets of a balanced Senate (figure 4.3) and those of the imbalanced House (figure 4.2) is striking and yields several implications. First, sectional equilibrium dramatically transforms the shape of the winset, removing the long "petal" of policies representing major changes along the slavery dimension. Put simply, *sectional equilibrium in the Senate implies that the political controversy excludes slavery.* Although proposals to alter slavery might have succeeded in the House, they could not pass the Senate. By manipulating the representation in the national institutions, elected officials were able to influence which policies could command a majority in these institutions.

Second, this approach shows why the territories were so critical to Southerners. As the principal mechanism protecting rights in slaves, *sectional equilibrium could be maintained only by expanding slavery.* The new economic history (NEH) has demonstrated that the South's direct *economic* motives for fostering the expansion of slavery were questionable and furthermore that these motives cannot explain why Southerners consistently and passionately pursued territorial expansion (Passell and Wright 1972; Wright 1978:130–35). My approach demonstrates that the South had significant, rational *political* reasons to pursue expansion, ones directly tied to the political foundations of the slavery economy. Failure to maintain equal representation would transform the political situation in the Senate to that of the imbalanced winsets of figure 4.2, allowing slavery to be threatened. *Protecting themselves from national political mischief thus required Southerners to favor the expansion of slavery.*[8]

The final implication of the analysis concerns the agreements over the territories and the absorption of more states into the Union. The theory suggests that the veto would serve its purposes on a day-by-day or year-by-year basis, that is, by preventing the national government from challenging rights in slaves. Over the long run, however, the most critical times concerned expansion. Because the country was growing, each new generation had to renew the

---

[8] Although the difference between figures 4.2 and 4.3 illustrates this principle with three and four senators, the result is general: a discontinuous change in the winset occurs with this configuration of senators when the two groups are of any size and the balance is broken by adding one voter to one side (see Weingast 1996:3-23–3-24). In particular, with thirty states and sixty senators, adding one free state to an existing set of equally balanced free and slave states has the effect of returning the eliminated petal to the winset.

TABLE 4.3
Northern Antislavery Measures in the House, 1800–60

Year	Measure
1804	Hillhouse Amendment sought to prohibit slavery in the Louisiana Purchase. Passed the House but failed in the Senate.
1818–19	Talmadge Amendment to the Missouri statehood bill sought to abolish slavery in Missouri. Passed the House but failed in Senate.
1836	Amendment proposed in the House to the Arkansas statehood bill that would have abolished slavery in Arkansas. Failed.
1836–44	Gag rules needed to prevent antislavery petitions.
1836–45	Northerners delay the admission of Texas for almost a decade.
1845	Motion in the House to suspend the rules to allow an amendment to the Texas statehood resolution that would split Texas into one slave state and one free state. Supported by a majority of 92–81, but failed to achieve two-thirds support required.
1846–50	Wilmot Proviso sought to prohibit slavery in the territory obtained from Mexico. Passed the House but failed in the Senate. Despite numerous attempts at compromise,[a] the House reaffirmed the proviso again and again over the next four years, creating deadlock.
1858	House defeated the Democrats' attempt to reinstate balance by admitting Kansas as a slave state.

a. Two examples of failed compromise proposals: (1) The 1848 attempt to resolve the sectional crisis by extending the 36°30' line to the Pacific failed in the House, which instead passed various antislavery measures, including the Wilmot Proviso. (2) The Clayton Compromise passed the Senate but failed in the House, which refused to recede from the proviso. This compromise sought to organize Oregon without slavery, to organize California and New Mexico without reference to slavery, and to refer all questions about slavery in the territories to the territorial courts, allowing appeal to the United States Supreme Court. For further discussion, see Potter (1976:63–89).

arrangements that began when the founding fathers created a system with strong constitutional protections for slavery.[9] These questions underpinned the principal crises of the Union, for the relative balance of power and the terms of exchange between the North and South were renegotiated during periods in which the renewal of the agreement was at stake. The controversies over Missouri (1819–20) and the Mexican War (1846–50) illustrate these themes.

At this point, it is worth pausing to suggest the veracity of an important prediction of the model, namely that antislavery measures should be able to pass the House of Representatives but not the Senate. Table 4.3 lists a series of antislavery measures over the course of the antebellum era, showing that Northerners regularly passed them. Most concern territorial or statehood politics, including the 1804 Hillhouse Amendment seeking to prohibit slavery in

[9]On the institutional protections for slavery provided by the Constitution, see Nichols (1963), North and Rutten (1987), Fogel (1989), Ransom (1989), Roback (1991), Finkelman (1996), and Rakove (1996).

the Louisiana Purchase; the 1818–19 Talmadge Amendment seeking to abolish slavery in Missouri; the 1846–50 Wilmot Proviso seeking to prevent the land gained in the war with Mexico from becoming slave territory; and the 1858 amendment defeating the attempt to admit Kansas as a slave state. In addition, Northerners attempted to abolish slavery in Arkansas during the consideration of its statehood in 1836. When the House considered the admission of Texas in 1845, Northerners sought to break it into two states, one free and one slave. Many of these votes were among the most critical of the era.

Of the several measures that passed the House, none passed the Senate. In the absence of sectional balance, had the North had a majority in the Senate, there is no reason to believe that these measures would have failed in that body. Put simply, Southern veto in the Senate was critical not only in theory for protecting Southern interests, but also in practice.

In short, the model shows that nothing inherent in antebellum politics produced parties that suppressed sectional motives. This finding, and other political features of the second-party system emphasized by the NPH (including the dominance of economic issues on the national political agenda), required the explicit construction of institutions in the form of the balance rule in the Senate.

Without this veto, rights in slaves would have been far less secure. Moreover, the many direct political assaults on slavery, passing the Northern-dominated House of Representatives on numerous occasions in the antebellum years, may well have gone further had the South not possessed its veto. To demonstrate this conclusion, we turn to a more explicit model of partisan policy choice under the second-party system.

Sectional Balance and the Suppression of Antislavery Initiatives in Antebellum America

The approach developed in the previous section contrasts with that of most historians, who emphasize that, prior to the 1850s, the issue of slavery in antebellum America was largely off the agenda. The principal national political issues were economic—focusing on tariffs, land policy, internal improvement, and banking—not sectional. Silbey (1985:xv, emphasis added) argues that "National political parties played a primary role in organizing, shaping, and giving life to antebellum politics, *not as reflectors of sectional forces but as direct and persistent alternatives to them*. . . . Partisan, not sectional, perspectives . . . controlled the American political landscape." Fogel (1989:281, emphasis added) focuses on a different aspect of the absence of slavery as a sustained issue during the antebellum years: "Politicians were initially unwilling to make the abolition of slavery an issue of national politics *because they believed that the Constitution enjoined them from doing so.* That interpretation of the Constitution was reaffirmed by Congress so often during the first half century after its ratification that it became a 'federal consensus,' a consensus as prevalent among politicians of the North as of the South." Looked at in this way, the problem of explaining the Civil War requires that we explain how the consensus supporting slavery fell apart and how slavery came, by the end of the 1850s, to dominate national politics.

My approach interprets the problem differently. No consensus supporting slavery existed in the sense that most Americans favored or believed they should support slavery. Instead, slavery was always a potentially divisive political issue. The observations that economic issues dominated national politics and that the party system appeared to suppress rather than foster sectional issues are part of the phenomena to be explained. Silbey's emphasis on parties, at least under the second-party system, represents an important piece of the puzzle, although it only partially explains why parties played that role.

As shown earlier, some Northerners had specific reasons to raise slavery as an issue, and a purely Northern coalition opposing the South on both economic and slavery issues remained a threat throughout this period. Southerners, concerned about their property and their institutions, required a system to protect themselves as a minimal condition for participating in the nation. The balance rule was the solution.

Sectional balance in the Senate afforded each region the power to veto policies inimical to its interests. My claim is that the balance rule underpinned a series of political phenomena in antebellum America: the federal character of the Union with a national government strongly limited in scope, a party system that suppressed slavery as an issue, and the lack of sustained political attention to slavery. The appearance of a "consensus" over slavery did not reflect a uniform interest throughout the country in preserving slavery. Rather it reflected strong incentives that prevented those who would oppose slavery from doing so.

The purpose of this section is to demonstrate the plausibility of these claims, particularly the suppression of antislavery initiatives.[10] Central to my approach are the implications of the balance rule, which works via off-the-path behavior. Because antislavery initiatives were costly, their failure implied the inability to capture benefits to counterbalance the costs. The veto implied by sectional balance thus proved central to forestalling antislavery initiatives. As a result, these initiatives were relatively infrequent during the antebellum years prior to 1850. But that does not imply that antislavery mesasures might have arisen at just any time. The apparent consensus emphasized by Fogel was a product of the deliberate design of institutions to prevent the success of those with an interest in advancing antislavery initiatives. The expectation of failure—off-the-path behavior in equilibrium—prevents antislavery initiatives, not the lack of desire for them.

[10]Substantiating them requires a much longer treatment (see Weingast 1996:4-1-4-34, 5-1-5-25, 7-1-7-15).

Sectional Balance, Off-the-Path Behavior, and the Protection of Slavery

The following two games portray both the national threat to slavery from unconstrained national politics and the value of the balance rule for precluding this threat. The first game is between a potentially antislavery party, AP, and the pivotal national voter, P (a voter in the Northwest), who holds the balance of political power between the two national parties.[11] The second game adds a third player, the South (S), who is granted a veto over national policy. Although S is not a player in the first game, its utility is affected by the outcome of the game. There are two additional "dummy players" who make no choices in either game but whose interests are affected by the outcome of both games: the majority party, MP, and a Northern nonpivotal voter (representing the Northeast, NE). Finally, uncertainty affects how the players view the two parties. To make this circumstance concrete, I assume that uncertainty concerns the economy: the country may experience economic good times or be in an economic panic.[12]

The purpose of this exercise is to show the behavioral implications of the veto, particularly its effect on antislavery initiatives and the majority party. The game is a highly stylized representation of antebellum politics. For example, it ignores decisions made by AP's political opponents and the voting decisions by the two nonpivotal voters. Nonetheless, the stylization captures a critical component of antebellum national politics.

GAME 1: NATIONAL ELECTORAL CHOICE IN THE ABSENCE OF
A SOUTHERN VETO

Understanding the game's implications for national politics requires calculation of the equilibrium outcomes. To begin this step, consider the sequence of choices made by the players. The game represents uncertainty over the economy by a nonstrategic player called Nature, N, who has the first move (figure 4.4). With probability π, Nature chooses good economic times; with probability $1 - \pi$, Nature chooses an economic panic. The state of the economy need not literally be the result of a lottery, as a move by Nature suggests. The move by Nature represents a convenient way to express the uncertainty facing the second player, who must choose prior to knowing the state of the economy.

---

[11]The pivot reflects the following idea. In a nation where 40 percent of the people voted for one party nearly all the time and another 40 percent voted for the other party nearly all the time, the remaining 20 percent held the balance of power and determined which party would be in the majority. For this reason, we call these voters pivotal.

[12]The evidence that economic performance affects the fate of incumbents is remarkable: the worse the economy, the less likely incumbents will win reelection. The period in question is no exception. See the evidence from such diverse contexts as U.S. presidential elections (Tufte 1978) and developing states in transition to democracy (Haggard and Kaufman 1995).

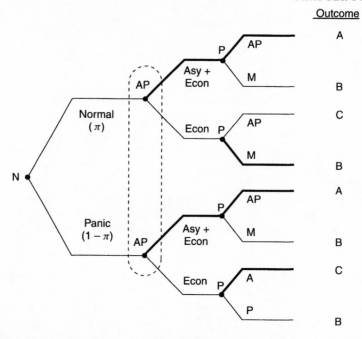

FIGURE 4.4. National policy choice without a Southern veto (game 1).

After Nature moves, AP moves and may advocate either antislavery policies along with its economic program or its economic program alone. These choices are labeled Asy + Econ and Econ, respectively. The dashed ellipse around AP's two decision nodes in figure 4.4 indicates that AP does not know the state of the economy (technically, Nature's choice) at the time of its decision.

P moves third and must decide whether to support AP or MP. To simplify the decision tree, I ignore the policy choice of the electoral winner, assuming in both games that the winner implements the policy it advocated. As to the information assumptions: I assume that the party has to commit to its candidate and platform well in advance of the election. Voters therefore have more information about the state of the economy on election day than do the parties when they make their decisions. I represent this by assuming that AP must choose in ignorance of the state of the economy (hence the dashed ellipses around its two decision nodes) while P knows the state of the economy when it must choose.

The outcomes are summarized as follows. If AP wins the election on a platform of Asy + Econ, the outcome is A; if it wins on a platform of Econ alone, the outcome is C. If MP wins the election, the outcome is B.

The preferences of P and S are given in figure 4.5 (ignore for now the outcome 0 in the rankings).[13] The two parties care only about winning, obtaining 1 if they

---

[13]The preference orders are derived from a more extensive and less stylized analysis (Weingast 1996:4-1–4-34, 5-1–5-25).

P_N	P_P	S
A	A	B
B	C	C
C	B	0
0	0	A

FIGURE 4.5. Players' preference rankings.

win, 0 if they lose. The pivot's preferences depend on the state of the economy. During normal times, P (P_N) prefers AP's combined policies of economics and antislavery (A) to MP's Econ policy (B) to AP's economic policies alone (C). During an economic panic, however, P (P_p) prefers AP's economic policies to MP's policies, ranking the three outcomes as follows: AP's combined policies of economics and antislavery (A) are preferred to AP's economic policies alone (C), which are preferred to MP's Econ policy (B). S ranks the outcomes as B, C, A regardless of the state of the economy.

To determine the outcome of the game, we solve for a subgame-perfect equilibrium, requiring that an action be specified for each decisionmaker at each node of the game. This solution is constructed through backward induction. Thus consider P's choices at the four nodes just prior to the end of the game. The relative attractiveness of the two parties for P depends in part on the state of the economy. During normal times, P prefers AP's combination of policies to MP's economic policies, so if AP offers both Asy + Econ, P prefers it to MP; if instead AP advocates only Econ, P prefers MP. During economic panics, P prefers AP to MP regardless of AP's choice of Asy + Econ or Econ. This leads to the following behavior by P: during normal times, P chooses AP if AP advocates Asy + Econ, otherwise P chooses MP; during a panic, P always chooses AP.

P's behavior sets the stage for AP's decisions. AP does not know whether there will be a panic. Because it wins regardless of its decision if there is a panic, and because it wins during normal times only if it chooses Asy + Econ, it will choose Asy + Econ. This allows AP to win under all economic circumstances.

In this game, AP is able to attract the pivot. Its combination of antislavery and economic policies allows it to dominate national elections. Both S and Southern slavery are therefore in trouble!

GAME 2: NATIONAL ELECTORAL CHOICE UNDER A SOUTHERN VETO

The sequence of action in the second game adds a fourth move by S to the three moves in the first game. In the additional move, S may veto the entire set of policies (figure 4.6), resulting in a payoff of 0 to P, S, and NE. Notice that players P and NE prefer all outcomes to the result of a veto, 0 (figure 4.5). Although S prefers B and C to 0, it prefers 0 over A. The players' preferences are otherwise unchanged from those in game 1.

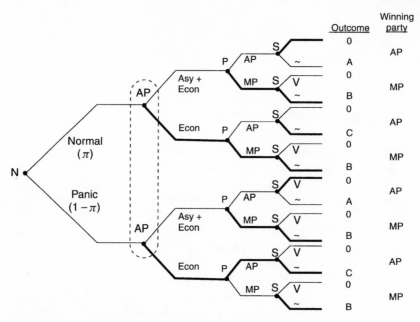

FIGURE 4.6. National policy choice under a Southern veto (game 2).

We again solve for the equilibrium by backward induction. Although this game has sixteen end nodes, there are only four possible outcomes, making it relatively easy to solve.

In the game's last move, S must choose between the outcome arrived at by the previous moves or, by exercising its veto, 0. Because S prefers 0 only to outcome A (Asy + Econ), it will exercise its veto only when the previous moves yield A. In all other circumstances, a veto would make S worse off. The following contingent rule for exercising its veto summarizes S's behavior at its eight decision nodes: S exercises its veto if and only if P chooses AP when AP has chosen Asy + Econ. This implies that S exercises its veto only at its first and fifth decision nodes (numbering the nodes from top to bottom).

Working backwards, the next set of decision nodes requires a choice by P, who takes S's behavior as given. Consider normal economic times. If AP advocates the combined policies, then choosing AP results in a veto and a payoff of 0 for P, whereas choosing MP yields a payoff of B. If instead AP advocates Econ, choosing AP yields outcome C, whereas choosing MP yields outcome B. In both cases, P prefers MP's policies to AP's.

An economic panic alters P's calculus. If AP advocates the combined policies, then choosing AP results in a payoff of 0, whereas choosing MP yields a payoff of B. If instead AP advocates Econ, choosing AP yields outcome C, whereas choosing MP yields outcome B. Hence, during a panic, if AP advocates

Asy + Econ, P chooses MP. Alternatively if during a panic AP advocates Econ, P will choose AP (because it prefers C to B). To summarize: taking S's behavior as given, P chooses MP during normal times, whereas during a panic it will choose AP if AP advocates Econ.

Next consider AP's decision at the first node. Taking P and S's behavior as given, observe that P never chooses AP during normal times, whereas during a panic P chooses AP if AP advocates Econ. AP can never win an election by advocating Asy + Econ, but it can win if there is a panic and if it advocates Econ. So AP will choose Econ as long as the probability of a panic, π, exceeds zero.

In the equilibrium of this game, MP dominates elections when the relative frequency of panics is low (that is, when $\pi < 0.5$). In the face of a Southern veto, AP has strong incentives to temper its potential antislavery initiatives. Although the pivotal voter prefers antislavery initiatives, S will veto them, making the pivot worse off. This results in a paradox: S's behavior deters the pivot from supporting AP if it advocates the very initiatives P prefers. The pivot's behavior, in turn, prevents AP from advocating these initiatives. S's veto is therefore critical to preventing antislavery initiatives. Put differently, the veto proves essential for self-enforcing limits on the national government's policy toward slavery.

The equilibrium of game 2 parallels outcomes in antebellum America, where Democrats dominated elections under the second-party system. Nonetheless, sometimes things went awry and the voters threw out the incumbents, for example, because of economic downturns, unpopular foreign events, or scandals.[14]

These games reveal the critical importance of the South's veto. In the absence of a veto, AP would dominate elections. AP's combined policies allow it to win under all circumstances, reflecting the result, established previously, that a purely Northern coalition could win national elections. Slavery is unstable under these circumstances and cannot survive in the national system.

Game 2 demonstrates that the outcome changes dramatically when the South holds a veto over national public policy. Because the South will veto AP's policies when AP attempts to implement a combined antislavery and economic policy, P prefers MP to AP when AP advocates ASY + ECON. This leads to a change in AP's behavior, and it instead advocates only its economic policies. AP's behavior under balance implies that P prefers MP over AP during good times but AP over MP during bad times.

Implications

The two games studied in this section have significant implications for the relative absence of antislavery initiatives under the second-party system. Assaults

---

[14]Moreover, in economic downturns, the Whigs' promotional economic policies were more attractive to voters than at other times, just as today the Democrats' economic interventionism becomes relatively more attractive than the Republicans' economic policies during recessions.

on slavery were relatively few, not because a consensus supported slavery or no one cared about slavery, but because of the deliberate construction of institutions designed to make it too costly for interested parties to attack slavery.

Games 1 and 2 demonstrate that Northerners had reasons to act against slavery for their own political purposes. Were they in control of the government—and were the South without a veto—Northerners would act on their preferences (game 1). In this game, the natural majority coalition is sectional. Northern preferences in game 2 are identical to those in game 1: the Northern pivotal voter still prefers assaults against slavery. Nonetheless, antislavery initiatives are no longer attractive. The Southern veto alters the implication of antislavery choices, changing Northerners' incentives. The veto implies that the pivot prefers MP rather than AP if the latter's choices will result in S's veto. Consequently, AP will not advocate these policies. Moreover, the veto has powerful behavioral consequences, decisively switching the majority party from AP to MP.

These games demonstrate how the suppression of sectional issues depended on more than just the behavior of parties and American political culture under the second-party system. Had the veto not been engineered to prevent Northern assaults on slavery, there would have been more assaults then actually observed, and some might have succeeded. The Southern veto in the senate made assaults on slavery relatively rare.

Political culture—the behavior of mass publics and elites—cannot be treated as indelible characteristics of the underlying electorate, as many analysts assume. My approach shows how that behavior, and hence important aspects of political culture, also depends upon political institutions and the incentives they create for political actors.

The emergence of a "consensus" that slavery was protected by the Constitution and not fair political game—central to Fogel's (1989:281–87) work—was neither the product of a fixed American political culture nor the result of a preference among nearly all Americans that slavery be protected. The appearance of a consensus under the second-party system was instead constructed, the result of political institutions that prevented those with an incentive to assault slavery from doing so.

Similarly, as Silbey has emphasized, parties were important suppressors of sectional initiatives. But the behavior emphasized by Silbey did not simply follow from the preferences of the electorate. Game 1 suggests that preferences alone would have led a Northern majority to attack slavery. The partisan suppression of sectional issues also hinged on the existence of the balance rule. Because balance implied that antislavery initiatives could not succeed, it dramatically altered the ability and inclination of elected officials to pursue such goals.

Let me end this discussion with the observation that contemporaries understood the implications of sectional balance in the Senate. First, Thomas

Jefferson clearly understood this principle and its implications as early as the 1780s. During the debates on the territories in 1784–87, Jefferson's plan envisioned an absence of slavery and far more new Northern states than Southern states. The prohibition on slaves in the new territories failed, however, and the prescribed number of new states was brought back into rough parity. As Nichols (1963:66–67) observed, "The arrangement for political expansion of the American [state], perfected in 1787 by the Constitution and later by the Laws of 1789 and 1790, had operated in such a way that an equal number of slave and free-labor states had been carved out of the original [Northern and Southern colonies plus the Northwest and Southwest territories], and an equilibrium was maintained between them in the Senate, where each state was equal to every one of its fellows."

Second, contemporaries under the second-party system clearly understood sectional balance, calling it "sectional equilibrium" (Carpenter 1930). In each of the major national crises, all over slavery (i.e., in 1820, 1846–50, and 1854–61), this notion was clearly articulated. Carpenter (1930:104) reports that during the debates over the Compromise of 1850, David Yulee provided "a convincing argument to prove that the South, in renouncing its constitutional claim to the protection of slavery in all the territories, received in return a guarantee of a sectional equilibrium in the Senate."[15]

Finally, John C. Calhoun, a much-misunderstood prophet of the South, understood this principle. In 1850, the faster growth of the North implied that sectional balance was harder to maintain. His proposal for a "concurrent majority," published after his death in 1850, sought to alter the Constitution so that there would be two presidents, one elected in the North and one elected in the South, each with the power to veto national legislation. The concurrent majority would accomplish the same end as sectional balance. By granting the South a veto, the concurrent majority would work exactly as did the Southern veto granted by the balance rule.

A Test of the Hypothesis about the Demise of Sectional Balance

My argument rests on the notion that sectional balance in the Senate allowed Southerners to protect their slave economy by granting them a veto over

---

[15]Carpenter (1930:103) further quotes Jefferson Davis as suggesting that "it is essential that neither section have such power in Congress as would render them able to trample upon the rights of the other section of this Union. It would be a blessing, an essential means to preserve the Confederacy, that in one branch of Congress the North and in the other the South should have a majority of representation . . . if legislation was restricted and balanced in the mode I have suggested, Congress would never be able to encroach upon the rights and institutions of any portion of the Union, nor could its acts ever meet with resistance from any part of it."

national policymaking. This interpretation works reasonably well for most of the second-party system, specifically from the late 1820s through 1850. But what accounts for the breaking of sectional balance with the admission of California in 1850 without a balancing slave state? Because the balance rule is central to my argument about both American democratic stability and the preservation of slavery under the second-party system, a discussion of its demise is essential.

Although Congress deviated from sectioinal balance in the Compromise of 1850, it did not undo the balance rule. Democrats fully expected to make good on their promise of reestablishing balance at the first opportunity. Unfortunately for Southerners and Democrats, the unforeseen disaster of the Kansas-Nebraska Act meant that there were never enough Democrats in the North to make good on this promise.

Explanations of this sort are logically unattractive. Because it is *always* possible to argue that "things failed to work out as anticipated," why should we have any faith in this one?

To investigate my hypothesis that the shift in representation away from the Democrats in the North prevented them from making good on the promise of 1850, I study the attempt to admit Kansas as a slave state under the Lecompton Constitution in early 1858. The case of admitting Kansas is especially relevant to our problem. The violence induced by the popular sovereignty provisions of the Kansas territory combined with the obvious electoral fraud surrounding the proposed proslavery Lecompton Constitution made supporting the Democratic Party's initiative difficult for large numbers of Northern Democrats (Nichols 1948; Nevins 1950; Potter 1976; Holt 1978). Nonetheless, the Democrats proposed to admit Kansas—and almost succeeded.

To provide evidence for my hypothesis about political expectations in 1850, I investigate the 1858 vote. The analysis is based on the assumption that decisionmakers in 1850 would have assessed the possibilities for future votes based in part on their experience with similar votes over the previous years. I then construct what the 1858 vote would have been had the Democrats retained their historic level of representation in the North rather than lost significant support after the Kansas-Nebraska Act of 1854. The construction shows that the Democrats' 1858 proposal would have passed had they experienced levels of support in the North typical of the second-party system.

The 1858 Vote to Admit Kansas as a Slave State

The principal vote defeating the proposal took place in the House of Representatives. In spite of the controversy surrounding Kansas and the Lecompton Constitution, President Buchanan strongly pushed the measure, and it easily passed the Senate, 35–25. In the House, where Northerners held a large majority, antislavery forces introduced a substitute measure that sought to force a new

TABLE 4.4

Proportion of Congressmen Voting to Admit Kansas as a Slave State, by Party and Region, 1858

Region	Democrats	Republicans	Americans
South	1.00	—	0.86
	(58)		(7)
Border	1.00	—	0.29
	(15)		(7)
Northwest	0.29	0.00	—
	(21)	(31)	
Northeast	0.78	0.00	—
	(32)	(60)	

Source: Poole and Rosenthal (1990).

and fair referendum on the constitution before Kansas could be admitted. The substitute passed on a close vote of 120–112. Had just four more Northern Democrats supported their party—fewer than 2 percent of those voting—Kansas would have become the sixteenth slave state.[16]

Although in 1858 Democrats held a proportion of the House near their historic average, their strength was provided largely by Southerners, a situation unusual by historical standards. Since 1850, the number of Northern Democrats had fallen while the number of Southern Democrats had risen. In this Congress, the Democratic Party held only 37 percent of all Northern districts, markedly below its historic average of 50 percent.

Table 4.4 presents the relative frequency of the various groups of congressmen supporting Kansas statehood under the proslavery constitution. Nearly all congressmen from slave states (93 percent) voted for the measure. As was typical of the antebellum era, support by Northern congressmen was partisan (Silbey 1967; Weingast 1996:5-1–5-25, 7-1–7-15). A majority of Northern Democrats (58 percent) voted in favor whereas all Republicans voted against.

In principle, there are two ways to reconstruct these votes. The most defensible way employs statistical models to analyze patterns of voting and then uses these patterns to project what the vote would have been had there been a different mix of congressmen. Unfortunately a logistic regression cannot estimate a model when a linear combination of the independent variables perfectly discriminates between categories of the dependent variable. In my model, the problem occurs because all Republicans voted against the measure and all Southern Democrats voted for it.[17]

---

[16]It is worth emphasizing at the outset that this analysis is *not* intended to suggest what might have happened had Kansas been admitted as a slave state. Instead, the vote on admitting Kansas as a slave state provides a good indication about the ability of the Democratic party to have made good on its promise in the compromise.

[17]A further complication is that one independent variable, Poole and Rosenthal's X score, is a nearly perfect predictor of how Northern Democrats voted.

The second method involves a simple and direct calculation. Both methods suppose that the Democrats in the North had, in 1858, retained their historic strength of 50 percent of all Northern congressional districts. This would have increased the number of Democrats in the Northwest from twenty to twenty-six and in the Northeast from thirty-two to forty-six.

To reconstruct the vote, I assume that the additional Northern Democrats would have voted in favor of the Lecompton Constitution with a frequency equal to that actually observed among other Democrats from their region. All Southern Democrats favored the Lecompton statehood. Among Northern Democrats, 29 percent in the Northwest and 78 percent in the Northeast supported the bill that ultimately failed. All Republicans opposed the measure.

The assumption that the Democrats retained their historic representation implies that we substitute Democrats for six Republicans in the Northwest and fourteen in the Northeast. To compute how the twenty new Democrats would have voted, I assume that 29 percent of the six new Democrats from the Northwest and 78 percent of the fourteen new Democrats from the Northeast voted for the measure. Rounding to the nearest whole vote, this calculation implies a net transfer of thirteen votes from the substitute measure to the Lecompton measure. Thus, had the Democrats retained their historic strength in the North, the Lecompton Constitution would have passed by a vote of 125–107 rather than failing 112–120.[18]

Implications

The evidence in this section shows that reasonable expectations in 1850 held that the Democrats would succeed at restoring balance at the next opportunity. Although the South's accepting of the breaking of the balance became in part

---

[18]Weingast (1996:10B-14–10B-20) provides a second set of counterfactual investigations. The analysis presented in the text takes the voting behavior of Northern Democratic House members as given. Yet recent events (the Kansas-Nebraska Act, the armed conflict between free-soil and proslavery settlers in Kansas, and the Supreme Court decision in the *Dred Scott* case) had led Democrats in the Northwest to vote disproportionately against their party in the Kansas vote. On many of the previous critical Democratic proslaverry measures (for example, the organization of the Utah Territory without restrictions on slavery during the Compromise of 1850, the vote to admit Texas in 1845, and the Kansas-Nebraska Act), House Democrats in the Northwest favored their party's position on average by more than 2 to 1. This historic average, rather than the actual frequency of support in 1858, would have been relevant for elected officials in 1850 trying to project the next critical vote on slavery.

For purposes of the second counterfactual, had Democrats in the Northwest in 1858 split evenly (rather than only 29 percent voting in favor), five more Democrats in the Northwest would have voted in favor instead of against. This implies that the measure to admit Kansas as a slave state would have passed, 117–115. Furthermore, if this second effect is combined with the effect studied in the text, the vote to admit Kansas would have passed by a large margin, 130–102.

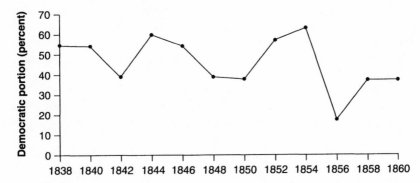

FIGURE 4.7. Democratic portion of the Northern House delegation, 1837–61. *Source:* Martis (1989).

its undoing over the next decade, Southerners could not know this at the time of the compromise. In 1850 they did not know, as we do now, that the Democratic Party's hegemony and the second-party system would soon meet their end. Nor did they know, as we do now, that the decade would end in sectional strife and civil war. Instead they would have seen far more continuity in their world than later events would suggest. For example, reactions in the two elections following the Compromise suggested that the Democrats would maintain their electoral dominance. Indeed, in the House of Representatives elected in 1852, Democrats fielded their largest delegation ever in the North (figure 4.7).[19] In the previous years since the Jackson presidency (1837–50), the Democrats had averaged a little above 50 percent of Northerners in the House. After the 1852 election, they held 63 percent of the House. Following the Kansas-Nebraska disaster, however, their percentage fell to 18 percent. Although Northern Democrats recovered somewhat in the next two elections, they never again regained their historic average of 50 percent of the Northern House delegation.

To gain a sense of the likelihood of experiencing a fall in representation as large as Democrats experienced in the 1854 elections, suppose that the Democratic share of the Northern House delegation is a normal random variable with a mean and standard deviation equal to their observed values. The mean proportion of Northern House members who were Democratic from the twenty-fifth to the thirty-third Congress was 51.3 percent, with a standard deviation of 0.099. The proportion of Democrats in the Northern House delegation following the Kansas-Nebraska Act was 16.3 percent, or a drop of 3.535

---

[19]Notice that figure 4.7 reports each House for the year of its main session, i.e., the year of the *next* congressional elections. Thus the size of the Democratic delegation to the House elected in 1852 is labeled in the year 1854.

standard deviations below the mean. Given these assumptions, the probability of observing such a large drop is about 0.0002 or 1 in 5,000. Put simply, this drop was an unlikely occurrence.

Nonetheless, even as late as 1858—after the Kansas-Nebraska Act, the so-called War in Kansas, and the *Dred Scott* decision—the Democrats almost succeeded in restoring balance. The vote reconstructions in this section show that, had the Democrats not experienced these political disasters, retaining their historic level of support in the North, their promise to restore balance would have succeeded.

Conclusions

Because political officials establish the rights and rules governing the economy, the economic and political systems are intimately related. Property rights that are potentially controversial are politically insecure. This conclusion holds for a range of economic rights, whether rights in slaves in antebellum America or rights underpinning the newly privatized markets of the former socialist states. Sustaining vulnerable rights requires that the government provide a credible commitment to these rights, that is, provide incentives for political officials to honor and protect those rights (North 1990; Weingast 1995). Without credible commitments, the potential vulnerability may be actualized, destroying these rights and the assets and society they protect.

Institutions that create credible commitments are thus central to the political foundations of an economy; the American slave system was no exception. As the new economic historians amply demonstrate, slavery was enormously profitable, especially in growing cotton.[20] On the eve of the Civil War, the economic value of slaves was on the order of the gross national product of the United States. Maintaining this wealth required that rights in slaves be protected from political interference. Given the huge magnitude of the slave economy, even small policy changes would have had a substantial effect throughout the South. In the face of this political uncertainty over their rights, Southerners sought protection for their economic system and their way of life.

A range of antebellum political institutions was designed to protect the slave economy from national political interference. Most obviously, the constitutional system of separation of powers provided a degree of durability by raising the costs of altering national policy. Federalism, underpinned by a constitutional jurisprudence of states' rights, provided further protection for Southerners. States' rights placed decisions about slavery with the states, not with the national government.

---

[20]For recent reviews with an eye toward the politics of slavery, see Fogel (1989:17–198), Ransom (1989), and Wright (1978).

But federalism was not self-implementing. It is true that many if not most Americans preferred action by local governments that were more readily controlled and adapted to their interests than action by a remote national government. Nonetheless, these preferences alone were insufficient to sustain American federalism (Weingast 1995). Doing so required the construction of self-enforcing limits on the national government. The result was a series of institutions beyond the Constitution's separation of powers and federal framework—for example, a set of intersectional political parties and sectional balance in the Senate—designed to maintain limits on the national government. As the models presented earlier in this chapter show, these institutions made limits on the national government self-enforcing by altering the incentives facing national political officials.

These institutions protected slavery from potential encroachment by the national government. Although many Northerners had the interest to pursue antislavery initiatives, sectional balance in the Senate allowed Southerners to veto these attempts. Indeed a series of antislavery initiatives passed the House of Representatives, where the North held majorities throughout the era. As the theory predicts, these all failed in the Senate.

Sectional balance also had more far-reaching effects, of which I mention two. First, beyond allowing Southerners to veto onerous measures, it dramatically reduced the Northerners' incentives to produce and support antislavery measures. Second, in a dynamic, growing nation, sectional balance required that the sections grow in parallel (Nichols 1963; Potter 1976). Sustained faster growth by one section would make sectional balance hard to maintain. For most of the first half of the nineteenth century, balanced growth occurred. When opportunities for Northern growth began to outpace Southern growth in the 1840s, the Democratic Party embraced "manifest destiny" as a way of expanding the area devoted to the slave economy, first by annexing the Texas Republic in 1845 and then by initiating the war with Mexico a year later. The result was not as the Democrats intended, however. The prospect of acquiring vast new territories for slavery made many Northerners nervous, leading to a prolonged sectional conflict over the territory gained in the Mexican War, settled only by the Compromise of 1850.

Economic historians have shown that, during the first five decades of the nineteenth century, Northern expansion was in part tied to Southern expansion and thus the international demand for cotton (see, e.g., North 1961). Parallel economic and territorial growth characterized the two sections. Parallel growth did not continue through the 1850s. Although both the Northern and Southern economies expanded, only the North expanded territorially. Moreover, the Northern economy increasingly became integrated, as more trade traveled along an east-west axis than along a north-south axis (Kohlmeier 1938; North 1961:101–21; Fogel 1989:302–12; see also Moore 1966:111–55). Economic and political constraints on the extension of slavery seemed to place an iron grip on Southern expansion while Northern expansion remained unfettered.

The importance of maintaining sectional balance in a growing economy helps explain the periodic antebellum crises. Because sustaining balance required balanced growth, ambiguity about future growth often meant potential advantage for one section. Each of the major crises—1820, 1846–50, and 1854–61—centered on the future of the territories and the implications for sectional balance. The first two crises were resolved by compromise among the moderates in both sections (Potter 1976). Yet the third crisis was not, resulting in an escalating sectional conflict and, ultimately, secession and war.

The Crisis That Led to War

Why could Americans resolve the crises of 1820 and 1846–50 but not that of the 1850s? My perspective points to three factors differentiating the third crisis. First, as noted previously, the South had become hemmed in by economic and political constraints. Given the high price of slaves in the early 1850s, slavery was not economically viable in any of the territories into which slaveholders could legally expand. Although many Northerners had in the past been willing to help Southerners pass measures expanding the territory for slavery, the costs of doing so were rising. Not only did slaveholders in the 1850s want access to land already designated as free by the long-standing Missouri Compromise, they also wanted access to exactly the same areas that Northerners sought to settle. In contrast, the costs to Northerners of granting Southerners access to land not yet designated as free or slave, and that Northerners did not then want, had been far lower in 1820.

Second, two significant structural changes altered the identity and preferences of the pivotal voter in national elections, a voter who had been a Democrat throughout the second-party system. First, the huge wave of immigration beginning in the mid-1840s greatly changed the Northern polity and economy (Holt 1978; Silbey 1985; Fogel 1989). In 1800 the two sections each had roughly two million people. In 1860, the North was nearly twice as big, with a population of twenty million compared with the South's eleven million, four million of whom were slaves. The asymmetric growth reflected immigration toward the end of the second-party system, beginning in the mid-1840s (Fogel 1989).

As the NPH emphasizes, immigration had profound political implications. Low-wage immigrants displaced large numbers of natives from their jobs, ultimately dislodging many native workers from their parties. This was especially true of the Democratic party, which tended to absorb the immigrants. Furthermore, by expanding the size of the Northern electorate, immigration diminished the need of Northerners to court Southern votes. Put another way, immigration lowered the costs of organizing a purely Northern party.

The second structural change involved the growing integration of the Northern economy, which increased the economic and political ties between the

Northwest and the Northeast. In 1820, settlers moving west to the frontier frequently tended to become self-sufficient farmers. In the mid-1850s, settlers moving west to the frontier often expected to participate in an international economy, growing grain to be shipped east and thence bound for Europe (Calomiris and Schweikart 1991). As manufactured goods were shipped west and food east, the Northern economy became increasingly independent of the Southern economy (North 1961:101–21).

The final factor hindering resolution of the third sectional crisis was the lack of understanding by most Americans at the time of the political implications of the structural changes. In this sense, the structural effects reinforced one another. Both implied that the pivotal Democratic voters in the North were less committed to the party's agenda than before.[21] Although politicians at the time could not readily observe this change, we now know that the Democrats' hold on their hegemonic position was weaker in the early 1850s than at any time during the previous two decades (see Poole and Rosenthal 1997:95–100).

In 1853 and 1854 Democratic leaders set out to do what Democratic leaders had always done, namely make a deal between Northern supporters of the party and the South for the protection and expansion of slavery. This strategy had worked many times in the past. Yet the Democrats' strategy failed in the mid-1850s. The structural changes imply that the pivotal Northern Democrat was not nearly as strongly Democratic as he had been during the second-party system. When faced with the Kansas-Nebraska Act's repeal of the Missouri Compromise, seemingly giving away Northern lands to slavery, pivotal Northern voters deserted the Democratic Party. At the same time, many natives in the Northeast also deserted the Democrats. In the wake of the Democrats' disaster, political entrepreneurs of several stripes sought to organize Northern voters, with the Republicans as frontrunners in the Northwest and the Americans as frontrunners in the Northeast. By the 1856 elections, however, the Republicans had surpassed their competitors, combining a mild nativist stand with a strong antislavery and especially anti-Southern stand (Holt 1978:139–81).

Part of the Republicans' success rested on the multiple appeals of their free-soil policy, which advocated a halt to the expansion of slave territory. Although free soil most obviously appealed to the relatively small group of abolitionists, its political appeal extended well beyond this group. As Foner (1970) emphasizes, free soil appealed to native workers. Free soil also appealed to a group of former Democrats in the North who sought to stem the influence of the slave economy, especially to keep the Northern economy expanding

---

[21]With the aid of hindsight, we understand these implications better today than did contemporaries. Our interpretations rest on more than a century's historical research. One reason we know more is that we can draw inferences after the fact from the unintended consequences of the choices made by contemporary leaders and voters.

and free from competition from the South. From the perspective of potential Northern settlers in Western territories, such as Kansas, free soil implied less competition from Southerners. That in turn implied more rapid ties to Eastern markets through railroads and, importantly, lower land prices.

In the face of these factors, the Democrats' attempts in the mid-1850s to reinstate sectional balance failed miserably, producing an effect opposite to that intended. The Democrats' major initiatives of the 1850s lost them their hegemonic national electoral position, ultimately driving many Northerners to the Republicans. As a consequence, they proved unable to reinstate sectional balance.

The absence of sectional balance combined with the rise of a new and potentially hegemonic Republican Party to threaten the South as never before. Because Republicans drew their electoral support solely from the North, their majority depended on neither the continued health of the slave economy nor the cooperation of the South. The resulting political incentives to the Republicans to cooperate with the South were just the opposite of those observed by Silbey (1967, 1985) during the second-party system. As Silbey suggests, the need to maintain Southern support meant that parties during the second-party system were moderating influences, helping to suppress divisive sectional issues. The incentives to the purely Northern Republicans were just the opposite, namely to distinguish their vision from that of the Democrats by focusing on policies beneficial largely to Northerners. Put simply, the absence of balance combined with a potentially new Republican majority to put the South at risk as never before.

Historians (e.g., Nichols 1963; McPherson 1988:66), have recognized balance as a principle underlying the territories but most do not recognize its far-reaching consequences. Balance was more than one principle among many influencing antebellum politics; it was the main principle underlying broad aspects of those politics. In the short run, Southerners had the veto to protect themselves. Over the long run, however, Southerners had to worry about maintaining it. This concern required that Southerners pay constant attention to economic and territorial expansion and, often, that they attempt to manipulate expansion.

The fights over the territories were not simply symbolic fights about unimportant issues, as some historians seem to suggest. Consider statements by two eminent historians of the era, David Donald and Don Fehrenbacher: "If it is true that the hottest issue of the 1850s was . . . not the future of slavery itself but the spread of slavery into the few remaining territories of the United States, do we not have to inquire why public opinion, North and South, grew so sensitive over what appears to be an abstract and unimportant point?" (Donald 1961:215). "Historians for more than a century have pondered the sectional struggle over slavery in the territories, trying to explain how it came to be invested with an emotional intensity that seems far out of proportion with its practical significance" (Fehrenbacher 1980:27). These comments at once downgrade the importance of the territorial issue and suggest that it can be separated from the larger controversy over slavery. My perspective instead suggests that they are two aspects of the same problem. Maintaining sectional balance in a growing nation implied that the territories represented the future of slavery. To the extent that balance protected slavery, the territorial issue was neither "abstract and unimportant" nor of low "practical significance" in comparison with the problem of slavery. The controversies over the territories were invested with so much "emotional intensity" precisely because they were about the future of slavery.

This chapter provides an analytical narrative of the growing sectional hostility. In addition to a narrative, it provides a model of two related and central aspects of the sectional controversy. First, the model reveals the threat from national politics to the Southern slave society: rights in slaves remained potentially insecure owing to uncertainty over the national politics of slavery. Only a minority of the nation valued slavery. An antislavery—or more accurately, an anti-Southern—majority therefore remained a possibility throughout the antebellum era, potentially threatening the nation's existence. Second, because most Americans in both sections valued the nation, a series of institutional compromises was devised to protect slavery via the sectional balance.

Two aspects of the approach demonstrate how sectional balance protected slavery. The first, utilizing a spatial model of political choice, shows that balance made antislavery initiatives infeasible. The second, using a simple sequential game, shows how the Southern veto altered the incentives of Northerners. Put simply, balance made self-enforcing the limits on the national government's ability to consider antislavery initiatives. In short, sectional balance protected Southern slavery and induced cooperation between the sections.

Although my account does not attempt to encompass the election of Lincoln, Southern secession, or the Civil War, it provides considerable insight into the rising sectional controversy. Sectional balance was undone temporarily in 1850. The Democratic Party's policy disasters—including the Kansas-Nebraska Act and the attempt to admit Kansas as a slave state—were a product of its attempts to reinstate balance. These policy disasters, particularly the Kansas-Nebraska Act, unexpectedly destroyed the Democrats' ability to reinstate balance. Finally, the rise of the sectional Republicans, in the absence of sectional balance, deeply threatened the South—*more so than at any previous time in American history.* Of course, that a threat is possible does not imply that it is realized. In principle, the sections could have resolved their differences, as they had on previous occasions. This chapter therefore does not offer an explanation for either secession or the Civil War. My more limited goal has been to explain why the stakes were so high. And here my approach suggests that virtually the entire Southern economy and hence society were at stake.

As the introduction to this volume suggests, many of the central assertions of an analytical narrative are not testable. In the case of the model presented in this chapter, untested assertions include the conclusions that sectional balance underpinned American political stability and that the demise of sectional balance in the 1850s was critical for the final sectional crisis. Nonetheless, aspects of the approach can be tested. Elsewhere I test a range of hypotheses and predictions about the spatial model (Weingast 1996:5-1–5-25, 7-1–7-15). This testing includes, first, demonstrating that members of Congress voted in the manner hypothesized by the model; second, showing that members of Congress had preferences over the issues corresponding to those assumed by the model; and third, using voting data to construct a winset for both the House and the Senate, showing that balance has precisely the effect hypothesized in the model.

This chapter also provides evidence in favor of one of the model's central conclusions. Because of the centrality of sectional balance, my argument requires an explanation for why Southerners allowed sectional balance to be broken in 1850, never to be restored. I argue that the South allowed the balance to be broken in part because the Democrats made a credible promise to restore balance or die trying. Most Democrats in 1850 expected to make good on this promise. The reason the Democrats failed to make good on their promise is that few Americans understood the structural changes that had weakened the party system and, in particular, the ties of the pivotal Northern voter to the Democratic Party. The Democrats' attempt to restore balance failed because they unexpectedly lost their hegemonic electoral position. In a sense unappreciated by most historians, the Democratic Party lost its hegemonic electoral position because of its imperative to restore sectional balance. This imperative underpinned many of the principal political events of the decade. These attempts included the opening up of new territory for slavery by repealing the Missouri Compromise in the Kansas-Nebraska Act and the attempt to admit Kansas as a slave state under fraudulent circumstances. The Democrats' loss of their hegemonic electoral position in national politics, in turn, removed their ability to restore balance.

A central weakness of this argument is that unforeseen circumstances can always be invoked to "explain" why events did not turn out as expected. So why should we take this explanation seriously? To address this question, I provide evidence supporting my view by examining the 1858 vote to admit Kansas as a slave state. I show that, had the Democrats not experienced their unexpected loss of Northern support following the Kansas-Nebraska Act, this measure would have easily passed. This finding provides evidence that the expectations held in 1850—that the Democrats would make good on their promise—were reasonable.

A New Synthesis

This chapter helps resolve a long-standing controversy among Civil War historians. Traditional historians offer explanations of the Civil War focused on national politics and the issue of slavery. New political historians argue that this focus is misplaced, and they emphasize instead the importance of local politics. My view suggests a new synthesis.

First, my approach encompasses the major findings of the NPH about the second-party system, namely that economic and not sectional issues dominated the second-party system; that many if not most people cared more about local politics than national politics; and that each party had strong incentives to suppress sectional measures. Exponents of the NPH are right to emphasize the incentives of parties to avoid purely sectional policies. As these historians point out, electoral pressures pushed parties away from divisive sectional stands, for these would alienate their supporters in the other section.

The models presented in this chapter show that parties alone could not suppress sectional measures. Sectional balance was also necessary. Paralleling the NPH argument about elections, my argument shows how the Southern veto in the Senate dramatically altered the incentives of Northerners who wished to pursue sectional issues. The incentives created by both sectional balance and elections kept sectional issues off the everyday agenda. As a consequence, the main issues under the second-party system remained economic.

Finally, the approach suggests how sectional balance, along with the Democrats' states' rights philosophy, helped maintain federalism. In the presence of a national government subject to strong limits on its powers, many if not most Americans had the luxury of ignoring national politics much of the time. But this type of federalism cannot be taken for granted. Rather it was in part the result of institutions designed for that purpose. The balance rule helped maintain limited national government and thus American federalism.

This perspective helps explain the periodic national crises. Although the crisis in the 1850s is central to the new political historians' approach, their explanation, suggesting that the crisis had its roots in the political reactions to immigration, does not extend to the previous two crises. My account suggests that all of the crises resulted from conflicts over how to extend balance beyond the limits of present agreements. The crisis over Missouri centered on whether the South would obtain an edge in national politics. The subsequent compromise not only balanced Missouri with Maine but also designated the remaining territory as free or slave. It also made the balance rule explicit, assuring that states would be brought in as pairs for the next thirty years. The crisis over the Mexican territory was also in large part about the potential for breaking the balance in favor of Southern dominance. Finally, the crisis initiated by the Kansas-Nebraska Act in 1854 involved in large part attempts to create new slave states.

During these crises, the limits on the national government were at risk. And, per the theory, nearly everyone in the nation turned their attention at these times to national politics. Between crises, as already noted, most people had the luxury (if they so chose) to focus on local politics while remaining ignorant of national politics. This behavior was not an abiding characteristic of antebellum America, but a product of institutions that protected people from a remote national government. Yet whenever these institutions began to break down, interest in national politics mushroomed.

Something further is missing from the NPH approach. Although the NPH provides important new insights about the breakdown of the second-party system—particularly regarding issues such as immigration and nativism—new political historians do not have a well-developed explanation of the breakdown of national politics in 1860.

My focus parallels that of traditional historians in an important respect: it places slavery and the territories at the center of the sectional conflict. Balance was a pervasive feature of the antebellum era. In addition to being the center of each national crisis during the antebellum years, it played a significant role in the Democrats' loss of their hegemonic electoral position in the 1850s. Historians in both camps have failed to understand that the major Democratic disasters— notably the Kansas-Nebraska Act, the subsequent "bleeding Kansas," and the 1858 attempt to admit Kansas as a slave state—all centered around the Democrats' attempts to restore sectional balance. This perspective helps explain why the Democrats pursued these policies, seemingly recklessly.

Arguing that slavery was at the center of the sectional conflict does not imply that my perspective embraces that of traditional historians. As the NPH observes, they have ignored a series of important local phenomena, including the importance of federalism in antebellum America. Furthermore, as the NPH observes (Silbey 1967; Swierenga 1975), some historians have tended to suggest an inexorableness to the sectional conflict, one of mounting tension from, say, 1846 to 1861. Nothing in my account suggests an inexorable rise in sectional tension.

This chapter provides a new explanation for the sectional crisis of the 1850s. My argument rests on an interpretation of antebellum American history involving the demand by most Americans for a national government strongly limited in scope. Beyond the Constitution, sectional balance proved a major element in making a credible commitment to limited national government. In particular, sectional balance reduced the incentives of many Northerners to attack slavery, thus providing incentives for cooperation between the sections. The sectional crisis of the 1850s was driven in large part by the Democrats' attempts to adapt the system of sectional balance to the new and unexpectedly different political circumstances of the 1850s.

References

Aldrich, John H. 1995. *Why Parties? The Origin and Transformation of Party Politics in America.* Chicago: University of Chicago Press.
Almond, Gabriel, and Sidney Verba. 1963. *The Civic Culture.* Boston: Little, Brown.

Austin, Erik W. 1986. *Political Facts of the United States Since 1789.* New York: Columbia University Press.

Brady, David W. 1988. *Critical Elections and Congressional Policy Making.* Stanford, Calif.: Stanford University Press.

Calomiris, Charles W., and Larry Schweikart. 1991. "The Panic of 1857: Origins, Transmission, and Containment." *Journal of Economic History* 51 (December): 807–34.

Carpenter, Jesse T. *The South as a Conscious Minority, 1789–1861* (1930; reprinted Columbia: University of South Carolina Press, 1990).

Cole, Donald P. 1984. *Martin Van Buren and the American Political System.* Princeton, N.J.: Princeton University Press.

Dahl, Robert. 1966. *Political Oppositions in Western Democracies.* New Haven, Conn.: Yale University Press.

Donald, David. 1961. "An Excess of Democracy." In his *Lincoln Reconsidered.* New York: Vintage.

Enelow, James, and Melvin Hinich. 1984. *The Spatial Theory of Voting: An Introduction.* New York: Cambridge University Press.

Fehrenbacher, Don E. 1980. *The South and the Three Sectional Crises.* Baton Rouge: Louisiana State University Press.

Finkelman, Paul. 1996. *Slavery and the Founders: Race and Liberty in the Age of Jefferson.* Armonk, N.Y.: M. E. Sharp.

Fogel, Robert W. 1989. *Without Consent of Contract: The Rise and Fall of American Slavery.* New York: Norton.

Foner, Eric. 1970. *Free Soil, Free Labor, Free Men: The Ideology of the Republican Party before the Civil War.* New York: Oxford University Press.

Haggard, Stephan, and Robert R. Kaufman. 1995. *The Political Economy of Democratic Transitions.* Princeton, N.J.: Princeton University Press.

Hartz, Louis. 1955. *The Liberal Tradition in America.* New York: Harcourt Brace Jovanovich.

Hinich, Melvin J., and Michael C. Munger. 1997. *Analytical Politics.* New York: Cambridge University Press.

Holt, Michael F. 1978. *The Political Crisis of the 1850s.* New York: Norton.

Hughes, Jonathan, and Louis Cain. 1998. *American Economic History,* 5th ed. Reading, Mass.: Addison-Wesley.

Kohlmeier, Albert Ludwig. 1938. *The Old Northwest as the Keystone of the Arch of the Federal Union.* Bloomington, Ind.: Principia Press.

Lindstrom, Diane. 1970. "Southern Dependence upon Interregional Grain Supplies." In *The Structure of the Cotton Economy of the Antebellum South,* edited by William Parker. Washington, D.C.: Agricultural History Society.

Lipset, Seymour Martin. *Political Man: The Social Bases of Politics* (1960; reprinted Garden City: Anchor Books, 1963).

———. 1963. *The First New Nation: The United States in Historical and Comparative Perspective.* New York: Basic Books.

McPherson, James M. 1988. *Battle Cry of Freedom: The Civil War Era.* New York: Oxford University Press.

Martis, Kenneth C. 1989. *The Historical Atlas of Political Parties in the United States Congress, 1789–1989.* New York: Macmillan.

May, Robert E. 1973. *The Southern Dream of a Caribbean Empire, 1854–1861.* Athens: University of Georgia Press.

Meinig, D. W. 1993. *The Shaping of America: A Geographic Perspective on 500 Years of History,* vol. 2: *Continental America, 1800–1867.* New Haven, Conn.: Yale University Press.

Moore, Barrington. 1966. *Social Origins of Dictatorship and Democracy.* City: Publisher.

Moore, Glover. 1953. *The Missouri Controversy: 1819–1821.* University of Kentucky Press.

Nevins, Allan. 1950. *The Emergence of Lincoln.* 2 vols. New York: Charles Scribner's Sons.

Nichols, Roy Franklin. 1948. *The Disruption of American Democracy.* New York: Collier.

———. 1963. *Blueprints for the Leviathan: American Style.* New York: Athenaeum.

North, Douglass C. 1961. *The Economic Growth of the United States: 1790–1860.* New York: Norton.

———. 1990. *Institutions, Institutional Change, and Economic Performance.* New York: Cambridge University Press.

North, Douglass C., and Andrew R. Rutten. 1987. "The Northwest Ordinance in Historical Perspective." In *Essays on the Old Northwest,* edited by David C. Klingaman and Richard V. Vedder. Athens: Ohio University Press.

Passell, Peter, and Maria Schmundt. 1971. "Pre–Civil War Land Policy and the Growth of Manufacturing." *Explorations in Economic History* 9 (Fall): 35–48.

Passell, Peter, and Gavin Wright. 1972. "The Effects of Pre–Civil War Territorial Expansion on the Price of Slaves." *Journal of Political Economy* 80 (November–December): 1188–1203.

Poole, Keith T., and Howard Rosenthal. 1990. Vote View computer software and data set. Pittsburgh: Carnegie-Mellon University.

———. 1997. *Congress: A Political-Economic History of Roll Call Voting.* New York: Oxford University Press.

Potter, David M. 1972. *The South and the Concurrent Majority.* Edited by Don E. Fehrenbacher and Carl N. Degler. Baton Rouge: Louisiana State University Press.

———. 1976. *The Impending Crisis: 1848–1861.* Edited and completed by Don E. Fehrenbacher. New York: Harper and Row.

Rakove, Jack. 1996. *Original Meanings: Politics and Ideas in the Making of the Constitution.* New York: Knopf.

Ransom, Roger L. 1989. *Conflict and Compromise: The Political Economy of Slavery, Emancipation and the American Civil War.* New York: Cambridge University Press.

Remini, Robert V. 1957. *Martin Van Buren and the Making of the Democratic Party.* New York: Columbia University Press.

———. 1972. *The Age of Jackson.* Columbia: University of South Carolina Press.

———. 1981. *Andrew Jackson and the Course of American Freedom, 1822–1832,* vol. 2. New York: Harper and Row.

Roback, Jennifer. 1991. *An Imaginary Negro in an Impossible Place: The Territories and Secession.* Princeton, N.J.: Princeton University Press.

Riker, William H. 1982. *Liberalism against Populism: A Confrontation between the Theory of Democracy and the Theory of Social Choice.* San Francisco: W. H. Freeman.

Rustow, Dankwart A. 1970. "Transitions to Democracy." *Comparative Politics* 2 (April): 337–63.

Shepsle, Kenneth A., and Mark S. Bonchek. 1997. *Analyzing Politics.* New York: Norton.

Silbey, Joel H. 1967. *Shrine of Party: Congressional Voting Behavior, 1841–52.* Pittsburgh: University of Pittsburgh Press.

———. 1985. *The Partisan Imperative: The Dynamics of American Politics before the Civil War.* New York: Oxford University Press.

Swierenga, Robert P. 1975. *Beyond the Civil War Synthesis.* Westport, Conn.: Greenwood Press.

Taylor, George Rogers. 1951. *The Transportation Revolution: 1815–1860.* New York: Holt, Rinehart, and Winston.

Tufte, Edward R. 1978. *Political Control over the Economy.* Princeton, N.J.: Princeton University Press.

U.S. Department of Commerce, Bureau of the Census. 1975. *Historical Statistics of the United States, Colonial Times to 1970.* 2 vols. Washington, D.C.: U.S. Government Printing Office.

Weingast, Barry R. 1995. "The Economic Role of Political Institutions: Market-Preserving Federalism and Economic Development." *Journal of Law, Economics, and Organization* 11 (April): 1–31.

———. 1996. "Institutions and Political Commitment: A New Political Economy of the American Civil War Era." Unpublished manuscript, Hoover Institution, Stanford University.

Wright, Gavin. 1978. *Political Economy of the Cotton South.* New York: Norton.

Five

The International Coffee Organization:
An International Institution

ROBERT H. BATES

CURRENTLY worth roughly $10 billion per year, coffee exports stand next to those of oil as the most valuable from the tropics. For many developing nations, coffee constitutes a major source of foreign exchange (see table 5.1).

From 1962 to 1989, the International Coffee Organization (ICO) regulated the world's exports of coffee. The organization was formed under the terms of the International Coffee Agreement, and its members accounted, on average, for 90 percent of the world's total consumption. The consuming nations that remained outside the ICO included the socialist countries of Asia, Eastern Europe, and the Soviet Union, which lacked the convertible currencies so desired by tropical exporters, and the Middle Eastern countries, which possessed such currencies but consumed little coffee (see table 5.2).

The ICO set target prices for coffee. In the later years of its existence, the target lay between $1.20 and $1.40 a pound. The agency then set quotas for coffee exports so as to force market prices into the target range. When its indicator of market prices rose above $1.40 a pound, quotas were relaxed; when it fell below $1.20 a pound, they were tightened. At times of extreme increases in prices, such as after major frosts in Brazil, quotas were abandoned altogether, until production returned to normal levels and trading resumed within the target range.

Quick calculations highlight the domestic significance of the ICO. Consider, for example, Uganda, one of the major suppliers of robusta coffee: for the coffee

The materials in this chapter are drawn from Bates (1997). The chapter was written while I was at the Center for Advanced Study in the Behavioral Sciences, Stanford, California. I acknowledge the support of Harvard and Stanford Universities as well as the National Science Foundation for its grants to the Center for Advanced Study in the Behavioral Sciences (SES-9022192) and to Robert H. Bates (SES-8821151). I am also grateful for the comments and criticisms received from Mihir Desai, Roberta Gatti, Avner Greif, Margaret Levi, Ronald Rogowski, Jean-Laurent Rosenthal, Fritz Scharpf, and Barry Weingast and the superb research assistance I have received on this project from Laura Alvarez, Rosalba Capote, Carlos Contreras, Amy Curry, Gina Dalma, Catherine Elkins, John Hall, Donald Da-Hsiang Lien, Brian Loynd, Andrew Mason, J. Muthengi Musunza, John Nye, Dixie Reeves, Daniel Restrepo, and Michael Thompson.

TABLE 5.1

Percent of Total Exports Composed of Coffee Exports in
Selected Countries

Year	Brazil	Colombia	El Salvador	Guatemala	Kenya	Côte d'Ivoire	Uganda
1950	63.7	77.8	88.9	66.9	17.4	50.0	28.8
1951	59.8	77.6	88.9	69.4	15.1	55.4	28.7
1952	73.8	80.3	87.9	75.6	24.1	62.6	25.8
1953	70.7	82.6	85.5	68.5	29.3	52.5	34.4
1954	60.7	83.7	87.6	70.8	25.2	64.9	32.9
1955	59.3	83.5	85.6	71.0	31.9	52.9	47.8
1956	69.5	76.9	77.5	75.3	41.5	63.7	37.9
1957	60.8	82.4	80.5	72.2	34.8	57.1	41.4
1958	55.3	84.9	72.5	72.6	31.3	59.6	39.6

Sources: International Monetary Fund (1980, 1990, 1992, 1993); Food and Agriculture Organization of the United Nations (1988–91).

year 1981/82, the ICO granted Uganda a quota of roughly 2.8 million bags (International Coffee Organization 1982:136, table VII-2).[1] Had members of the agency permitted Uganda a 5 percent higher quota, the country could have earned an additional $20 million per year in export markets.[2] Ten more bags of coffee, shipped out by a Ugandan peasant, would have generated an additional income of over $200,[3] an increase equivalent to the average annual per capita income in Uganda at that time.

This chapter presents a narrative of the birth, behavior, and collapse of the ICO. It then analyzes this narrative, employing a variety of analytic approaches. Of particular interest is that several of these approaches fail. Either they fail to fit important features of the empirical setting or, to succeed, they require conditions that are logically inconsistent with their premises. From observing the failure of various analytic approaches, however, we learn: we are driven to a new appreciation of the significance of features of the case materials and to revisions of our approach. The interplay between data and analysis (George 1979) promotes a refinement and deepening of our understanding of the political economy of the coffee market and of the origins and significance of its institutions.

[1]Throughout, I employ the standardized measure adopted by the ICO, according to which one bag contains 60 kilograms of green coffee.

[2]Based on an average price for robusta of $1.06 a pound. See the price data contained in Licht (1993:G.15).

[3]Even assuming that taxes, bribes, and transport consumed over 80 percent of the border price costs. A bag of coffee weighs 60 kilograms, or 132 pounds. With a price at the border of $1.00 per pound, ten bags would be worth about $1,320. The extent of government taxation is documented Sears et al. (1979).

TABLE 5.2
Exports and Imports (Millions of Bags) by Member and Nonmember Nations, 1972/73–1981/82

	1972/73	1973/74	1974/75	1975/76	1976/77	1977/78	1978/79	1979/80	1980/81	1981/82
World exports	61	58	57	57	53	55	64	61	59	64
Member exports (by origin)										
Brazil	18	15	15	13	15	9	13	14	16	17
Colombia	6	7	8	7	5	8	11	12	9	9
Other Americas	19	16	20	19	18	20	22	20	19	20
Robustas	16	18	15	18	14	14	16	15	15	17
Member exports (by destination)										
To members	54	51	50	50	48	46	57	54	52	52
To nonmembers	7	6	6	7	5	5	6	6	8	9
Exporting nonmembers	—	—	—	—	—	—	—	—	—	—
World gross imports	64	64	62	66	60	56	70	67	67	69
Members	57	57	55	59	53	49	63	60	59	61
USA	24	23	20	22	18	17	22	20	18	19
EEC	22	22	22	24	22	21	27	25	27	27
Other members	12	12	12	13	13	10	15	14	14	15
Member imports by origin	57	57	55	59	53	49	63	60	59	61
From exporting members	54	53	51	55	50	46	59	56	55	56
From importing members	3	3	3	3	3	3	4	4	4	4
From nonmembers	—	—	—	1	—	—	—	—	—	1
Importing nonmembers	6	7	7	7	7	6	7	7	7	8

Source: International Coffee Organization (1982:2, summary table).
Note: —, Less than 500,000 bags.

The Narrative: Part I

The origins of the ICO lie in the emergence of Brazil as a dominant producer and its subsequent efforts to influence prices in international markets. In the nineteenth century, Brazil became the primary producer of coffee. When leaf rust spread to the plantations of the Dutch East Indies, coffees from that region became scarce and their prices rose. As the supply of Brazilian coffees increased, their prices declined (Delfim Netto 1959:155). As the price differential between coffees from the two origins widened, consumers increasingly switched to Brazil's cheaper coffees. By the mid-1800s, 50 percent of the coffee purchased in world markets came from Brazil, a figure that rose to 70 percent by the early 1900s (figure 5.1). With the collapse of exports from the east, Brazil became a giant in the world coffee market. It became the dominant producer of the world's coffee (see Delfim Netto 1959; Holloway 1975; Bates 1997).

Brazil was quick to seize the opportunity offered by its market power. Led by political leaders from São Paulo, the largest of its coffee-producing states, Brazil in 1906 launched its famous valorization scheme, purchasing and stockpiling nearly eight million bags of coffee (Delfim Netto 1959; Holloway 1975). Brazil's efforts to "stabilize" the price of coffee soon attracted new entrants into the market, and Colombia soon became its major competitor. As shown in figure 5.2, Colombia increased its exports from fewer than three hundred thousand bags in the early 1890s to over three million bags in the early 1930s. In its efforts to exploit its power in the international coffee market, then, Brazil provoked entry.

In the mid-1920s, Brazil once again sought to determine the international price of coffee. Announcing a policy of "permanent defense," the government built warehouses, controlled the movement of coffee by rail and by sea, created a financial system to enable the purchase of the crop, and constructed a regulatory bureaucracy that superintended the stockpiling and movement of coffee, retiring it from the external market and thereby driving up its price in global markets. However, Brazil feared the entry of additional producers into the market. It therefore sponsored a series of international conferences at which it sought to secure agreements to limit the production of coffee for export. In these meetings, its diplomats repeatedly threatened economic sanctions should its rivals fail to restrict production and exports (Ramirez Ocampo and Perez Gomez 1986). When other nations failed to endorse a formal marketing agreement, Brazil acted on these threats: increasing monthly shipments by 50 percent, on November 8, 1937, Brazil dumped its stocks of coffee (Taunay 1943:60).

As a result of Brazil's actions and the loss of the European market in the late 1930s, Colombia and other Latin American producers joined with Brazil to limit exports and thereby stabilize the international price of coffee. The end of World War II led to a sharp upward shift in the demand for coffee. The resultant postwar rise in coffee prices was brought to a climax by the Brazilian frost of

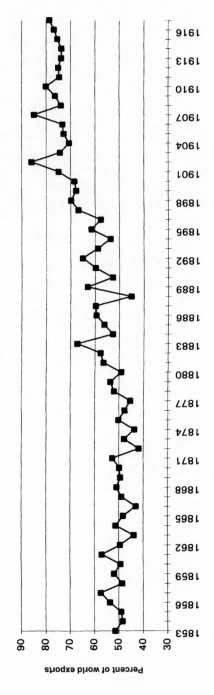

FIGURE 5.1. Brazil's share of world coffee exports by year, 1853–1917. *Source:* Beyer (1947, appendix, table V). Reproduced from Bates (1997).

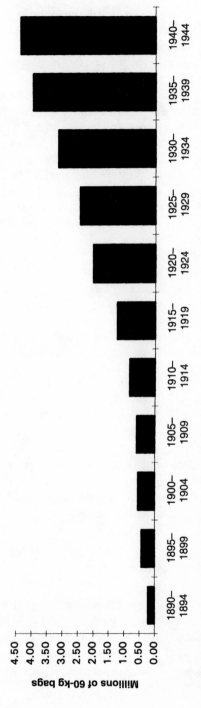

FIGURE 5.2. Colombia's entry into the world coffee market. *Source:* Bacha and Greenhill (1992, appendix, table 1.1). Reproduced from Bates (1997).

1953. Brazil once again sought to exploit the opportunity created by the shortage of coffee; by limiting shipments, it attempted to raise the price. In 1953 Brazil's minister of finance instituted a multiple exchange rate in which "coffee dollars" would be exchanged for cruzeiros at a rate far less favorable than that received by the importers or exporters of other commodities. Resources therefore shifted out of coffee production and the dollar price of coffee rose in world markets. The government also increased the price offered by its coffee agency from $0.56 to $0.90 a pound. As exporters could not earn profits selling coffee bought at this price, they abandoned the market to the government.

Just as Brazil's efforts as a price setter before the war had been threatened by entry, so too was its postwar intervention. In an effort to forestall a subsequent decline in coffee prices, the dominant producers, Brazil and Colombia, negotiated an international agreement, El Convenio de Mexico, that obligated coffee producers to withhold a percentage of their products from the international market. Under the terms of this agreement, the government of Brazil accumulated nearly twenty-five million bags of coffee—an amount equivalent to half of the world's total annual consumption—and the government of Colombia purchased over half a million bags per year and withheld them from the market.[4]

El Convenio de Mexico failed to raise the market price of coffee, however, for it failed to prevent entry. The data indicate that while Brazil and Colombia withheld a large fraction of their exportable production from world markets, small Central American nations—Costa Rica, El Salvador, and Guatemala—undercut the market (table 5.3). In addition, African producers remained outside the agreement and continued to expand their market share. During World War II, annual production in Africa had reached four million bags as Africa replaced Latin America in European markets; following the peak of the price rise in 1954, Africa's production more than doubled once again (figure 5.3). Although Brazil repeatedly threatened again to dump its coffee, it refrained from acting on its threat. With the failure of El Convenio de Mexico, the dominant producers sought a broader pact that would enable them to erect political barriers to coffee exports. The result was the creation of the ICO.

Analyzing the Narrative: Cut I

In order to understand better the circumstances that led to the creation of the ICO, we turn to game-theoretic models of imperfect competition and, in particular, to a canonical game: the so-called "chain store paradox" (Selten

---

[4]American Embassy, Bogotá, to Department of State, Dispatch 341, November 6, 1958, file 821.2333/11–658, United States Archives.

TABLE 5.3

Adherence to Quotas Under El Convenio de Mexico, 1958–61

	1958					1959					1960					1961				
	Exportable production (millions of bags)	Exports (millions of bags)	Addition to stocks (millions of bags)	Exports as percentage of exportable production	Percent of total exports	Exportable production (millions of bags)	Exports (millions of bags)	Addition to stocks (millions of bags)	Exports as percentage of exportable production	Percent of total exports	Exportable production (millions of bags)	Exports (millions of bags)	Addition to stocks (millions of bags)	Exports as percentage of exportable production	Percent of total exports	Exportable production (millions of bags)	Exports (millions of bags)	Addition to stocks (millions of bags)	Exports as percentage of exportable production	Percent of total exports
World total	46.20	36.50	9.70	79.00	100.00	52.00	42.60	9.40	81.92	100.00	66.40	42.50	23.90	64.01	100.00	52.40	43.70	8.70	83.40	100.00
Total Western Hemisphere	35.90	26.40	9.50	73.54	72.33	40.20	31.60	8.60	78.61	74.18	52.80	30.60	22.20	57.95	72.00	37.00	30.50	6.50	82.43	69.79
Brazil	20.80	12.90	7.90	62.02	35.54	26.00	17.70	8.30	68.08	41.55	37.00	16.80	20.20	45.41	39.53	22.00	17.00	5.00	77.27	38.90
Colombia	7.00	5.40	1.60	77.14	14.79	6.90	6.40	0.50	92.75	15.02	7.00	5.90	1.10	84.29	13.88	6.70	5.60	1.10	83.58	12.81
Mexico	1.50	1.30	0.20	86.67	3.56	1.20	1.20	0.00	100.00	2.82	1.50	1.40	0.10	93.33	3.29	1.40	1.50	-0.10	107.14	3.43
El Salvador	1.30	1.40	-0.10	107.69	3.84	1.40	1.30	0.10	92.86	3.05	1.50	1.20	0.30	80.00	2.82	1.30	1.40	-0.10	107.69	3.20
Guatemala	1.20	1.20	0.00	100.00	3.29	1.20	1.40	-0.20	116.67	3.29	1.40	1.30	0.10	92.86	3.06	1.30	1.30	0.00	100.00	2.97
Costa Rica	0.70	0.80	-0.10	114.29	2.19	0.80	0.70	0.10	87.50	1.64	0.80	0.80	0.00	100.00	1.88	1.00	0.80	0.20	80.00	1.83
Other	3.40	3.40	0.00	100.00	9.32	2.70	2.90	-0.20	107.41	6.81	3.60	3.20	0.40	88.89	7.53	3.30	2.90	0.40	87.88	6.64
Total Africa	8.90	8.80	0.10	98.88	24.11	10.40	9.70	0.70	93.27	22.77	11.90	10.70	1.20	89.92	25.18	13.30	11.30	2.00	84.96	25.86
Ivory Coast	1.80	1.20	0.60	66.67	3.29	2.40	2.00	0.40	83.33	4.69	2.50	2.40	0.10	96.00	5.65	3.20	2.60	0.60	81.25	5.95
Angola	1.30	1.30	0.00	100.00	3.56	1.40	1.50	-0.10	107.14	3.52	1.80	1.40	0.40	77.78	3.29	2.70	2.00	0.70	74.07	4.58
Uganda	1.40	1.30	0.10	92.86	3.56	1.50	1.50	0.00	100.00	3.52	1.90	1.90	0.00	100.00	4.47	1.90	1.80	0.10	94.74	4.12
Kenya	0.40	0.40	0.00	100.00	1.10	0.40	0.40	0.00	100.00	0.94	0.40	0.40	0.00	100.00	0.94	0.50	0.50	0.00	100.00	1.14
Tanganyika	0.40	0.40	0.00	100.00	1.10	0.40	0.30	0.10	75.00	0.70	0.40	0.40	0.00	100.00	0.94	0.50	0.40	0.10	80.00	0.92
Others	3.60	3.40	0.20	94.44	9.32	4.30	4.00	0.30	93.02	9.39	4.90	4.20	0.70	85.71	9.88	4.50	4.00	0.50	88.89	9.15
Total Asia and Oceania	1.40	1.40	0.00	100.00	3.84	1.30	1.30	0.00	100.00	3.05	1.70	1.40	0.30	82.35	3.29	2.10	1.70	0.40	80.95	3.89

Source: Rowe (1963:21).

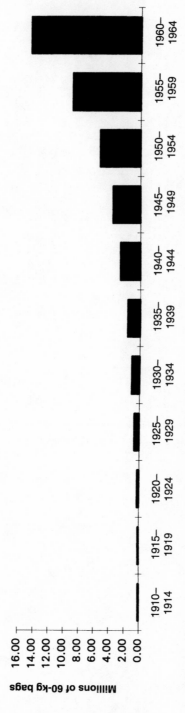

FIGURE 5.3. Africa's entry into the world coffee market. *Source:* Bacha and Greenhill (1992, appendix, table 1.8). Reproduced from Bates (1997).

1978; Kreps and Wilson 1982). Analysis of this game provides insight into the difficulties faced by the dominant producers in preventing entry.

The chain store paradox refers to competition between an established firm, a chain store, and a potential entrant. In order to retain its monopolistic status, the chain store seeks to deter entry; it therefore threatens to fight any firm seeking to enter the market. Fighting is costly. The new arrival, or entrant, can choose whether to enter the market or stay out. The incumbent firm can choose whether to incur the costs of fighting the new entrant, thereby retaining its monopolistic status, or let it enter and then share the market. The new firm moves first.

In figure 5.4, the new entrant is designated NE and the monopolist I (for incumbent). The new firm can enter (E) or refrain from doing so ($\sim$E, where $\sim$ signifies negation); the incumbent can then choose to retaliate (R) or not ($\sim$R). The payoffs to the entrant are listed first and those to the incumbent second. Should the incumbent deter entry, it then reaps monopoly profits (x). Should it fail to do so, the entering firm receives positive profits ($1 > y > 0$). Fighting inflicts costs of 1 on both firms.

The lessons of the chain store paradox come in two stages: those generated by the game when it is played a finite number of times and those generated when it is played an infinite number of times (or when it is terminated probabilistically).

Played once, the game yields a clear outcome: despite the incumbent's threats to retaliate, it will fail to deter entry. The monopolist will gain, should the new firm refrain from entry; but once the new firm has chosen to enter, the monopolist does better by acquiescing, for fighting is costly. The monopolist's threats are therefore not credible.

This result lays the foundation for the paradox. Intuitively, when the game is repeated, it would seem plausible that the incumbent would fight. A chain store, for example, might be expected to pay the costs of punishment in one market so that it could render its threats credible in others. But analysis of the game shows that such intuition is violated. In the last market, knowing that the incumbent cannot profit from fighting, the new firm enters. So too in the penultimate market. Through backward induction, the process then unravels, such that in the first market the chain store chooses to share the market rather

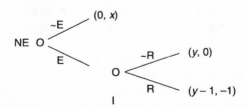

FIGURE 5.4. A stage in the chain store game. *Abbreviations:* NE, new entrant; I, incumbent; E, enter; $\sim$E, not enter; R, retaliate; $\sim$R, not retaliate.

than to contest entry. Knowing that no future periods of monopoly profits await it in other markets, the incumbent will not incur the costs of fighting in the first. The dominant firm—the chain store—is therefore, paradoxically, powerless. Even in repeated play, its threats are not credible.

When the game is infinitely repeated (or randomly terminated), however, then the analysis suggests that for a sufficiently high discount factor, the dominant producers will fight to deter entry. The costs of fighting will yield a stream of benefits over a sufficiently long period that, if not heavily discounted, will more than compensate for the short-term losses. In the face of an infinite (or uncertain) time horizon, the monopolist might therefore be willing to pay the cost of fighting (Fudenberg and Maskin 1986). The dominant producer will treat the costs as an investment in creating a valuable reputation. Knowing that it will fight, potential competitors refrain from entry; they are deterred from competing in the market.

In applying this analysis to the coffee market, we can note that Brazil, Colombia, and other producers were locked in an infinitely lived game, or one that would be terminated only through a random act of fortune—such as by the diseases that had earlier befallen the East Indies. And yet, although the incumbent, Brazil, sought to deter entry in the 1930s, it refrained from doing so in the 1950s. The logic of the model thus fails to find confirmation in the data. However, its failure proves fruitful; it motivates us to return once again to the narrative and to a reappraisal of the case materials.

One possible lesson is that governments possess interests that differ from those of nations. The producing countries may be infinitely lived, but their governments are not. Governments may therefore not be willing to incur short-term costs to achieve gains that will accrue over time. The more politically insecure the government, the more heavily it will discount the future. Such reasoning highlights the significance of domestic politics to the international behavior of nations. It highlights in particular the importance of the political insecurity of the government of Brazil and especially of its pressing need for foreign exchange (Bates 1997). But this attempt to render the analytics consistent with the narrative runs afoul of an obvious difficulty: the fact that the Brazilian governments of the 1930s were surely as insecure as those of the 1950s, but nonetheless contested entry.

We are thus driven to take yet another look at the data. In both the 1930s and the 1950s, Brazil constituted the dominant producer in the international coffee market. In the 1930s, when Brazil faced competition from Colombia, it faced prospective, but not present, threats from Africa as well. After World War II, however, Brazil actually faced competition from that quarter: during the war, African producers had expanded their plantations and captured a large portion of the European market. They had already entered the coffee market.

Returning to the logic of the model, we rapidly gain an appreciation of the political significance of these economic facts. Coffee production involves high fixed costs. Prior to the late 1960s, coffee trees required five to seven years to reach full production, and variable inputs, such as pesticides and labor, constituted less than 30 percent of the total costs of production. After producers incurred such high fixed costs, they would naturally be reluctant to close down production in response to a fall in price; in this case, they would be reluctant to uproot their plantations, and instead would simply reduce their inputs of labor. The implication for the model is that when a region enters production, the game becomes a one-period game; for any reasonable rate of discount, the new player must be viewed as infinitely lived. The chain store model demonstrates that with finite repetition (such as one period of play), entry cannot be deterred by costly threats; in such settings, threats lack credibility. Changes that took place during the 1940s thus rendered the market of the 1950s the equivalent of a single-shot game.

In studying the origins of the ICO, we have taken recourse to one theory of imperfect competition: a theory of entry deterrence. From it, we have gained a deeper appreciation of the political significance of the economics of the coffee industry and, in particular, of the way in which the technology of production influenced the strategic behavior of the producing nations. We have also gained insight into why dominant producers failed in their attempts to cartelize the market and why they therefore sought an alternative way of restricting market competition—one based not on entry deterrence, but rather on third-party enforcement.

Return to the Narrative

When Brazil and Colombia realized that they were unable to prevent free riding on the part of small producers, they turned to the dominant consumer, the United States, to police the agreement by imposing restrictions on coffee imports. In so doing, they were aware that economic arguments would not work. The United States was a consumer, not a producer, of coffee. Brazil and Colombia therefore based their appeal for U.S. cooperation on the threat of communism.

In January 1959, Castro entered Havana; by the middle of 1960, he had made clear his opposition to the United States and his commitment to a Marxist-Leninist philosophy. In the presidential elections of 1960, John Kennedy and Richard Nixon competed to see who could pose as the greater crusader against communism and, in particular, "Castroism," its local variant. The governments of Brazil and Colombia were able to link the defense of coffee prices to the defense of hemispheric security. Indeed the United States' statement of support for the coffee agreement was incorporated into the proclamation of the Alliance for Progress, the Kennedy Administration's principal response to the communist threat in Latin America.[5]

---

[5]The best treatments of these events are contained in Fisher (1972). See also Wagner (1970) and Levinson and Onis (1970).

For the United States to become a member of the ICO, the executive branch's support for an international coffee agreement was a necessary, but not a sufficient, condition, however. Membership required passage of a treaty, and thus action by the Senate. It also required the passage of enabling legislation by the House of Representatives, empowering U.S. customs authorities to monitor and police shipments by private firms (figure 5.5). Although the executive branch and the Senate may have been willing to trade off economic costs for political gains, the House was much less willing to do so. Indeed, because of its concerns with inflation and the growth of government regulation of private markets, the House first delayed and then defeated the legislation necessary for U.S. participation in the ICO. Only with the convening of a new Congress did it pass the legislation, after having delayed U.S. entry into the ICO for over two years. Even then, repeated assurances from major corporations that the regulation of the market would not harm their interests were necessary before the House would act.

The Department of State sought to regulate international trade in coffee so as to raise its price and thereby inject much-needed foreign exchange into the economies of Latin America. However, it lacked the expertise about commercial practices that would enable it to regulate trade effectively, and so it turned to the large coffee-roasting firms for information. These firms—General Foods, Procter and Gamble, and others—purchase "green" coffee from the coffee-producing nations, which they then roast, grind, and sell at retail in consumer markets. The executive branch also needed to secure the support of Congress, and the firms' cooperation proved critical for this purpose as well.

U.S. participation thus rested upon a domestic political coalition that included the executive branch—the White House and the Department of State—and Congress. The large firms played a major role in constructing that coalition. The consensus of all who have researched the history of the ICO is that, had the firms opposed the agreement in their testimony before Congress, the treaty would not have passed and the ICO would never have been created (Krasner 1971, 1973a,b; Bruchey 1987).

Analyzing the Narrative: Cut II

The Chicago School

Having employed one model—the chain store model of entry deterrence—to examine the origins of the ICO, we now turn to another: the model of third-party enforcement offered by the so-called "Chicago school" of regulation (Stigler 1971; Peltzman 1976). This approach stresses that cartels are inherently unstable; producers face grave difficulties in restricting entry and in restraining competition. In response, the argument holds, producers shift their efforts

	Executive branch	Congress
Necessary condition	+	0
Sufficient condition	+	+

FIGURE 5.5. Necessary and sufficient conditions for passage of executive policy in the United States. *Symbols:* +, supports; 0, does not object.

from the marketplace to the political arena. By marshaling public-interest arguments—such as the need to enhance quality or to protect public health—private firms secure government regulation of an industry. By thus bending the regulatory process to their own ends, they employ public power to secure private objectives: the cartelization of the market and the redistribution of income from consumers to themselves.

The Realist School

The argument of the Chicago school seeks to provide a neoclassical model of cartel formation. But when applied to the case materials, the argument confronts a major anomaly: the United States is a consumer, not a producer, of coffee.[6] Being neoclassical, the model requires rationality in individual choice. A major reason for applying models to narratives is to secure logically consistent explanations for events or outcomes. The United States' expenditure of costly effort to establish an agreement that raised prices to consumers violates the premises of the model.

As was the case in our discussion of the chain store paradox, this failure of analysis is nonetheless informative: it casts light upon important properties of the data. In this instance, the failure highlights the significance of the communist threat to U.S. security. Just as the public's concern with air safety today enables producers to secure the regulation of competition among airlines, so, by analogy, the United States' concern with the communist threat enabled the producers of coffee to secure the regulation of competition in the coffee market. Adding "political preferences" to the United States' objective function thus restores logical consistency; it highlights political benefits that compensate for the economic costs resulting from the formation of the cartel. The neoclassical model thus joins the set of explanations offered by the "realist" school of international relations, which treats states as rational actors and argues that large states, or so-called hegemons, willingly bear the private costs of providing the infrastructure that provides collective goods (e.g., Kindleberger 1973; Waltz 1979).

---

[6]With the exception of the relatively small amount of coffee production in Hawaii.

The facts of the narrative again intrude, however, and mark as premature such efforts at closure. The explanation is saved by noting the magnitude and intensity of threats to security. But the narrative discloses that even at the height of the cold war—even when the introduction of Soviet missiles into Cuba underscored the fragility of U.S. security and the dangers of communism— the Congress of the United States delayed and defeated the administration's efforts to implement the ICO. There is thus an awkward lack of fit. Given the supposed magnitude of the stimulus, the response was uncertain and long delayed; a major reason for the delay was that multiple domestic actors were responsible for foreign policy. Our attempt to preserve the neoclassical vision of policymaking by identifying political benefits thus fails to fit the data.

Turning to Domestic Politics

The performance of the Chicago model of cartels thus inspires us to search for a more decentralized model of politics. We shift from a unitary actor to a perspective based on collective choice. Phrased another way, we shift from a focus on international relations between presumably unitary states to a focus on the domestic politics of international policymaking.

The United States' entry into the ICO required subscribing to the terms of a treaty between states. Enabling legislation was required to implement the treaty, and participation in the ICO therefore required the concurrence of both houses of Congress. To model the behavior of the United States, we can adopt a spatial framework: one that adheres to the premise of rationality in choice but that analyzes how collective policy emerges from the strategic interplay among decentralized interests.

Spatial models are neoclassical; they locate the preferences of actors as points in a policy space, which represent ideal or bliss points, i.e., points of maximum utility. Policy outcomes can also be represented as points in that space, and their distance from an ideal point can be interpreted as a measure of utility losses, the extent of the loss being proportional to the distance. As security could be purchased by paying higher coffee prices, the policy space can be cast in one dimension: a greater interest in security implies a greater willingness to pay for coffee imports.

In figure 5.6, I construct a spatial portrait of the interactions among the executive branch (E), the Senate (S), and the House of Representatives (H). The status quo (SQ) denotes the level of security generated by prevailing policies. International security constitutes the underlying dimension; more specifically, the dimension depicts the willingness to commit resources to counter the threat posed by communism. Panel A represents the distribution of preferences in the early 1950s. The location of the ideal points of the House, Senate, and executive branch suggests a low concern with security, the executive branch being the most concerned. The point labeled "ICO" signifies the level of resources that would be channeled into the fight against communism by entering into the ICO. Panel A suggests that the executive branch would be most inclined to join the ICO. Its ideal point lies midway between the status quo and the ICO policy outcome. The ideal points of the House and Senate, however, lie closer to the status quo than to the ICO, suggesting that, given their low assessment of the significance of the communist threat, they would not be willing to shift to the new policy.[7]

Panel B suggests the change brought on by the rise of Castro. The executive branch now shifts to supporting the ICO, as does the Senate. Some members of the House likewise reappraise the significance of the communist threat; some remain unwilling to ask American consumers to finance the war against communism by paying higher consumer prices. But the median of the House does shift to the right; its preferences track those of the large roasters, who have now come out in favor of the international agreement. As the two houses of Congress as well as the executive branch now prefer the outcome under the ICO to that under the status quo—i.e., as their ideal points lie closer to the point marked ICO than to the point marked SQ—the necessary conditions for the adoption of the policy now prevail and the collective choice now shifts in favor of the agreement.

In seeking an explanation for the formation of the ICO, we have thus moved from the study of entry deterrence (or its failure) to the study of cartel behavior. Although it provided a useful starting point, the Chicago model of regulation encountered a major anomaly, one that challenged its neoclassical foundations. To fit the narrative, while also preserving logical consistency, we recast the model,

---

[7]It is important to justify the specification of preferences. One way is by appealing to case materials. As described by Krasner (1971), Bruchey (1987), and Bates (1997), the passage of the ICO was managed in the Senate by the Foreign Affairs Committee, whose members were deeply concerned with international relations. Prior to addressing the question of the ICO, the committee had investigated and reported upon the origins of political instability in Brazil, and in doing so it had emphasized the destabilizing impact of low commodity prices and shortages of foreign exchange. In the House of Representatives, the Ways and Means Committee introduced the legislation. Little concerned with foreign affairs, the committee focused instead on domestic taxation.

Another way of justifying preferences is by appealing to reason. A senator is elected for a six-year term, a congressman for two. One-third of the Senate is up for election every two years, but all members of the House stand for reelection on that schedule. Economic shocks are therefore more likely to have an impact upon the elections of a majority of the members of the House than upon those of a majority of the members of the Senate. The House is thus more likely to pay attention to economic issues. Moreover, it is easier to launch a presidential campaign from the Senate than from the House. Motivated by ambition, senators might be more willing than members of the House to endorse costly programs that yield enhanced national security. It is notable, in that regard, that several of the senators on the Foreign Affairs Committee at the time of its endorsement of the ICO—for example Senators James W. Fulbright and Hubert H. Humphrey—were maneuvering for places on the national ticket of the Democratic Party.

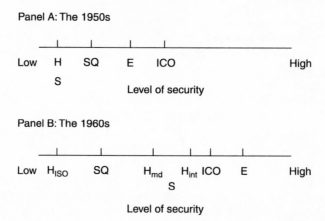

FIGURE 5.6. A spatial analysis of U.S. domestic politics. *Abbreviations:* E, executive branch; H, House; H_{int}, House internationalists; H_{iso}, House isolationists; H_{md}, House median; ICO, policy outcome under ICO; S, Senate; SQ, policy outcome under the status quo.

rendering it a variant of "realism." But this effort also foundered on anomalies in the data, forcing us to move from a form of international relations theory to a decentralized neoclassical model—one that focused on domestic politics.

In the domestic political game, it was the roasters that helped to put in place the conditions necessary for U.S. support for the ICO. They brought the House of Representatives into the coalition between Congress and the executive branch. To explore the role of these large firms, we turn once again to case materials.

Return to the Narrative

The largest players in the industry, General Foods and Procter and Gamble, are well-managed, dynamic, and expansionary firms that have access to large amounts of capital (see, for example, Harvard Business School 1987). The rivalry between them is intense. Competition takes the form of the introduction of new forms of coffee: soluble in the 1950s, freeze-dried in the 1960s, and decaffeinated in the 1970s, for example. It also takes the form of introducing new brands, such as Taster's Choice, Brim, International Coffees, High Point, and Mellow Point. In addition the firms compete in penetrating regional markets. Historically, General Foods' Maxwell House has tended to dominate markets in the East, Procter and Gamble's Folgers, markets in the West. However, when Folgers invested heavily in advertising and promotional campaigns to capture selected markets east of the Mississippi, General Foods retaliated, cutting its prices and concentrating its advertising in the "home base" from which Folgers had launched its expansion (Harvard Business School 1987; Hilke and Nelson 1989).

Though intense, this rivalry between the firms is not competitive, in the strict meaning of the term. At the time that the United States sought to enter the ICO, the top four firms accounted for roughly 60 percent of the domestic sales of coffee (table 5.4).

In their study of the U.S. coffee industry, Gallop and Roberts (1979) grouped the over 160 coffee roasting firms by size, assigning one large firm (General Foods, one must presume) to a category of its own, the five next largest firms to a second group, and the remaining 150 or so, each with less than 1 percent of the market, to a third. They then calculated the reaction functions of firms in each category. The small firms, they found, behaved as if taking into account the behavior of larger firms, and the leading firms chose levels of production as if anticipating the behavior of firms in every size class. This behavior, they concluded, was consistent with "dominant firm leadership" (p. 326) in a market characterized by imperfect competition.

Being locked in strategic interrelationships with other roasters, the large firms thus possess incentives not only to compete but also to cooperate. In the marketplace, cooperation can take the form of refraining from entering into a particular market or from cutting prices in an effort to increase market share. In the political realm, it can take the form of providing public goods, as by seeking to influence public polices toward the industry.

When the executive branch turned to the coffee industry, it approached the National Coffee Association (NCA), an organization that represented the interests of importers, roasters, and distributors of coffee. As control over the making of policy toward international commodities moved from the Treasury Department, with its commitment to free trade, to the Department of State, with its preoccupation with national security, the NCA organized a Foreign

TABLE 5.4
Characteristics of Six Leading Coffee Roasting Firms

	Market share (percent)			
Firm	1955	1961	1968	1970
General Foods	21	34	36	28
Proctor and Gamble	9	12	15	3–15
Standard Brands	6	6	5	< 10
Hills Brothers	8	6	9	> 90
Nestlé	4	3	4	20–30
A&P	NA	NA	7	< 10
Total	48	61	69	—

Source: Krasner (1973b:503).
Notes: NA, not available. All totals exclude A&P.

TABLE 5.5
Members of the Foreign Affairs Committee of the National Coffee Association,
1960–63

Year	Six largest roasters	Six largest green coffee firms	Small firms
1960	3	0	3
1961	3	0	4
1962	3	1	3
1963	4	1	1

Source: Krasner (1971:255).

Affairs Committee to monitor and advise the government as it prepared to intervene in coffee markets. The committee intensified the association's efforts to educate the bureaucracy about the economic and commercial realities of these markets. It communicated by letter,[8] by dispatching delegations to the Department of State,[9] and by hosting Department of State representatives at business conferences.[10] At the department's invitation, the Foreign Affairs Committee of the NCA participated in the Coffee Study Group, a committee organized by the Department of State to develop the regulations that constituted the framework for the International Coffee Agreement.[11] As shown in table 5.5, the large roasting firms held half or more of the positions on the Foreign Affairs Committee.

The industry was active not only in the United States but also in Latin America. Even a casual reading of the commercial press and the minutes of organizations within the Latin American coffee industry yields an appreciation of the prominence of its executives. The arrival in a producing country of, say, George Robbins, head of the coffee division of General Foods, amounted to a state visit, with formal receptions, ceremonial dinners, and extensive coverage by the national press on the political, economic, and society pages. And Robbins did visit, regularly touring the great coffee centers: Rio, Santos, São Paulo, Manizales, and Bogotá.[12]

One of the most significant of his visits took place in Bogotá in July 1963. The treaty had been ratified by the U.S. Senate in December 1962. General

[8] See, for example, the correspondence between Edward Aborn, president of the NCA, and the secretary of state, contained in file 821.2333/1–1653, United States Archives.

[9] See the discussions in Fisher (1972) and Bruchey (1987:103ff).

[10] The NCA holds an annual conference in Boca Raton, Florida, to which it invites government officials from the United States and abroad.

[11] Information on the organization of the Coffee Study Group is contained in file 398.2333/2–1955, United States Archives.

[12] So constant was the presence of Robbins that I failed to record each notice of his arrival. For a Brazilian example, see the coverage given his 1948 visit in *Revista do Comércio de Café de Rio de Janeiro,* February and March 1948. For examples from Colombia, see Actas No. 38 and 42–44, October 30–December 18, 1952, in Comité Nacional (1952). See as well records of the visit of his successor, Paul Keating, to Manizales in Federación Nacional de Cafeteros (1980).

Foods had participated in the trade advisory committee that had helped to draft the accord in Washington and in the delegation that helped to negotiate its ratification by member nations. Its executives also served on the delegation representing the United States at meetings of the ICO. In the meetings in Bogotá in July 1963, Robbins, formerly a member of the U.S. delegation, entered into direct commercial negotiations with the managing director of Colombia's coffee agency. And the executive committee of that agency convened a series of secret sessions to discuss his proposal.[13]

In the early 1960s, General Foods was purchasing 1,800,000 bags of Colombian coffee annually, or nearly one-quarter of Colombia's total production and nearly two-thirds of its exports to the United States. It now offered to increase its annual purchases by 500,000 bags, with a commitment to continue at this increased level for three years. In exchange, General Foods wanted a reduction of $0.02 a pound in the price charged for the additional bags purchased, over and above its usual discount of 10 percent. It also offered to launch a new brand of coffee, to be called Yuban, that would feature "pure Colombian" coffee.

The leaders of Colombia's coffee industry treated General Foods' offer with great caution. They had long sought to build consumer loyalty to Colombian coffee in the United States and had even paid a leading advertising firm to promote it; General Foods' offer to feature a "pure Colombian" label would, they felt, inspire emulation by other roasters, and so give a boost to their marketing campaign. However, they also saw disadvantages to the proposal. One was the danger of becoming even more dependent on General Foods; another was the risk of being seen by other producers as cutting the price of coffee, just as an accord to stabilize prices was being put in place. In the end, the executive committee decided to go ahead with the deal. They did so, I believe, in order to strengthen, not weaken, the international agreement.

Shortly after the initiation of postwar efforts to build an accord, the dominant producers had signed bulk contracts with the large coffee roasting firms. Colombia appears to have signed its first such contract with General Foods in 1959; Brazil followed suit in May 1960.[14] The evidence suggests that similar contracts were signed with other major roasters: Nestlé, Rotfus, and Procter and Gamble. The contracts committed the roasters to the purchase of fixed amounts of coffee per quarter—450,000 bags, in the case of General Foods in the early 1960s—in exchange for discounts on the price of coffee. Under the terms of each contract, the discount was applied to the costs of future purchases. Because the discount was not paid immediately, but rather rebated in subsequent periods, the market for coffee was transformed from a spot market. Under the terms of the bulk contracts, the producers and roasters entered into long-term relationships.

---

[13]This account is drawn from Federación Nacional de Cafeteros, Comité Nacional (1963).

[14]Acta No. 4 de la sesión del día 28 de enero de 1960 and Acta No. 18 de la sesión del día 12 de mayo de 1965 in Comité Nacional (1960, 1965).

Of course, financial costs and benefits constitute a significant component of the exchange between the dominant producers and the large roasting firms. The $0.02 per pound price reduction in the purchase of Colombian coffee enabled General Foods to pay nearly $2 million less for its 1,500,000 bags of coffee and Colombia to generate a 17 percent increase in its sales in the North American market. But Colombia got even more out of the bargain. As part of its relationship with General Foods, it also secured political services.

General Foods and the other large roasters were not merely purchasers and processors of coffee. They were also lobbyists and members of national delegations. They provided the executive branch with the information necessary to maintain and to regulate the coffee trade and testified before Congress on behalf of U.S. intervention. From Colombia's point of view, the discount in the price of coffee to General Foods bought compensating advantages: the help of a large roaster in securing the United States' enforcement of the International Coffee Agreement, thereby checking opportunistic behavior by the competitive fringe—and raising the average price of coffee.

In turn General Foods and the other large roasters who had signed bulk contracts received major economic advantages. The large roasters operated in the national market. Taking into account their costs for advertising, distribution, and promotion, the purchase of raw materials constituted a comparatively small portion of their expenses. However, for the small, regional roasters with whom they competed—Chock Full O'Nuts in Baltimore and Atlanta or Breakfast Cheer in Pittsburgh—the price of raw materials constituted a relatively larger percentage of total costs (Hilke and Nelson 1989; Sutton 1991). By structuring the regulation of the market so as to increase the price of raw materials, and by securing rebates from the dominant producers of those raw materials, the larger roasters were able to increase the costs of raw materials to their competitors, thereby achieving a cost advantage.[15]

Analyzing the Narrative: Cut III

In describing the behavior of the major coffee firms, this narrative has portrayed behavior analyzed by Oliver Williamson and others: a form of market rivalry in which one firm seeks to maximize its profits by raising the costs incurred by its rivals.[16] Within the United States, the large roasters backed the cause of the agreement. Insofar as the U.S. government enforced it, it raised the costs of raw materials to all coffee firms; however, insofar as the large roasters received discounts from the producers, the increase in costs affected only their competitors. They thus secured a cost advantage.

---

[15]The situation most clearly resembles the Penington case (Williamson 1968). The impact of the industrywide shift in the costs of production on competitors in the industry is magnified in this instance by the rebates (Salop and Scheffman 1983).

[16]See Williamson (1968) and Salop and Scheffman (1983).

A major question then arises: why would such an agreement be stable? As suggested in the logic highlighted by the entry-deterrence game, the answer must lie in the credibility of the threats that support it. This reasoning focuses attention on the relationship between those who demanded the agreement (the large coffee producers) and those who organized its supply (the coffee roasting firms). Examining the outcome of their behavior in a collusive equilibrium, we find that when a large roaster, like General Foods, helped the U.S. government to police illicit shipments of coffee from the competitive fringe—say, Central America—it drove up the price of those coffees. The differential between the price of Colombian and other coffees then declined. Given the differentials in quality between Colombian and other mild coffees, buyers switched to Colombian coffee. As more buyers turned to Colombian coffee, Colombia's dependence on any one given buyer of its coffee declined. The strategies pursued by the parties in the collusive equilibrium thereby lowered the costs to producers of implementing threats to the roasting firms. The reduced costs to Colombia of canceling its contract with any given firm rendered Colombia's threats—but this time, against firms—more credible. The collusive agreement could therefore become self-enforcing.

In an interview (October 27, 1982) with the head of the coffee division of Procter and Gamble, the second largest roaster of coffee in the United States, I gained insight into the extent and nature of the fears that deterred movement away from the collusive equilibrium. Procter and Gamble cultivates a reputation for a strong commitment to "all-American" values: patriotism, capitalism, and competitive markets. Yet when I questioned the head of its coffee division about the agreement he indicated that "the free market would be O.K." "We may in fact testify in Congress against [the agreement]," he added. "How about Brazilian reprisals?" I asked. "Would they be likely to punish you by canceling your contracts?" There was a long pause before the executive replied, "Don't even breathe that possibility to anyone else. I will have to explain to our Chief Executive that the Brazilians may force us on board. I would be less than honest if I didn't say this to him. The Brazilians price coffee so attractively to us—we go with that contract and buy big and use it. We buy all we can get. But then they can put the screws on us."

The chief executive officer of Procter and Gamble preached the virtues of the free market; the head of its coffee division had to deal with the realities of the coffee market. I take the latter's comments as confirmation of his beliefs as to what would happen were his company to stray from the path of collusion and violate the terms of its relationship with the organizers of the accord.

In seeking an analytic framework for the narrative offered by the ICO, I have reached for models of imperfect competition. Most fail, but each does so in an interesting and informative manner. As with the chain store paradox and the Chicago model of regulation, their failures highlight important features of the data—features whose significance has thus far been insufficiently appreciated. Their failures also inspire important reformulations of the models, either to improve their goodness of fit or to restore consistency in their logic. Economic models of collusion become models of political economy, or, as with the realist school, models of international relations give way to models of domestic politics.

In the end, we arrive at a complex vision, albeit still one of a cartel. Formally the ICO constituted an agreement among sovereign states. In reality it was a political and economic alliance engineered at the subnational level. The ICO represented a coalition among bureaucrats, politicians, and firms that used the power of states to restructure markets. The result was enhanced political security for public officials and the enhanced profitability of firms, which secured wealth in return for political service.

The ICO as an Institution

Thus far we have explored the creation and maintenance of the ICO.[17] We now turn to its behavior.

Effectiveness

It is difficult to measure directly the impact of the ICO. Being unable to generate reliable estimates of the impact of the ICO, I have therefore settled for a less direct assessment of its impact. For the ICO to work, it needed to fulfill two necessary conditions: it had to restrict arbitrage between the member and nonmember markets and competition among the producers of coffee. The evidence suggests that it succeeded at both.

RESTRICTING ARBITRAGE

Figure 5.7 presents evidence concerning the effectiveness of the ICO. The horizontal axis displays years, including the dates during which quotas were in effect: August 1965 to October 1972 and October 1980 to August 1985. The vertical axis records the ratio between coffee prices in the markets of member

---

[17]The operations of the ICO create three measurement problems. The imposition of quotas limits supplies when prices are declining, thus censoring the data and biasing estimates of the determinants of market prices; market forces determine prices when they lie above the target range and quantity restrictions when they enter that range, thus imposing a change in regime; and prices can induce a change in quotas, just as quotas can induce a change in prices, thus creating a problem of endogeneity. The attempts of other scholars to assess the impact of the ICO have failed to address these issues. I therefore could not use their estimates. My own attempts to construct a properly specified model of the regulated coffee market foundered on the absence of data on key variables, especially in monthly time series.

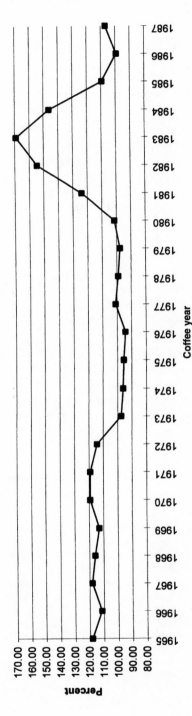

FIGURE 5.7. Price of coffee exported to members as percentage of price of coffee exported to nonmembers. Quotas were in force during the periods August 1965 to October 1972 and October 1980 to August 1985. *Source*: Monthly price data from the files of the ICO. Reproduced from Bates (1997).

and nonmember nations, expressed as a percentage.[18] When the ratio exceeds 100 percent, then prices in member markets exceed those in the markets of nonmembers; arbitrage has been prevented and barriers to trade effectively put in place. The evidence in figure 5.7 suggests that when the ICO imposed quotas it was able to enforce them, yielding a higher price in the coffee markets of member nations.

Although visually satisfying, were these effects statistically significant? To answer this question, I calculated the means and variances of coffee prices in member and nonmember markets during periods in which the ICO did and did not impose quota restrictions.[19] I constructed a variable, *D*, which measures the difference in the mean value of prices in the member and nonmember markets in each period. *D* can be transformed into a test statistic that possesses a *t*-distribution. The null hypothesis is that the mean of *D* is 0, or that there is no statistically significant difference between the mean of the prices in the two markets. We can reject the null hypothesis if the test statistic falls into a critical range—a range within which its value would be highly unlikely (one chance in one hundred) to fall were it determined by chance. In this instance, I chose a critical range appropriate to a one-tailed test; I wished to reject the null when the value of the test statistic was highly and significantly positive, i.e., when the mean price of coffee in the member market exceeded that in the nonmember market by a level significantly greater than would be likely by chance. Given the number of observations available, the critical region in which one can reject the null hypothesis begins at 2.33. The results of the test, presented in table 5.6, enable us to reject the hypothesis of no difference in the mean price of coffee in the two markets at the .01 level of confidence. The imposition of quotas appears to generate a significantly higher price in member markets.[20]

RIVALRY

Thus far I have focused on the impact of the ICO on average prices. At least as important is its impact on relative prices, for competition between coffee

---

[18]The measure of coffee "prices" is actually the unit value of exports, as recorded in International Coffee Organization, W.P.—Agreement No. 1/88, Rev. 2.

[19]With the help of Ms. (now Dr.) Dixie Reeves, my research assistant. For a development of the method followed, see Larsen and Marx (1990:486–87, 496–97).

[20]As seen in figure 5.7 and table 5.6, when quotas were not in place, prices in member markets fell below those in the markets of other countries. At such times, exporters sought hard currency earnings and competed for sales in Europe and the United States.

The greater tendency for producers to sell low-quality coffees in the nonmember market constitutes a plausible alternative explanation of the price differentials. Research by economists at the Department of State concluded, however, that this behavior could not account for the magnitude of the differential (interview, Washington, D.C., June 1990). And a reanalysis of the data underlying table 5.6 suggests that the differential was as great for each quality of coffee, i.e., as great for robusta as for milds.

TABLE 5.6
Testing for the Impact of the Coffee Quota

	Number of observations	Mean for D	t-Statistic
Periods in which quotas were in place			
August 1965 to October 1972	600	2.342	5.295
October 1980 to August 1985	299	18.742	6.571
Periods in which quotas were not in place			
November 1972 to September 1979	420	−1.516	−1.264
September 1985 to August 1988	240	−9.150	−1.923

Source: Monthly price data from the files of the ICO.

producers takes the form of competitive price cutting by producing nations. The market appears to recognize four qualities of coffee. Colombian milds, a washed arabica, are positioned at the top of the market.[21] Then come the other milds, the washed arabicas produced in Central America. Brazil's unwashed arabicas occupy the third rung in the quality rankings.[22] Africa's robustas slot in at the bottom of the market.[23] Despite the quality differences, consumers are willing to substitute among these varieties, given sufficient incentive. A competitive cut in the price of other mild coffees would therefore produce a lowering of the price of Colombian coffee, for consumers would be willing to switch from Colombia's high-quality coffee, given a sufficient price differential.

A second test of the effectiveness of the ICO, then, is its impact on relative prices. Figure 5.8 illustrates the pattern of relative prices for a period during which quotas were in effect. By and large, price differentials remained stable. The pattern contrasts with that exhibited in figure 5.9, which portrays relative prices in a period during which quotas were suspended following a catastrophic frost in Brazil. Given Brazil's size in the market, the frost produced a massive rise in prices (compare the prices on the vertical axes of figures 5.8 and 5.9). It also produced a massive distortion in relative prices. After recovering, Brazil sought to reposition its coffee at a price level intermediate between that of the other milds and that of robusta coffees. But, as can be seen in figure 5.9, African producers resisted, cutting their prices to keep Brazil from closing the gap. So did the producers of other milds, who lowered their prices below those charged by Brazil. This competitive response posed a challenge to Colombia as well, for the growing price differentials between other milds and Colombian coffee encouraged consumers to abandon the higher-quality

[21] The vast bulk of which are produced in Colombia, of course. But Kenya and the Kilimanjaro region of Tanzania also produce coffees classified in this group.

[22] Ethiopia also produces unwashed arabicas; its crop is insignificant by comparison with that of Brazil.

[23] Indonesia is also a major producer of robusta coffees.

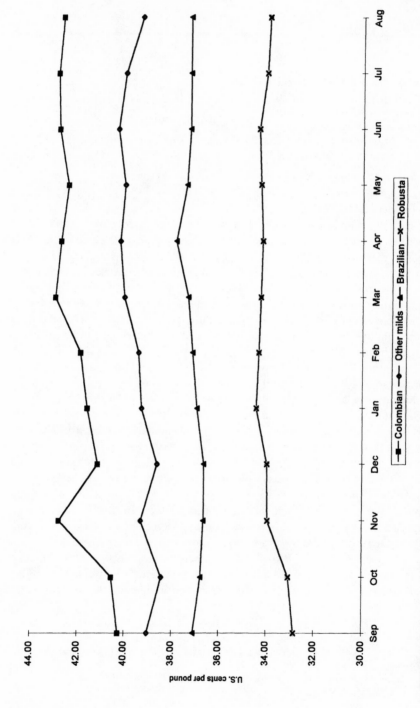

FIGURE 5.8. Coffee prices, 1967–68. *Source*: Monthly price data from the files of the ICO. Reproduced from Bates (1997).

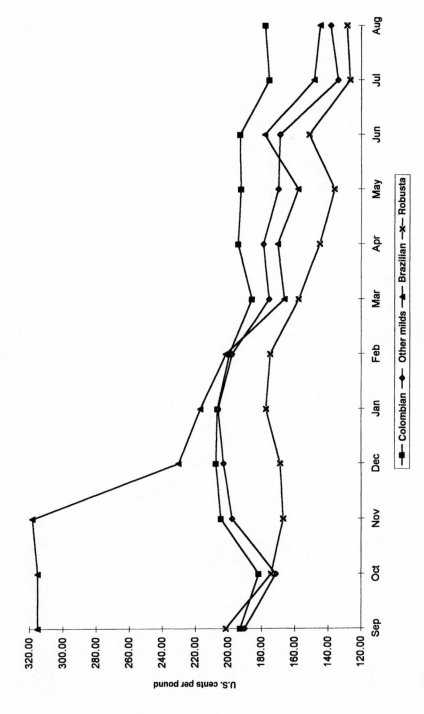

FIGURE 5.9. Coffee prices, 1977–78. *Source:* Monthly price data from the files of the ICO. Reproduced from Bates (1997).

Colombian product. Colombia therefore joined in the price cutting. In the face of the kind of competitive behavior portrayed in figure 5.9, the dominant producers sought to reimpose the quantity constraints that would generate the evenly spaced price differentials exhibited in figure 5.8. They succeeded in doing so.

The ICO thus appears to have worked. It was apparently able to prevent arbitrage across markets and competition between producers of different kinds of coffee. It appears to have been able to regulate behavior in the coffee market in ways that enabled it to achieve higher average prices. Indicative of this power is the behavior of coffee prices following the breakup of the ICO. As will be recounted in the narrative that follows, in June and July 1989 the ICO collapsed. As seen in figure 5.10, when the ICO broke up, coffee prices plummeted. The spot price for Colombian milds, for example, fell from $1.80 a pound in June to less than $1.00 by July—and stayed below $1.00 a pound for several years thereafter.

Operations

In addition to having been able to regulate the coffee market effectively, the ICO appears to have been rule governed. The best-documented example of the impact of the rules comes from the negotiations that led to the assignment of quotas in 1982.[24] Quotas had been suspended when prices rose above the target range because of shortages resulting from the Brazilian frost of 1975. As prices returned to the level at which the ICO would seek to defend them, Brazil proposed a new set of quotas. Under this proposal, Brazil would secure over 33 percent of the market, a share held in the 1960s but long since lost, particularly since the frost of 1975. The primary victim of Brazil's proposal would have been Colombia, which would have been constrained to less than a 19 percent share of the market, after having captured over 22 percent of it following the frost. Colombia therefore set out to block Brazil's proposal by crafting one of its own.

Under the rules of the ICO, quotas had to be voted upon, and Article 13 of the International Coffee Agreement governed the allocation of votes. Under Article 13, the proportion of total exports for the period 1976/77 to 1979/80 accounted for by a given producer, i (call them P_{1i}, where 1 stands for the time period above, i for the producer, and P for export performance) determined the proportion of the votes controlled by that producer (call that proportion W_i). This rule can be represented as

$$W_i = f(P_{1i}) \qquad (1)$$

[24]This section draws heavily upon Bates and Lien (1985) and Lien and Bates (1987). The articles contain the data underlying this analysis. For treatments of closely related issues, see Fielding and Liebeck (1975) and Hosli (1993).

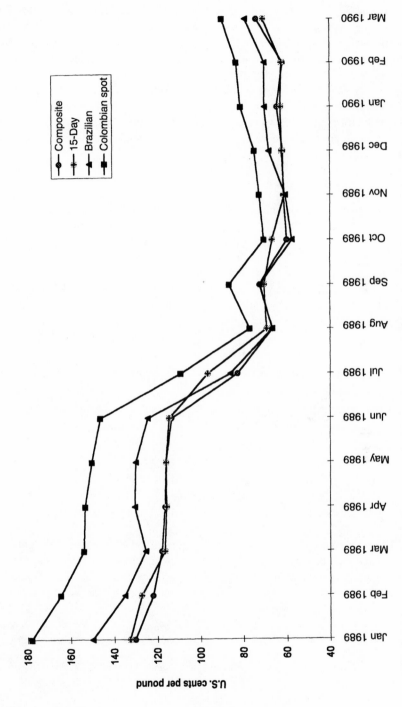

FIGURE 5.10. The breakup of the ICO, July 1989. *Source:* Monthly price data from the files of the ICO. Reproduced from Bates (1997).

Article 30 of the agreement governed the allocation of quotas. Claims for quotas, this article stated, were to be based on average exports over one of two three-year periods: 1968/69 to 1971/72 or 1976/77 to 1979/80.[25] Claims for quotas were transformed into actual quotas only when voted upon, however; quotas were set by a (distributed) two-thirds majority vote of the member nations. Article 30 can therefore also be represented in the form of a function, wherein the quota assigned to a particular nation, $i(q_i)$, is a function of past export performance (P_{2i}, where the subscript 2 refers to the time period noted in this paragraph, rather than that used in the allocation of votes, as discussed earlier) and of votes (W_i). Thus

$$q_i = g(P_{2i}, W_i) \tag{2}$$

Rule-governed environments produce opportunities for sophisticated behavior. In the presence of voting rules, actors can behave strategically. In majority-rule environments, they can convert endowments of votes into political power by converting coalitions into political majorities. Given a set of rules that defines a winning majority, the Shapley value of an actor provides a measure of that actor's power: the percentage of all coalitions among members of the group which that actor, given its allocation of votes, can convert into a winning majority.[26] Once again, the reasoning can be summarized:

$$S_i = h(W_i) \tag{3}$$

where S_i stands for the Shapley value of nation i and W_i for its endowment of votes, as noted previously.

The rules that governed the assignment of the quotas by the ICO thus can be recast as a system of equations:

Equation	Justification
1. $W_i = f(P_{1i})$	Article 13
2. $q_i = g(P_{2i}, W_i)$	Article 30
3. $S_i = h(W_i)$	Behavioral assumptions

In effect, this system constitutes a model of how quotas (q_i) would be assigned under the rules of the ICO, were actors making sophisticated use of the powers conferred upon them by those rules. An advantage of this formalization is that it suggests a way of estimating the impact of the rules. We can estimate

---

[25]The producer nations could choose either period. Brazil, for example, chose the first and Colombia the second, as the former lost market share following the frost of 1975 while the latter gained.

[26]For a discussion, see Luce and Raiffa (1957). For illuminating critiques and discussions, see Roth (1988).

the parameters of the model, and thus the impact of the rules of the agreement, by using a two-stage least squares approach, in which the constant terms, P_1 and P_2, are used as instruments to eliminate the correlation between S_i and q_i indirectly produced through their association with export performance.[27]

Equation (4) presents the results for the allocation of the quota proposed by Colombia:

$$q_i = -0.2279 + 0.8281 P_{2i} + 0.2175 S_i \qquad (4)$$
$$\underset{(0.214)}{} \quad \underset{(0.0674)}{} \quad \underset{(0.0746)}{}$$

The figures in parentheses represent standard errors of the estimated parameters. The standard errors of the estimated coefficient relating Colombia's Shapley value to its quota is one-third the value of the estimated parameter, and it is therefore statistically significant.

These results can be interpreted as suggesting that Colombia took cognizance of the rules and their effect on the distribution of power and allocated quota entitlements so as to accommodate the voting power of particular nations. Indeed documentary evidence underscores the hypothesis that the Colombian delegation counted votes and crafted its proposal accordingly.[28] The rules thus appear to have shaped the behavior of member nations, and, in particular, the allocation of rights to export in international markets.

By creating the ICO, the dominant producers sought to erect a governance structure that enabled them to reduce the risks of opportunistic behavior—risks that undermined their capacity to incur costs with the certainty that they, and others, would reap the benefit of higher coffee prices. The results of the estimates also provide a test of their ability to do so. The Shapley value provides a measure of the ability of a nation to convert coalitions into winning coalitions, i.e., into ones that command electoral majorities. Under the rules of the agreement, bigger producers were endowed with greater numbers of votes; intuitively they should therefore have possessed more power. Equation (5) provides the test we seek. As seen in that equation, the relationship between the voting strength of a nation and its Shapley value is indeed nonlinear; it is quadratic, such that as the number of votes controlled by a nation increases, its Shapley value rises more than proportionately:

$$S_i = 0.8227 W_i + 0.0152 W_i^2 \qquad (5)$$
$$\underset{(0.0031)}{} \quad \underset{(0.0018)}{}$$

The lesson is clear: by controlling more votes, larger nations gained more "Shapley power," as shown in equation (5) and therefore could extract greater quotas, as shown in equation (4). This estimate of the impact of the rules thus

[27]Da-Hsiang Donald Lien and I have performed this analysis (Bates and Lien 1985).

[28]Memorandum No. 001, enero 22 de 1982, pp. 1–2, Convenio International de Café, *Copiador Memorandos*, 1982.

underscores the ability of the ICO to offer the large producers the assurance that were they to restrict exports, they need not fear predation by the smaller exporters.

The values of the parameters estimated from the model provide a further measure of the economic significance of the political rules put in place by the ICO. They suggest, for example, that had Kenya possessed but one vote more in 1982, it could have increased its quota such that it could have earned an additional $168.5 million each year throughout the 1980s. We can thus see how the rules of this government of coffee affected the wealth of nations.

In this section, we show that the ICO was rule governed. Earlier in this chapter, we have argued that its rules became self-enforcing. The rules were so regularized that they could be modeled and the model tested against data generated by the behavior of states. Where the rules of an organization are so precise that they can be formalized, and where the tests of the resultant model suggest that the rules in fact shape the conduct of actors, then I, for one, am willing to call that organization an institution.

Return to the Narrative

Narratives describe a birth, a life, and a death. In the preceding sections, we have provided an account of the birth and life of the ICO. In this section, we describe its demise. The collapse of the organization represents a shift in outcomes—a change in the value of endogenous variables. It also implies that the values of the variables that we posited as exogenous themselves change. It therefore provides a test of our explanation.

The ICO, I have argued, constituted a coalition among firms and bureaucrats that used states to regulate international markets. A key to the ability of the producers to secure third-party enforcement was the willingness of coffee roasters and security specialists in the United States to elicit the enforcement of the agreement. The mix of coffees demanded by consumers changed, but, given the binding nature of the quotas, the mix of coffees supplied by the producers did not. In the United States, consumers switched from soluble coffees, which intensively employed robustas, to ground coffees, with a higher percentage of arabicas. In seeking to respond to changes in consumer preferences, the roasters confronted the supply constraints imposed by the ICO.

Because the ICO worked, it resulted not only in a fixed proportion of coffees of different types but also in large price differentials between member and nonmember markets. As the price differential increased, so too did the fears of the large roasting firms, who worried that competitors would secure low-cost coffee, illicitly importing it from nonmember countries. The cooperation of the large firms remained knife edged: each was willing to cooperate only so long as it was certain of the cooperation of others. Insofar as the agreement worked, then, incentives to elude the administrative barriers strengthened, and so too did the readiness of key actors to abandon the agreement.

In the 1980s, two changes appear to have triggered defection. One was the large-scale movement of European roasters to Berlin, attracted by favorable tax policies. The other was the entry of a European firm, Nestlé, into the North American market, through its purchase of Hills Brothers. The large U.S. roasters now faced a competitor with possible access to cheap coffee, purchased in the nonmember markets of Eastern Europe.

In response to the constraints imposed by the ICO on the mix of coffees available in the market and their relative prices, and to the entry of Nestlé into the U.S. market, the Foreign Affairs Committee of the NCA shifted from a supporter to a critic of the ICO. In February 1988 it indicated that it had detected

two severe weaknesses in the operation of the current agreement . . . :

1. The sale of coffee to non-members . . . at prices substantially below the price at which . . . coffee is offered to members of the Agreement. This practice has created a so-called "two-tier" market that is not only economically unfair to member states, but also encourages various illegal or clandestine diversions of coffee. . . .

2. The inflexibility of the quota system in making coffee of the origins or types required by consumers available to the market.

The committee therefore concluded and resolved "that the interests of the United States coffee . . . industry are best accommodated by free and unrestricted trade of coffee."[29]

The Department of State, we have argued, constituted a second key element in the domestic coalition underpinning the ICO. The department was concerned with international security; in particular it was concerned with the threat of communism. But in the late 1980s, the communist threat collapsed. The left no longer posed a political threat in Brazil, and, in a variety of industrial and agricultural markets, Brazil had come to resemble more closely a mature economic rival than a struggling developing nation. Another key element of the ICO's domestic support coalition, the Department of State, therefore defected.

The structure of policymaking in the United States requires that the executive branch push for the agreement and that it secure the consent of Congress. Essential to the latter is the backing of the coffee roasting firms. The support of both the Department of State and the coffee roasters for the ICO had weakened. In terms of our spatial model, we can think of the changes that took place in the 1980s as representing a shift from panel B to panel A in figure 5.6. The executive branch and the House, deferring to the preferences of the roasters,

[29]"Report of the Foreign Affairs Committee, Board of Directors, National Coffee Association," February 1988, p. 4.

shifted their policy preferences away from the ICO and toward the free market policies that had formed the earlier status quo.

The collapse of the ICO marks the last stage of this narrative. The institution did not endure. But our understanding of it appears to have survived the test posed by its demise. Changes in the value of explanatory variables acted decisively, and in expected ways, upon the politics of the coffee market.

Conclusion

As a political institution that regulated international markets, the ICO was very rare indeed; few other bodies have effectively governed the behavior of states in the global arena. As with other rare occurrences, the history of the ICO can be described; it possessed a birth, a life, and a death. In analyzing this case, however, I have sought to move beyond mere narration. I have sought to extract systematic knowledge.

In an effort to do so, I have sought to fit analytic frameworks to the history of this institution. One framework was that of noncooperative game theory and, in particular, the chain store model of entry deterrence. Like the narrative, the game analyzed actors and choices. Being starker than the narrative itself, it highlighted features of the narrative. It sharpened our understanding of the logic underlying the events and heightened our awareness of what was problematic and therefore in need of explanation. It also provided an engine of discovery, directing our attention to important features of the data.

The analysis also drove us to recognize that the creation of the ICO was not the result of purely economic behavior, but rather of political and economic choice making. In keeping with the Chicago theory of cartel behavior, I sought to see why a third party—the government of a consuming nation, the United States—would provide enforcement for a collusive agreement among producers. Using the tools of spatial analysis, I explored the politics of coalition formation and isolated the domestic political coalition that explained why the government of a consumer nation should support a cartel.

The last part of this chapter emphasized an additional advantage of moving from historical accounts to analytic narratives: the transformation helps to render such accounts amenable to testing. Models explicitly separate exogenous from endogenous factors and specify the causal linkages between them. They constitute a claim that changes in the exogenous variables should, of necessity, generate changes in those that are endogenous. Models therefore set the stage for testing. One way is by estimating relationships between variables. Another is by making observations of data generated by events that take place outside the original sample. Thus did the death of the ICO provide an opportunity to assess our account of its creation.

References

Arango, Mariano. 1982. *El Café en Colombia, 1930–1938.* Bogotá: Carlos Valencia.

Bacha, Edmar, and Robert Greenhill. 1992. *150 Years of Coffee.* Rio de Janeiro: Marcellino Martins and E. Johnston.

Bates, Robert H. 1997. *Open Economy Politics: The Political Economy of the World Coffee Trade.* Princeton, N.J.: Princeton University Press.

Bates, Robert H., and Da-Hsiang Donald Lien. 1985. "On the Operation of the International Coffee Agreement." *International Organization* 39: 553–59.

Beyer, Robert Carlyle. 1947. "The Colombian Coffee Industry: Origins and Major Trends, 1740–1949." Ph.D. diss., Department of History, University of Minnesota.

Bruchey, Stuart. 1987. *American Business and Foreign Policy.* New York: Garland.

Comité Nacional. Various years. *Actas, Acuerdos, Resoluciones.*

Delfim Netto, Antônio. 1959. *O Problema do Café No Brasil.* São Paulo: University of São Paulo.

Federación Nacional de Cafeteros. 1980. *II Seminario Sobre Economía Cafetera.* Manizales, Colombia: Corporación Autonema Universiatria de Manizales.

Federación Nacional de Cafeteros, Comité Nacional. 1963. *Actas II* (July-December).

Fielding, Geoff, and Hans Liebeck. 1975. "Voting Structure and the Square Root Law." *British Journal of Political Science* 5: 249–63.

Fisher, Bart. 1972. *The International Coffee Agreement: A Study in Coffee Diplomacy.* New York: Praeger.

Food and Agriculture Organization of the United Nations. Various years. *Trade Yearbook.* Rome: Food and Agriculture Organization of the United Nations

Fudenberg, Drew, and Eric Maskin. 1986. "The Folk Theorem in Repeated Games with Discounting or with Incomplete Information." *Econometrica* 54 (3): 533–54.

Gallop, Frank M., and Mark J. Roberts. 1979. "Firm Interdependence in Oligopolistic Markets." *Journal of Econometrics* 10: 313–31.

George, Alexander L. 1979. "Case Studies and Theory Development." In *Diplomacy: New Approaches in History, Theory, and Policy,* edited by P. G. L. Lauren. New York: Free Press.

Harvard Business School. 1987. *United States National Coffee Market.* Cambridge, Mass.: Harvard University Press.

Hilke, John C., and Philip B. Nelson. 1989. "Strategic Behavior and Attempted Monopolization: The Coffee (General Foods) Case." In *The Antitrust Revolution,* edited by John C. Kwoka and Laurence J. White. New York: Scott Foresman.

Holloway, Thomas H. 1975. *The Brazilian Coffee Valorization of 1906.* Madison: State Historical Society of Wisconsin for Department of History, University of Wisconsin.

Hosli, Madeline O. 1993. "Admission of European Free Trade States to the European Community: Effects of Voting Power on the European Community Council of Ministers." *International Organization* 47 (4): 629–43.

International Coffee Organization. 1982. *Quarterly Statistical Bulletin, July-September 1982.* London: International Coffee Organization.

International Monetary Fund. Various years. *International Financial Statistics.* Washington, D.C.: International Monetary Fund.

Kindleberger, Charles. 1973. *The World in Depression, 1929–1939.* Berkeley: University of California Press.

Krasner, Stephen D. 1971. "The Politics of Primary Commodities: A Study of Coffee 1900–1970." Ph.D. diss., Department of Government, Harvard University.

———. 1973a. "Manipulating International Commodity Markets: Brazilian Coffee Policy 1906 to 1962." *Public Policy* 21 (4): 493–523.

———. 1973b. "Business-Government Relations: The Case of the International Coffee Agreement." *International Organization* 27 (4): 495–516.

Kreps, David, and Robert Wilson. 1982. "Reputation and Imperfect Information." *Journal of Economic Theory* 27: 253–79.

Larsen, Richard J., and Morris L. Marx. 1990. *Statistics.* Englewood Cliffs, N.J.: Prentice Hall.

Levinson, Jerome, and Juan de Onis. 1970. *The Alliance That Lost Its Way.* Chicago: Quadrangle Books

Licht, F. O. 1993. *International Coffee Yearbook, 1993.* Ratzeburg, Germany: F. O. Licht.

Lien, Da-Hsiang Donald, and Robert H. Bates. 1987. "Political Behavior in the Coffee Agreement." *Economic Development and Cultural Change* 35 (3): 629–36.

Luce, Duncan, and Howard Raiffa. 1957. *Games and Decisions.* New York: John Wiley and Sons.

Peltzman, Sam. 1976. "Toward a More General Theory of Regulation." *Journal of Law and Economics* 19 (2): 211–40.

Ramirez Ocampo, Jorge, and Silervia Perez Gomez. 1986. *83 Años de Política Cafetera Internacional y la Participación de Colombia en este Proceso.* Bogotá: Federación Nacional de Cafeteros.

Roth, Alvin E. 1988. *The Shapley Value: Essays in Honor of Lloyd S. Shapley.* Cambridge: Cambridge University Press.

Rowe, J. W. T. 1963. *The World's Coffee.* London: Her Majesty's Stationery Office.

Salop, Steven C., and David T. Scheffman. 1983. "Raising Rivals' Costs." *American Economic Review* 72 (2): 267–71.

Sears, Dudley, et al. 1979. *The Rehabilitation of the Economy of Uganda,* vol. 2. London: Commonwealth Secretariat.

Selten, Reinhart. 1978. "The Chain-Store Paradox." *Theory and Decision* 9: 127–59.

Stigler, George. 1971. "The Theory of Economic Regulation." *Bell Journal of Economics and Management Sciences* 2 (1): 3–21.

Sutton, John. 1991. *Sunk Costs and Market Structure: Price Competition, Advertising, and the Evolution of Competition.* Cambridge, Mass.: MIT Press.

Taunay, Afonso de E. 1943. *Taunay, Historia do Café No Brasil,* vol. 15. Rio de Janeiro: Departamento Nacional do Café.

Wagner, Harrison R. 1970. *United States Policy toward Latin America.* Stanford, Calif.: Stanford University Press.

Waltz, Kenneth N. 1979. *Theory in International Politics.* Reading, Mass.: Addison-Wesley.

Williamson, Oliver E. 1968. "Wage Rates as Barriers to Entry: The Penington Case in Perspective." *Quarterly Journal of Economics* 83 (1): 85–116.

Conclusion _____

THE CHAPTERS in this volume have explored the sources of political order, the origins of conflict, and the interplay between international and domestic political economy. Throughout their discussion of such themes, they have focused on the nature and significance of institutions. Because the chapters engage such fundamental issues, they are of general significance. Those seeking insight into state formation, the political foundations of development, and the role of institutions can read them with profit. But although the themes and insights are general, the generality of the *explanations* is far less apparent. It is to this issue that we now turn.

Postdiction

Green and Shapiro (1994) criticize the literature on rational choice for failing to be empirically grounded. We hope that these chapters offer a convincing rebuttal. But in eluding this charge we may run afoul of another. Insofar as users of rational choice theory address empirical evidence, Green and Shapiro contend, they construct models that simply account for the original evidence. Mere exercises in "curve fitting," such efforts do not offer adequate tests of theory.

In the introduction, we provide one rejoinder: that in constructing our theories, we were often driven to the discovery of new features of our data. Thus Greif was compelled to move from the domestic to the international level, Levi found it necessary to consider the distinction between rural and urban populations in their response to military recruitment, and Weingast had to address the revision in Southern expectations following the Democratic Party's loss of the House elections. The chapters themselves provide another rejoinder: in some, the models fail. Bates, for example, was compelled by the evidence to discard, or reconfigure, a variety of approaches to the analysis of cartels. Greif began with a model derived from the spatial literature on voting (Hinich and Munger 1997)—an approach that he was forced to abandon. Levi had to reconsider a model in which changes in conscription followed directly from expansions in suffrage. In addition, models posit relationships among variables that render them subject to testing. In Rosenthal's chapter, for example, the conditions that make it rational to launch wars suggest relationships between the fiscal power of elites and the returns from fighting, thereby providing a means for evaluating his explanation.

When models highlight features of the data that hitherto have escaped attention; when they can be contradicted by the evidence; and when they predict relationships that must hold, if their equilibria capture the processes that generate the phenomena of concern—then we are well beyond postdiction. As they furnish deep insights into particular cases, these chapters are not mere exercises in "curve fitting."

Going Further?

Can we claim more? In particular, do game theoretic models of a particular case furnish explanations that, being general, can be applied to, and tested in, other settings?

These questions can be addressed from two perspectives. One is that of comparative statics; the other, research design. The two are closely related, for the method of comparative statics generates relationships among variables that can then be tested through the appropriate selection of cases. When addressed from these perspectives, the questions yield, upon reflection, a guarded response: yes—but with important limitations.

Comparative Statics and Research Design

We have already noted that the conditions that define the equilibrium of a particular model yield testable hypotheses; they predict relationships among variables and so are subject to testing. Ideally we would want to go further. As we can often do when analyzing maximization under constraints, we would like to be able to manipulate the conditions that define the equilibrium, so that we could observe how changes in exogenous variables generate changes in the variables whose value they determine. The investigation of such comparative statics yields testable hypotheses and thus further opportunities for testing (Henderson and Quandt 1971).

Such a strategy can be applied, given appropriate conditions. Most relevant here is that the model possess but a single equilibrium. When this is the case, then we can vary particular exogenous variables and derive from the model propositions about how the value of endogenous variables should alter. Of the chapters in this volume, Rosenthal's most closely approximates the requirements for the use of this method. The conditions that define the equilibrium of his model suggest that as the elite gains fiscal control, the crown should lose policy autonomy. Using the method of comparative statics, Rosenthal is thus able to formulate hypotheses and to test them with data gathered from England, where elite control over fiscal policy was greater than in France.

When thus moving "out of sample" to test an analytic narrative, we confront issues of research design. For Rosenthal to test his model of France using data drawn from England requires that the cases be homogeneous, in the sense that the expected value of the dependent variable (i.e., the policy autonomy of the crown) be the same in both cases when the explanatory variable (i.e., elite fiscal control) takes on a particular value. Much therefore turns on Rosenthal's assumption that England was sufficiently similar to France that the two cases could be treated as homogeneous.[1]

In other instances, behavior in equilibrium may be influenced by more than one exogenous variable. The application of comparative statics then becomes more difficult. In exploring the determinants of political order in Genoa, for example, Greif needed to expand the time profile of his case study so as to secure variation in one variable—such as external threat—while controlling for the other—the profitability of commerce. Alternatively, Greif could have located other cases: ones that would have enabled him to control for one variable while varying the other. He too would then wish to take counsel from the students of research design, who offer important guidelines for case selection.

Multiple Equilibria

Thus far we have discussed the possibilities offered by analytic narratives whose models yield unique equilibria. Difficulties arise, however, when the conditions necessary for uniqueness fail to prevail. Such is commonly the case in game theoretic models.

In strategic environments, changes in the value of an exogenous variable can alter the equilibrium choice of strategies.[2] Phrased one way, changes in exogenous variables therefore can alter the set of equilibria. Phrased in a way that more directly addresses a central theme of this book, changes in the value of the exogenous variable can lead to changes in institutions. Viewed either way, under such circumstances neither the method of comparative statics nor case selection offers a straightforward means of assessing the general validity of the model.

To illustrate the difficulty, recall Bates's analysis of the coffee market. In the absence of global political tensions, a neoclassical model of market competition worked: the cartel was unstable and subject to free riding. When the value of the exogenous variable changed, however, and global security was threatened, then the competitive outcome no longer prevailed. Third-party enforcement became rational and facilitated collusion among producing nations. *The change in the*

---

[1]More precisely, much turns on the assumption that the two countries do not differ in ways that correlate with the independent variable. Were France to differ from England in ways that related to elite control over fiscal policy, then inferences regarding the impact of fiscal control over policy autonomy would be subject to error.

[2]This is not always the case. Equilibria may be robust, and therefore subject (within limits) to comparative statics. The analysis of the robustness of equilibria forms an important part of the literature on industrial organization (see, for example, Laffont and Tirole 1987).

value of a critical exogenous variable thus produced a change in the equilibrium outcome. An obvious implication is that propositions derived from a model of the coffee market prior to the cold war period could not be tested with data drawn from that period. The institutions that shaped trade strategies altered; there was a shift to a new equilibrium. The behavior of producers therefore altered in the two periods, and different processes generated prices in international markets. It is therefore difficult to test explanations employing data from outside the original sample.

Weingast offers an additional example. Political stability in the nineteenth-century United States, he argues, was conditioned by the credibility of the balance rule. Once the rule had been broken, incentives changed, and actors therefore altered their political strategies. As the counterfactual test of his argument dramatically illustrates, the model that fit behavior in the one period failed to fit it in the other.

When there are multiple equilibria, the logic that drives strategy choices, given one value of an exogenous variable, may not be the same as the logic that shapes choices, given other values. When the value of an exogenous variable alters, people may recompute their best strategies and new strategy combinations may come to form equilibria. Conventional comparative statics, which explores relationships between exogenous and endogenous variables, therefore cannot be applied to generate propositions about variables that are testable out of the original sample. For the same reasons, investigators may find it difficult to test their explanations by applying the canons of research design to select additional cases.

One response is to concede the obvious: that analytic narratives are refractory to some of the most commonly employed research methods. They therefore often yield outcomes that tend to be "one off" and that are relatively rare and infrequent. Many crucial historical events exhibit such characteristics. Phrased more positively, by capturing the mechanisms that account for such properties, analytic narratives deepen our understanding of why such events evade understanding by "normal" scientific methods.

A second response is to offer an alternative interpretation of our approach. Rational choice theory (and in particular the theory of games) offers a theory of structure: it suggests a way in which structures create incentives that shape individual choices and thereby collective outcomes. Insofar as a game yields multiple equilibria, it may be difficult to test its explanatory power. But the "force" of a game may lie in the properties of structure that it highlights and in the strategic problems to which it gives rise. And whereas the specific game may not be portable, these other attributes may offer opportunities for comparative analysis. They may yield explanations that can be tested in many different settings.

Examples of common strategic problems would include the following:

Collective action problems. Students of class conflict (Elster 1985; Przeworksi 1985), ethnicity (Laitin 1992, 1995; Hardin 1995), and social movements (Chong 1991; Kuran 1995; Golden 1996) focus upon such problems, as do students of sectoral politics (Frieden 1991) and conflict between town and country (Bates 1981; Varshney 1992).

Principal agent problems. Researchers into the politics of central planning (Kornai 1995), public sector enterprises (Waterbury 1993), and relations between the legislature and bureaucracy (Ramseyer and Rosenbluth 1993; Cowhey and McCubbins 1995) concentrate upon the political problems resulting from agency, as do researchers into the internal politics of political parties (Michels 1962; Ramseyer and Rosenbluth 1993; Cowhey and McCubbins 1995).

Problems of credible commitment. A series of recent studies focuses on the ability or inability of nation-states to bind themselves to international agreements (Eichengreen 1991; Simons 1994; Bates 1997). Researchers have also focused on problems of credibility in the making of domestic economic policy (North and Weingast 1994).

Two-level games. Tsebelis's (1990) study of domestic politics in Europe and Putnam's (1988) research into interstate policymaking stress the strategic dilemmas arising from the necessity of actors to compete in more than one political arena.

Certain structural features of strategic settings also commonly occur, and game theoretic analyses suggest their significance for collective outcomes. These too provide opportunities to focus on diverse cases from a common vantage point. Such key features would include the following:

The power of the pivot. The pivotal decisionmaker is that individual or group whose choice decides the outcome.[3] In his chapter, Bates utilized a commonly employed measure of the capacity of individuals to pivot by rendering coalitions winning, given the rules of the game (the Shapley value; see Shubik 1985); he employed this measure to analyze the allocation of export rights among members of the ICO. Greif's discussion suggested that by creating the *podestà* the Genoese created an agent that possessed the incentive to side with whichever party was attacked by another. Because his support decides which side wins a conflict, the *podestà* is pivotal. Levi's discussion suggested how electoral changes in the nineteenth century changed the identity of the pivotal voter (e.g., from the elite to the rural propertied and urban bourgeoisie), in turn altering the policy outcome. Pivots also played a role in Weingast's account of the demise of the Democratic Party's hegemonic position in antebellum America.

Gatekeeping authority. Gatekeeping authority is the power to initiate or to block consideration of proposals within a particular jurisdiction (Shepsle and Weingast 1981; Denzau and Mackay 1983). This authority is typically apportioned by institutions and helps to determine the way in which they shape

---

[3]In a voting contest over a one-dimensional issue space, the pivot is simply the median voter. In more complex issue spaces, however, a single median may not exist.

political outcomes. Gatekeeping authority conveys the power to prevent an alteration of the status quo. Thus Bates showed how the rules of the ICO enabled the major producers to limit predation by the small, by endowing the former with sufficient votes to block proposals to alter quotas in the ICO. Weingast demonstrated how the power of the Senate to prevent issues from being deliberated at the national level helped to keep slavery from becoming a defining issue in the second-party system. In Schattsneider's phrasing, the power of the gatekeeper thus helps to account for the institutionalization of bias in political systems (Schattsneider 1960).

Veto points. Many political systems endow several actors with the right to veto a policy change in a particular area (Immergut 1992a,b; Tsebelis 1995). Weingast's chapter explores the political significance of such veto points. The balance rule transformed the vetoes endowed by the Constitution to the House and the Senate into a dual set of vetoes for both North and South. The dual veto placed self-enforcing limits on the national government, helping to maintain the constitutional system of states' rights and federalism—and also helping to preserve slavery. Rosenthal's distinction between parliamentary and absolutist regimes hinges on the differential ability of elites to veto the initiation of war in the two political systems, whereas Levi's concern with democratization emphasizes the changing political locus of veto power.

Conclusion

The contributors to this volume have sought to construct analytic narratives and so extract deeper insights from case materials. In so doing, we have gained a heightened awareness of the intimate links between theoretical reasoning and empirical research. At least in the world of strategic behavior, we have learned, theory with narrative is stronger than theory alone. And narrative with theory is more powerful than narrative alone. Analytic narratives offer a method for moving from the context-rich world of events and cases to explanations that are logically rigorous, illuminating and insightful, and, if handled with care, subject to empirical testing.

References

Bates, Robert H. 1997. *Open Economy Politics*. Princeton, N.J.: Princeton University Press.
———. 1981. *Markets and States in Tropical Africa*. Berkeley: University of California Press.
Chong, Dennis. 1991. *Collective Action and the Civil Rights Movement*. Chicago: University of Chicago Press.

Cowhey, Peter F., and Mathew D. McCubbins, eds. 1995. *Structure and Policy in Japan and the United States*. Cambridge: Cambridge University Press.

Denzau, Arthur, and Robert Mackay. 1983. "Gate Keeping and Monopoly Power of Committees." *American Journal of Political Science* 27: 720–62.

Eichengreen, Barry. 1991. *Golden Fetters*. New York: Oxford University Press.

Elster, Jon. 1985. *Making Sense of Marx*. Cambridge: Cambridge University Press.

Frieden, Jeffery A. 1991. *Debt, Development and Democracy*. Princeton, N. J.: Princeton University Press.

Golden, Miriam. 1996. *Heroic Defeats*. New York: Cambridge University Press.

Green, Donald P., and Ian Shapiro. 1994. *Pathologies of Rational Choice Theory*. New Haven, Conn.: Yale University Press.

Hardin, Russell. 1995. *One for All*. Princeton, N.J.: Princeton University Press.

Henderson, James, and Richard Quandt. 1971. *Microeconomic Theory: A Mathematical Approach*. New York: McGraw-Hill.

Hinich, Melvin J., and Michael C. Munger. 1997. *Analytic Politics*. Cambridge: Cambridge University Press.

Immergut, Ellen. 1992a. *Health Politics*. Cambridge: Cambridge University Press

———. 1992b. "The Rules of the Game: The Logic of Health Policy-Making in France, Switzerland and Sweden." In *Structuring Politics: Historical Institutionalism in Comparative Analysis,* edited by Sven Steinmo, Kathleen Thelen, and Frank Longstreth. Cambridge: Cambridge University Press.

Kornai, János. 1995. *The Economics of Shortage*. Amsterdam: North-Holland Press.

Kuran, Timur. 1995. *Private Truths, Public Lies*. Cambridge, Mass.: Harvard University Press.

Laffont, Jean-Jacques, and Jean Tirole. 1987. "Comparative Statics of the Optimal Dynamic Incentive Contract." *European Economic Review* 31: 901–26.

Laitin, David. 1992. *Language Repertoires and State Construction in Africa*. New York: Cambridge University Press.

———. 1995. "National Revivals and Violence." *Archives Européenes de Sociologie* 36: 3–43.

Michels, Robert. 1962. *Political Parties*. New York: Collier.

North, Douglass, and Barry Weingast. 1994. "Constitutions and Commitment." In *Monetary and Fiscal Policy,* vol. 1: *Credibility,* edited by Torsten Persson and Guido Tabellini. Cambridge, Mass.: MIT Press.

Przeworksi, Adam. 1985. *Capitalism and Social Democracy*. Cambridge: Cambridge University Press.

Putnam, Robert. 1988. "Diplomacy and Domestic Politics: The Logic of Two-Level Games." *International Organization* 42: 427–60.

Ramseyer, Mark J., and Frances Rosenbluth. 1993. *Japan's Political Marketplace*. Cambridge, Mass.: Harvard University Press.

Schattsneider, E. E. 1960. *The Semi-Sovereign People*. New York: Holt, Rinehart and Winston.

Shepsle, Kenneth A., and Barry R. Weingast. 1981. "The Institutional Foundations of Committee Power." *American Political Science Review* 81: 85–104.

Shubik, Martin. 1985. *Game Theory and the Social Sciences*. Cambridge, Mass.: MIT Press.

Simons, Beth. 1994. *Who Adjusts.* Princeton, N.J.: Princeton University Press.

Sutton, John. 1991. *Sunk Costs and Market Structure.* Cambridge, Mass.: MIT Press.

Tsebelis, George. 1990. *Nested Games.* Berkeley: University of California Press.

———. 1995. "Decision Making in Political Systems: Veto Players in Presidential-ism, Parliamentarianism, Multicameralism, and Multipartyism." *British Journal of Political Science* 25: 289–325.

Varshney, Ashutosh. 1992. *Beyond Urban Bias.* London: Cass.

Waterbury, John. 1993. *Exposed to Innumerable Delusions.* Cambridge: Cambridge University Press.

Appendix _____

THE PURPOSE of this appendix is to provide an example of a full-information game in extended form and to introduce the notions of (subgame-perfect) equilibrium, the equilibrium path, and credible threat. The stylized example is designed to meet the immediate needs of the reader. For further information about game theory, the reader is advised to consult more extensive treatments, such as Morrow (1994).

Consider figure A.1, which displays the peacetime army game. The home nation (player H) decides whether to have a large or a small army (L or S), and an opponent (player O) decides between maintaining peace and initiating war (P or W).

Payoffs are determined as follows. For the home country:

   a. An army costs 10.
   b. Life without being conquered is worth 25.
   c. Defending in war costs 5, if there exists a large army.
   d. If no large army exists, then H is overrun if O initiates war, and H receives the payoff 0.

For the opponent:

   a. Overrunning H in war is worth 10.
   b. Initiating war but failing to overrun H costs 20.
   c. The payoff is 0 otherwise.

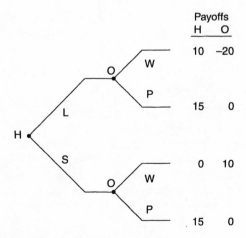

FIGURE A.1. The peacetime army game.

TABLE A.1
Payoffs in the Peacetime Army Game

Outcome (H move, O move)		Payoff to H	Payoff to O
Large army, war	(L, W)	10	−20
Large army, peace	(L, P)	15	0
Small army, war	(S, W)	0	10
Small army, peace	(S, P)	15	0

The payoffs are displayed in figure A.1 and in table A.1, which lists the payoffs for each combination of possible actions. Thus, in the first line, H chooses a large army (L) and the opponent chooses to attack (W). Under the assumptions mentioned previously, the attack is repulsed and the payoffs to H and O are 10 and −20, respectively.

To analyze this game, reason backward from the end nodes (displayed in figure A.1), which show the payoffs to the two players. Moving last, player O will choose the alternative (W or P) that represents his best response to the choices of H. Should H choose L (i.e., to build a large army), O's best response is P (i.e., not to initiate war). If H chooses S (i.e., to build a small army), then O's best response is W (i.e., to initiate war). P and W thus represent best responses to L and S, respectively.

Player H now knows what player O, choosing rationally, will do. Continuing the backward reasoning, player H can now choose her best response to the anticipated actions of O. Player H now knows that she must choose between raising a large army, L, in which case O will choose P with a payoff to H of 15, or raising a small army, S, in which case O will initiate war, with a resultant payoff to H of 0. Given that the payoffs resulting from the choice of L exceed those resulting from S, player H's best action is L.

Thus far we have indicated how to reason through a full-information game in extended form. The equilibrium choice of strategies is denoted by the following set:

For H: L.
For O: P if H chooses L, and W if H chooses S.

The equilibrium set of strategies is composed of each player's best response to the anticipated actions of the other. Anticipations will be confirmed by the choices actually made. The equilibrium defines an outcome—wherein H builds a large army and O does not attack—with its attendant payoffs (15 to H, 0 to O).

Note that the equilibrium choice of strategies contains the actors' best responses at each decision node. In this game, each node is a singleton and so defines a subgame.[1] The strategy combinations are therefore not only Nash, they

---

[1]More precisely, a subgame contains a single node and all its successors. The originating node is a singleton in its information set, and none of its successors is connected by an information set to a node not in this subgame. As a consequence, the player who has to choose at this node knows that she is at this node and not at any other.

are also subgame perfect. The significance of this property becomes apparent when we inspect the lower branches of figure A.1, which include a portion of O's equilibrium strategy. The actual path of play is (L, P). H would not choose S. Why? Because O would then choose W; he would initiate war. Higher payoffs for O imply that he would initiate war were H to stray off the equilibrium path. O's decision to initiate war is credible, because H knows that were she to build a small army (i.e., choose S), O would profit from war (O's payoff from W is 10; that from P, 0). The credibility of O's initiating war when H chooses S thus renders the equilibrium self-enforcing; neither H nor O has any reason to stray from her or his choice of strategies, or to revise her or his expectations as to how the other will behave.

Note an additional property of this example. Consider a country with a large army that has never been attacked. Some citizens might argue that, because they have never been attacked, the resources going to the army are wasted. Others might argue just the opposite: the country has never been attacked, they assert, precisely because it possesses a large army. Two very different possibilities thus imply the same set of observations. But the observationally equivalent interpretations rest on markedly different theories of behavior.

To settle upon an explanation, we must move outside the game and investigate empirical materials. We must determine how the opponents' beliefs shape their behavior. This blend of strategic reasoning and empirical investigation helps to define the method of analytic narratives: the mixture between formal reasoning and the detailed exploration of case materials, and the ideographic and nomothetic forms of explanation.

Reference

Morrow, James D. 1994. *Game Theory for Political Scientists.* Princeton, N.J.: Princeton University Press.

Index

Entries suffixed by an f denote citations within figure captions; those suffixed by an n, within the note whose number immediately follows the n; and those suffixed by a t, within tables.

Robert H. Bates is the Eaton Professor of the Science of Government and Faculty Fellow of the Institute of International Development at Harvard University.

Avner Greif is Associate Professor of Economics at Stanford University.

Margaret Levi is Professor of Political Science and the Harry Bridges Chair in Labor Studies at the University of Washington, Seattle.

Jean-Laurent Rosenthal is Professor of Economics at the University of California, Los Angeles.

Barry R. Weingast is Senior Fellow at the Hoover Institution and Ward C. Krebs Family Professor of Political Science at Stanford University.